BUDDHA'S CHILD

BUDDHA'S CHILD

MY FIGHT TO SAVE VIETNAM

NGUYEN CAO KY
WITH MARVIN J. WOLF

ST. MARTIN'S PRESS ❧ NEW YORK

For all who were touched by the armed struggles of Indochina, and especially those who gave their lives in defense of freedom.

Library of Congress Cataloging-in-Publication Data

Cao Ky, Nguyen.
    Buddha's child : my fight to save Vietnam / Nguyen Cao Ky with Marvin J. Wolf.—1st ed.
        p. cm.
    ISBN 0-312-28115-3
    1. Nguyän, Cao Ká. 2. Vietnam (Republic)—Politics and government. 3. Vietnamese Conflict, 1961-1975. 4. Prime ministers—Vietnam (Republic)—Biography. I. Wolf, Marvin J. II. Title.

    DS556.93.N512 A3 2002
    959.704'3'092—dc21

                                                            2001058560

First Edition: May 2002

10 9 8 7 6 5 4 3 2 1

CONTENTS

ACKNOWLEDGMENTS

MANY thanks to our literary manager, Peter Miller of PMA Literary and Film Management Agency, for his tireless efforts in finding the best publisher for our work. We greatly appreciate the sensitivities and support offered our project by our editor, George Witte, and his principal assistant, Marie Estrada, as well as the efforts of Henry Yee, who created the graphics.

We are also indebted to Julie Wheelock for her work in transcribing dozens of interview tapes both rapidly and accurately. Retired Foreign Service Officer Douglas Pike was generous with his time and personal recollections. Dr. James R. Reckner and Dr. Ron Frankum of Texas Tech University provided several photos and allowed us access to much helpful historical material.

Archivist Mike Parrish of the Lyndon Baines Johnson Library in Austin, Texas, was especially helpful in locating declassified documents from the LBJ era.

John Taylor and Susan Naulty of the Richard M. Nixon Presidential Library in Brea, California, were courteous and most helpful in offering records and photos of Mr. Nixon's post-presidential contacts with General Ky.

Joseph and Barbara Treaster graciously offered the hospitality of their home during several visits to New York in connection with this book.

1
PREMIER

PLAYING with my toddler son and daughter, laughing and teasing and very much enjoying fatherhood, I was spending a rare quiet evening in my quarters at Tansonnhut Air Base. Then my wife beckoned me to the telephone, and the voice of an army officer told me that there was an emergency: The Armed Forces Council was to meet in the prime minister's office immediately. I threw on my uniform and hurried off. It would be a long time before I would again enjoy the leisure to roll around on the floor with my children.

In Prime Minister Phan Huy Quat's office I found several army generals, along with Quat and President Phan Khac Suu, South Vietnam's chief of state. I learned that Quat and Suu were determined to resign their posts.

Suu was a picture postcard of Vietnam's past. Although trained in France as an agricultural engineer, this goateed octogenarian, a member of the Cao Dai sect, wore the black silk robes and circular cap that in the colonial era had symbolized a mandarin, a learned official. Such dress had gone out of fashion in my father's time; to Americans of the 1960s, Suu looked like a character from a Charlie Chan movie.

Appearing equally obsolete, Dr. Phan Huy Quat, leader of the Dai Viet party, was looking like a frail, white-haired schoolmaster, then in his sixties. Together they were symbolic of Vietnam's biggest problem: too many leaders and not enough leadership.

In the eighteen months since an army coup d'état toppled

the repressive Ngo Dinh Diem in November 1963, five military-dominated regimes had held power in Saigon. After so much infighting, the military brass was sick of politics. The generals hoped that the Phans, who were not related, would lead a sixth and purely civilian government that would provide at least steady management of our nation's many urgent problems.

Diem had been toppled by a quartet led by Duong Van "Big" Minh, who made himself chairman of the Military Committee and ran things, after a fashion, for less than ninety days. General Nguyen Khanh's coup drove him from office, but Big Minh came roaring back nine days later. He lasted just thirty-six days, until Khanh's second coup. Five months later, Big Minh again maneuvered Khanh out and returned for a third try as boss. In between these successful coups were several that failed.

By the time Big Minh returned for the third time, the communist leaders of North Vietnam had taken full advantage of this boiling pot of political instability. Not content with supplying and controlling the Vietcong guerrillas who terrorized many of our rural areas, Hanoi had begun to move well-equipped regiments and divisions of its regular army into South Vietnam, especially into the thinly populated Central Highlands region. We had an invasion to repel, and so the Armed Forces Council, of which I was a junior but outspoken member, finally tired of Big Minh and Khanh and their game of musical chairs. Two months after Minh's last coup, we invited a pair of widely known, white-haired civilian politicians to take over. The army's leadership had hoped that this combination of Suu, a southerner, or Cochinchinese, and Quat, an Annamese from central Vietnam—both familiar political figures of the colonial era—would cancel some of the regional animosities that infused almost every Vietnamese political issue.

But just like the military, the civilians could not resolve their differences. When Premier Quat shuffled his cabinet following an attempted coup, two of the ministers he had dismissed refused to leave office. Chief of State Suu backed them, arguing that Quat had no authority to fire anyone without Suu's approval. When neither would back down, both decided to quit. Trying to patch things up, we pleaded and cajoled and discussed for hours, seeking ways to narrow the gulf between these two stubborn politicians, each beholden to relatively small but very different constituencies.

The problem went beyond the current impasse. Quat and Suu could not agree on anything. If President Suu wanted to do something, the prime minister, who held more power, vetoed it. If Prime Minister Quat tried to institute some activity that Suu objected to—which seemed to be every initiative that Quat held dear—the president used his influence to undermine, obstruct, or delay.

Personally, I was disgusted by both of these dinosaurs. They had learned their trade under French colonial rule, and their values and methods were inappropriate to a republic. South Vietnam was backed by the United States, a world power that sought to contain the spread of international communism. America had made a commitment to help defend our small, struggling nation, but along with their millions of dollars and the legions of young men who were prepared to die for *our* freedom came a thicket of restrictions and advice. I suppose that everything was too new for Quat and Suu, that they were too set in their ways to accommodate the change required by our situation. Nevertheless, like most of the other generals, I would have preferred them to continue in office. The military needed to focus on fighting.

"There is no use talking any more!" said Quat. "The military must now assume responsibility for the government." It was past two in the morning, and everyone was exhausted. Quat picked up the phone and in minutes a man with a tape recorder appeared. While we generals watched, Quat and Suu read resignation statements. The man with the tape recorder left for the government radio station, where the tape would be broadcast a few hours later. We scheduled an emergency session of the Armed Forces Council for 8:00 A.M., and I went home to sleep.

Our meeting convened in an enormous, air-conditioned conference room at the Saigon headquarters of General Le Nguyen Khang, commandant of the marines. Behind a table at the head of a room that seated 500 was General Nguyen Van Thieu, who as minister of defense was ranking officer. He was flanked by the Armed Forces Council's other leaders, four senior generals.

In a room almost half filled with generals and colonels, I sat in the cheap seats. Around me were the other so-called Young Turks, men in their thirties who commanded elite military units: Nguyen Chanh Thi, the airborne brigade commander; Khang, commandant of the marines; navy boss Commodore Chung Tan Cang; and army generals Nguyen Duc Thang and Nguyen Bao Tri. As a group we had tried to reform the military and had publicly opposed the excesses and corruption of many senior generals.

Thieu explained the situation with Suu and Quat and announced what we all knew: Because the civilian leadership had failed, it was now up to us, the military, to form a new government. No one had to say why; the failure of these two veteran politicians, who despite their limitations were the most able and popular of a contentious multitude of inept power-seekers, was proof enough that the military represented Vietnam's only organized power.

And we were at war. Someone must take the helm of our rudderless ship before it was overwhelmed by the elements and capsized. We could not afford a long lapse in leadership.

Thieu proposed that the assembled military leaders nominate one or more of the group to become the new prime minister, then put these nominees to a vote.

"Who will volunteer to serve as prime minister?" asked Thieu. The room fell silent. "If there is no volunteer, we will proceed to the next phase," he continued. "We will nominate someone, and then the whole membership will vote to approve him or not. At this time are there any volunteers?"

No one raised a hand. No one said that he wanted to become prime minister. And why would anyone? Six governments in eighteen months, and the Americans, never long on patience, were already irritated. Six governments in eighteen months, and none of the army officers who had served as prime minister or president still had a command. If you were one of the country's four corps commanders, you were the next thing to a warlord, with virtually total freedom within your fiefdom. Commanders of divisions, regiments, or brigades controlled thousands of troops and were free to run their commands much as they saw fit.

I certainly did *not* want to be prime minister. I detested politicians, whom I regarded, as a class, as corrupt sellouts. I hated politics. I had *no* political experience, no aspirations for power, no desire for any job but the one that I held. I commanded the Vietnamese Air Force, the VNAF, the largest and most important of my nation's elite services, and I felt then and now that it was the most enjoyable job that a man could ever wish for. I was at home in the sky, glad to be among the few who could carry the fight to the enemy by attacking the North, and I loved the challenge of building my service into a modern force. Our American friends had promised new jet aircraft, expansive base facilities, and far greater firepower, and I looked forward to many years in command of the VNAF.

Why risk losing all that for a position that might last nine weeks or nine months—or nine days?

I listened quietly for several minutes, until it was apparent that no one would volunteer to serve as prime minister. Then, because I was considered not merely one of the Young Turks but also their spokesman, first among equals, I got to my feet and raised my hand. "I nominate General Nguyen Van Thieu,"

I said. "He is the most senior of us. He has some experience with government."

Everyone applauded, and I sat down.

When the room quieted, Thieu shook his head. I tried to engage him in a dialogue, enumerating all the reasons why he was the best choice for the job.

Thieu was eight or nine years my senior, a trim, compact man just starting to bald. He had been among the generals who deposed Diem, though he concealed his role so well that few westerners ever knew it. We had had little contact, but even then I could sense that he was a wait-and-see type, very ambitious but even more cautious. After I nominated Thieu to serve as prime minister, he replied at length about all the reasons why he should not accept—but would not commit himself either way. When I politely pressed him, he replied in the negative. "No, no," he said. "Not me." I thought that perhaps he would like a chance to change his mind, that he wanted to be begged, but no, he declined. "I will not serve as premier, that is final," he said.

With Thieu at the head table were the army's other senior generals. When it was clear that Thieu would not accept the responsibility, each man at the table was nominated, in order of seniority. Each declined in turn, and all quite forcefully.

I looked over at Nguyen Chanh Thi, the tough paratroop commander. Five years earlier, a cabal of his junior officers had forced him into accepting the most visible role in the first attempted coup against Diem. The move had failed, in part because of Thi's lack of sophistication, and he had been forced into exile in Cambodia. Before he fled, however, during the brief moment when it looked like Diem would fall, Thi had declared himself head of a provisional government.

"I propose General Thi," I said. "He likes politics. He was among those who first tried to oust Diem."

Thi demurred and could not be coaxed.

Three more generals were nominated; one by one each declined, offering a variety of reasons.

What it came down to was that nobody wanted the risk of losing what he had in such an unstable and dangerous time. Maybe another time, but not now.

The posturing and speechifying and excuses consumed hours. At noon Thieu called a break and we adjourned to another room, where small tables had been set up. The marines had set up an American-style chow line with sandwiches and coffee, and we helped ourselves.

I took some food and went looking for a vacant table when Thieu, sitting with a group of five or six top generals, caught my eye. He waved me over.

"We have been talking," he said. "Everyone agrees that you are the one best qualified for this job."

This took me by surprise. But I was already convinced that we in the military were Vietnam's only hope. If we cared about our country, there was no other choice: We could expect dire consequences if we failed to name a new prime minister within twenty-four hours of Dr. Quat's resignation. It might well lead to the end of our nation, to the triumph of the communists.

Later I had many opportunities to think about this moment, about the heavy responsibilities that I was so casually asked to take upon myself. But at that instant, I thought of nothing but the problem at hand—and I did not feel as if I had any choice. "If you all think that I can do the job, then okay," I said. "I accept.

"But," I continued, "you must go back to the meeting and raise the matter again to the Armed Forces Council. If no one else will take the job, and if all the members want me to serve as premier, then I will accept this position as an assignment from the military."

When the meeting resumed, Thieu proposed me as prime minister, saying that he was certain of my fitness for this duty.

He asked if anyone objected, and instead everyone stood and applauded as if I had just won some important prize or donated a big sum to charity, and the meeting came to an end. At the time I was flattered that so many top officers had so much confidence in me. I have had thirty-six years to reconsider, however, and now, having dealt with many of those generals, I suspect that the older generation, those who had served the French and risen to power under Diem, approved my selection because they were sure that I would fail and, in failing, I would lose not only my command but also my life.

There were no reporters present at our meeting, and the only statement issued by the Armed Forces Council said that it had accepted the resignations of Dr. Phan Huy Quat and Mr. Phan Khac Suu and that Air Vice Marshal Nguyen Cao Ky, the new prime minister, would form a government. The Western news media, perhaps conditioned by our interminable coups or unwilling to consider the possibility of a peaceful transfer of power, reported that Thieu had headed a "Young Turk's coup" and made me prime minister. U.S. ambassador to South Vietnam Maxwell Taylor also wrote of a coup by Thieu in a telegram to President Lyndon Johnson. Now these diplomatic and press errors are enshrined as history in every American encyclopedia and history book. It is a mistake. Thieu was never a Young Turk, and there was no coup.

I became prime minister of the Republic of Vietnam on June 19, 1965. At thirty-four years of age I had never held office, never joined a political party, never commanded more than a few thousand men—and my impoverished nation was wracked with internal dissension and engaged in war against a pitiless and able foe.

American diplomats, generals, and journalists nattered about my preference for purple socks, noted that I wore my hair longer than a U.S. Marine Corps drill instructor, or reported, erroneously but often, that I packed a "pearl-handled" revolver. Others, including many well acquainted with bar girls and brothels, clucked over my reputation as a bon vivant and boulevardier. *Newsweek* reported that I was a lady killer, although it also reported my response to this accusation: "I've never killed a lady, but lots of ladies have killed me." William Bundy of the U.S. State Department concluded that I was "the bottom of the barrel," the last, worst choice of a desperate military. Author Frances FitzGerald wrote that I was a dupe, a tool of the ARVN corps and division commanders, "the one general who they felt confident lacked the capacity to take power himself." And, writing in 1991, a year before sometime saxophonist William Jefferson Clinton became president of the United States, journalist Stanley Karnow described me as "looking like a saxophone player in a second-rate nightclub."

There were shreds of truth in some of these observations, although I am only familiar with first-rate nightclubs. But I was not aware, then, of this outpouring of criticism. Instead I focused on my responsibilities: the welfare of more than 15 million of my countrymen, including the many who would be glad to see me fail. I might not survive the week, as practically every "informed observer" predicted, but I knew my duty. My office was a sacred trust, no less a charge from Buddha and my nation as from my military brethren, and I vowed that I would do as much for my country as my abilities and energies permitted. I might well fail, but it would not be for lack of effort or because I compromised my principles.

2
CHILDHOOD

AFTER a long, cold winter's journey up the Red River from Son Tay, my mother arrived at the foot of the mountain. It took her hours to climb the hundreds of stone steps leading to the summit, but she was desperate, and this visit to Huong Tich, the pagoda dedicated to Buddha that has welcomed pilgrims for more than a thousand years, was her last chance. A few months earlier, my father had begun negotiations to take a second wife, a young woman whom he hoped would bear a son to carry on the family line. Mother had presented Father with three daughters and two sons, but neither of these handsome, light-skinned boys had survived past early childhood. A trusted fortune-teller advised that it was not my mother's destiny to raise a son. Seeking to change her fate, Mother set out on her pilgrimage.

Near the shrine is a lake, and from its center jut several huge rocks where people come to pray. Mother found a sampan and paid the boatman two fares. The second was for the son whose soul, she hoped, would return with her. At the sacred stones, Mother prayed to Buddha for a son. Then she went home.

When I was born nine months later, I was considered Buddha's child. According to our custom, Mother had to give me away until I was no longer an infant. But every night Uncle Hoan, my mother's brother, placed my bed next to a window, so that she could see me while remaining outside his household.

And that is how my destiny was set. Many times death has taken those closest to me, but I was spared. No matter how great the peril I have encountered, I have emerged without harm. I am Buddha's child, and until my purpose in this life has been fulfilled, Buddha will protect me.

...

I like to tell jokes and to laugh. My father, Nguyen Van Hieu, had a very different sense of humor. His demeanor was serious and reserved, even in private, and though I was his only son, he was usually quite distant with me. Born in 1895 into a family of scholars and minor government officials, from the age of eight he was educated in the classic Chinese manner: After learning to write several thousand Chinese ideographs, the system of writing imposed on Vietnam after its third-century conquest by China, he turned his attention to the study of Chinese literature. He practiced calligraphy and read such classics as *The Book of Filial Piety, The Analects of Confucius, The Book of Maxims, The Book of Odes, The Book of History, The Book of Rites,* and *The Book of Changes.*

Father studied long and hard to prepare for the national civil service examination. If he achieved a high grade, as had my grandfather and uncles, he could look forward to a career as a government administrator. If his abilities permitted, in time he might have been appointed to a high position in some ministry, or perhaps have served as the top official in a province or district. This was the path that our ancestors had followed for generations. Our family was among Vietnam's tiny middle class. We owned a few hectares of land, on which we grew vegetables and rice and raised a few pigs and chickens. We were far from wealthy, yet we were relatively privileged. Most of our countrymen, including my mother's family, were peasants, subsistence farmers who survived from year to year at the whim of the rice harvest. I was well into my teens before I fully appreciated just how fortunate my family had been.

Although we Vietnamese had twice defeated invading Chinese armies, we did not finally rid ourselves of Chinese rule until the eighteenth century. By the middle of the next, Vietnam was a French colony. In return for bringing Christianity and European mores to what they called Indochina, the French set up plantations and took our tea, timber, tin, rubber, and rice, to say nothing of our labor and our nationhood. To ensure that there was a supply of cheap labor, they taxed small rice farmers until most had no choice but to sell their land. Under the principle of divide and conquer, the French exploited ancient regional animosities by establishing different political entities in the southern, central, and northern regions.

At about the time that my father expected to embark on his civil service career, the French, with the stroke of a pen, abolished both the Chinese-inspired education system and the written language that it employed.

In its place, the French governor-general imposed Quoc-Ngu, an alphabet that uses Roman characters and accent marks to indicate the six tones that we use in speaking. This alphabet was developed in about 1651 by Father Alexander de Rhodes, a Roman Catholic missionary, in an effort to win more converts. Along with mandatory Quoc-Ngu came the colonial version of the French education system, the lycée, with curricula more suited to the modern era of commerce and industry and to European cultural imperatives.

In fairness to the French, the Chinese writing system requires intensive study. Peasants, especially farmers whose lives were endless days of backbreaking toil, rarely found the time to learn even a hundred characters. Quoc-Ngu can be taught to children in a few hours of daily schooling, and its introduction made universal literacy possible. The French, however, did little to educate peasants and workers, and when they were eventually forced to depart, they left behind a nation woefully unprepared for self-rule.

My father had little to do with the French. He had had no inkling that he was of the last generation of Vietnamese who would learn Chinese as their primary written language, or that he also would be among the first forced to learn a foreign alphabet, a foreign language, and to absorb, if not embrace, French culture. His entry into adulthood was therefore a disagreeable disappointment. Instead of entering the civil service, he taught classical Chinese in a private college, a relatively unimportant position.

While this radical reversal of fortunes did not destroy him, surely it left him embittered. Father taught his classes with enthusiasm, but looked forward to vacations and school holidays when he could go hunting. He was often gone for weeks, pursuing game in the wild country near the border with China. It was only later that I discovered that although he did in fact hunt, he also pursued far more dangerous game: Father carried ammunition and messages between members of the resistance forces opposing French colonial rule.

As he grew older and more disenchanted with colonial government, my father drew upon his formal training to write poetry in the classical Chinese style. These beautiful verses were admired not merely for their elegant calligraphy but also for their wit and insight. Father used these often-humorous verses to lampoon the crooked, the foolish, and the ill mannered, especially the third-rate politicians whom the French routinely appointed to positions of authority. He sent his poems to the newspaper in our provincial city of Son Tay, west of Hanoi along the Red River; if the powerful cringed before his brush, he made few lasting enemies. Even those whom he skewered admired the way Father employed his words.

...

Like most Buddhist children, at birth I received both a Buddhist and a family name. According to tradition, however, no one calls me by my Buddhist name. Our family name, Nguyen, has no special meaning; it is just a name, and very common. In Vietnam, children of the same sex and generation within each family usually share a middle name. Mine, Cao, means high, and was not an unusual boy's name in my part of the country. The combination of Cao and Ky, however, is rare; I have met no other with that name. Ky means a flag or an emerald, depending on which Chinese character is used, so Cao Ky could mean a high flag or a precious emerald. It could also mean an aristocrat or a chess master, one who is very smart and able to think several moves ahead. By the time of my birth in 1930, however, all names were recorded in Quoc-Ngu, with its Roman characters. As a child I never thought to ask my father about such things. Today, guessing at what he might have been thinking, I lean toward "high-ranking person," but frankly, while I am a little curious, I am not one of those who think that a man's name is his destiny. Action is destiny.

When I was little, our household included two servants, a woman who helped clean and cook and a manservant. In the dim recesses of memory, I see this man hoisting me atop a calf that my mother bought for me to ride until I was big enough to get on a horse. I loved American cowboy movies, and astride the calf I rode the small pasture behind our house and tried to herd our pigs. Those swine usually had other ideas, but it was fun anyway.

As the only boy among four sisters, I was treated like a little prince and allowed to do whatever I pleased. My three older sisters tell me that when I was a toddler, the only thing that would make me stop crying and smile was to let me smash a dish or a glass against the floor. Few parents, I imagine, would have stood for this, but my mother bought boxes and boxes of the cheapest crockery. When I cried, someone handed me a few dishes to break, and soon I was again smiling.

Thinking back across the years, I have wondered if this familial tolerance helped shape my outlook, my view of myself and my place in the world. Some will call me arrogant, but I think now that it did not, or at most only a little. I am Buddha's child.

I was born with certain traits of character, and I don't think that the influences of family, friends, schools, or the military world affected me. For example, while it is usually true, as Lord Acton wrote, that "power corrupts, and absolute power corrupts absolutely," I am the exception to that rule. My heart is the Buddha's heart. I held nearly absolute power for more than two years—including the power of life or death over my countrymen—but it did not alter my sense of self, or my worldview, or the way that I treated others. It did not corrupt me in the slightest. And, while I have had many teachers and I have studied many subjects and learned about human nature and about the world through the trial and error of experience, while I have made my share of mistakes and misjudgments, I think that the fundamental nature of my character is as it was when I was born. If my parents had been stricter or even more tolerant, I don't think my upbringing would have changed my basic consciousness, my fundamental way of dealing with the world.

In the manner of his generation, my father left the running of his household to my mother. She was born Phung Thi Cac, the daughter of an educated farmer. Like many of his class and generation, Father could not be bothered about money, and so left that to Mother. And she did very well in business, importing different kinds of goods to sell in the marketplace. After I finished elementary school, we moved to Hanoi so that I could enroll in one of the city's two French-style lycées. Later on Mother established a bus line that hauled farmers to and from the city, and this business prospered for a time.

I was about nine when World War II began. Germany quickly defeated France and occupied the northern half of that vanquished nation. The Vichy government, based in the south of France, collaborated with Germany and continued to administer France's colonies, including all of Indochina, which included Laos, Cambodia, and Vietnam. Japan, allied with Germany, occupied Indochina in 1941 and began helping itself to our rice, minerals, and rubber. While the Japanese left the French colonial apparatus intact and allowed the appearance of Vichy control, the United States angrily ordered Tokyo to withdraw its forces. When the Japanese government refused, the United States cut off oil supplies, setting in motion the chain of events that culminated in Japan's attack on Pearl Harbor.

The war was unsettling to our life in Hanoi. I sometimes saw American bombers overhead, attacking Japanese ships using the Haiphong port. Often the explosions came too close, and our schools were closed. Several times, along with much of Hanoi's population, our family was evacuated to the countryside. In about 1943, after several interludes of moving as refugees from one village to the next for weeks or months, we relocated to Tuyen Quang, a small city about seventy miles from the Chinese border. Again my mother went into business, traveling north to China via river sampan, returning with goods to be sold in local markets.

Father found a position teaching Chinese, and while the pay was poor, the townspeople treated him with great respect, addressing him always as "Mr. Teacher." Soon all the desperation and hatred that had been gnawing at him surfaced. The French had made him feel irrelevant and useless, and finally he became open in his resistance to colonial rule. Father went into the mountains to join anti-French guerrillas. I am not sure what role, if any, this thoughtful man of letters played, but the following year, on Christmas Eve, a force under Ho Chi Minh's military deputy, Vo Nguyen Giap, attacked a French headquarters at nearby Phai Khat and killed many French soldiers. This battle marked the start of the revolution, and it established Giap's reputation as a fighter.

In my father's absence we moved back to Son Tay. About that time, the Allies liberated France, and the Japanese began taking active control of Vietnam. The noncom in charge of our local garrison was a Sergeant Takahashi, a bright, charming fellow with an ingratiating manner. My mother practically adopted him. She introduced him to a nice Vietnamese girl, whom he soon married. I began spending time at Japanese army head-quarters, sometimes eating with the soldiers. I participated in their games, singing, and other social activities, and learned a smattering of the Japanese language—enough, probably, to get into serious difficulties.

One day Takahashi gave the husband of my third sister, Hu-yen, a small Browning pistol, probably one taken from a downed U.S. aviator. My brother-in-law was very happy with such a fine gift and showed it to everyone in the family.

Even though I liked Takahashi as a man, as a Vietnamese I knew that we had to oust foreign occupiers. One day in late 1944, along with my nephew and a young pal, I decided that it was time for me to follow my father, to join the Resistance forces in the mountains along the Red River near the Chinese border. Everyone had heard how they ambushed Japanese patrols and raided Japanese outposts, that they were determined to restore Vietnam's independence. "My brother-in-law has a gun," I said. "We should take that with us when we join the resistance." My cohorts agreed, so I went home and took the pistol from its hiding place. We packed some clothes and all the food we could carry and slipped away during the night.

Our plan was to walk to the Red River, hire a sampan, and go north. The Resistance controlled much of the river traffic, and we hoped that when we got close to the border region they would stop our boat. Then we would tell them that we wanted to join their struggle. We hiked to one of the river towns, found a boat, asked the woman who owned it to take us north. But before we could embark, a powerful storm with strong winds swept down from China. The woman refused to sail. She said that we would have to wait until the storm had passed. So we waited, unaware that my worried mother had called Sergeant Takahashi. It was easy enough for him to find three young runaways; in a few hours we looked through the rain and saw the police, along with several Japanese soldiers, coming to take us home. Back in Son Tay, Takahashi told me that I had made my mother cry. He must have had some inkling of what we were up to, but he never asked me why. Many years later, when I became prime minister, I asked the Japanese government to help locate this kindly soldier, but they were unable to find him. He may have died in Borneo during the last weeks of the war.

A few months after this futile attempt to join the Resistance, word came that my father had died. He had contracted malaria, and in that remote, almost inaccessible jungle, with few doctors and little medicine, his kidneys failed as a result of the infection. He was fifty years old.

The war ended months later, and my family returned to Hanoi, where I resumed my studies at the Lycée du Protectorate. I had no clue at that time, but among my generation, graduates of the Protectorate and Hanoi's other lycée, the Albert Sarraut, would go on to become the vast majority—upward of 95 percent—of national leaders in both the North and the South, including communists. Because of my father's background, in addition to French and English and the other required subjects, for three years I studied Chinese. As a young man, I could write very beautiful Chinese characters, and even today I still recognize hundreds of Chinese words.

The British disarmed the defeated Japanese in Cochin, the south of Vietnam, and Chinese forces under Chiang Kai-shek did the same in the northern regions. Despite the pleas of Ho Chi Minh and other nationalist leaders that Vietnam's independence should be restored, the British and Chinese allowed their French allies to return.

Angry and disgusted, I joined much of my generation, perhaps a million young men and women, who left Hanoi and Saigon and Hue and the other cities under French control. Along with so many other young men and women, I went into the mountains and jungle with the Resistance, working to kick the French out and liberate our country. And the one name on my lips, as well as those of nearly everyone of my generation, was Ho Chi Minh, who had earned our admiration by opposing the French.

In what we called Liberated, or Free, Zones, where the French had little military presence, the Resistance took over. Everyone was required to have a kind of passport, a travel document, even to walk from one village to the next. To enforce this and other new regulations, the communists created what amounted to a police force. Virtually to a man those chosen for this work were the most ignorant and brutal peasants. I met none that could even read or write his own name, much less the mandatory travel documents.

I was sixteen years old, and any time one of these cadres heard my Hanoi accent he demanded to know my father's occupation. Upon learning that I was a student, he became suspicious. Among these communists, anyone with the slightest education was considered a potential enemy of the people, at the least a bad influence. I had no notion that this mind-set would in a few decades mature into the genocidal atrocities of the Khmer Rouge, but looking back, the path between beginning and end is now clear.

Like everyone in the Resistance, I was subjected to political indoctrination, but the cadres and their enforcers had yet to declare themselves communists. By the time their affiliation was clear, however, I had changed my mind about Ho Chi Minh. By observing the Resistance leaders and those who enforced their will, it was apparent that they were coarse, stupid, and ignorant. Their anti-intellectualism and brutal behavior made it clear that for them, the Resistance movement was not merely about expelling foreigners. It was about turning the tables, about becoming the rulers, about revenge. As often as landlords had exploited peasants, as often as Vietnamese were mistreated by the French and their surrogates, it was plain that if the communists came to power they would treat their former social betters much worse. It would never be enough for these communists to raise themselves up. They would not be satisfied until they had humiliated and brutalized the educated classes.

It may seem that I am an elitist, and perhaps this is so, but my family, and the others whom I knew before the war, always treated servants with consideration and dignity. We knew our places, they knew theirs, and each respected the other. I had been raised among people who valued civility and revered education, and I found the communists despicable and frightening in their ignorance and hatred.

Even so, I could not return to live under French rule. Like so many others, I was trapped between the devil and the abyss, and all I could do was try to survive, to hope that we would soon throw the French out. For the next two years, until 1948, I traveled the countryside, engaging in many different activities, getting a most unusual education.

As a schoolboy I always had a little money in my pocket, because I had only to ask my mother for it. My classmates' mothers were less generous, and so usually it was I who bought the sweets or soft drinks. My pals teased me that I came from a rich family. It was not so; we were all about the same. We all had the deep and genuine affection of parents who protected us and shielded us from life's miseries. Now, in the mountains and jungles, for the first time in my life I mingled with the children of poverty, boys my age who had grown up unloved, hungry, fearful. It was a shock to realize how easy my life had been and how many had not been so fortunate.

In those damp, malarial jungles, however, we were all equal. And all equally miserable. We rarely had enough to eat, and we shivered through long, wet nights, often sleeping on the ground without even a blanket, awakening to find hundreds of leeches clinging to our bodies, each fat and swollen from feasting on our blood.

One day, while I was visiting a guerrilla unit in the mountains, two of Vietnam's most famous poets and writers, Xuan Dieu and Huy Can, stopped by our camp. They had just returned from France, where they took part in talks between a delegation led by Ho Chi Minh and French leaders. We were so poor that we had no cash, not even for cigarette papers. All that we could offer our honored guests was tea and our homegrown tobacco to smoke in handmade pipes. We sat around for hours listening to talk about France, about the negotiations, about the international struggle for human rights and self-determination. It made a big impact on me.

I was too young to carry a rifle, and in truth there were few weapons among the Resistance. My duties included raising vegetables and livestock, preparing food, and cleaning up. Later I was assigned to a troupe of traveling actors and singers that promoted Resistance ideas to the farmers and peasants in ways that simple people could grasp, something like what the Soviet communists called agitprop—agitation and propaganda. Afoot and occasionally by river sampan, we traveled hundreds, even thousands of miles from one region to the next, visiting almost the whole country.

Walking down from the northern mountains toward Tuyen Quang, I fell ill with malaria. My comrades found me a place to rest for a few days and continued their journey. When I felt a little better I set out on foot for Son Tay. Only a few hours after I reached home I lapsed into a coma. I awoke three days later, my clothing and blankets soaked with sweat, in a sampan floating down the Red River toward Hanoi. I demanded that my mother stop the boat. I wanted to go back to the mountains, to rejoin the Resistance, but she refused. I was too weak to argue.

Within days, most of my family returned to Hanoi to take turns caring for me. For weeks I hovered between life and death, until Mother found a good doctor, one of very few in Hanoi at the time. He injected me daily for two years, until my blood was clear of the deadly parasite. After a few months back in Hanoi, my strength returned and I resumed my studies.

3

SOLDIER

I began my last year at the lycée in 1950 with hazy plans for what would come next. I supposed that I would go on to the university and after a few years would join my brothers-in-law working in the family business. Or perhaps I would go abroad to study. I wasn't sure.

Buddha, however, had definite plans for me and for my country. Under French domination, the nation called Vietnam had vanished from the map in the nineteenth century. Dividing and conquering, France controlled Vietnam's three diverse regions. Tonkin is the north; thickly populated Annam, which includes the former imperial capital of Hue, is the central region; and in the south, rice-rich Cochinchina. France administered each state in a different way. Tonkin has swift rivers that could be harnessed for hydroelectric power, and valuable mineral deposits, but when it comes to growing food, life is hard in my homeland. Apart from the Red River delta, there is little land suitable for large-scale farming. There were some large landowners, but even along the Red River, few peasant families owned or even leased more than about a third of an acre. Winters are cloudy and cool, and rice farmers must work very hard to grow enough to feed their families. Only the hardiest people survived, which is why, I suppose, we northerners have long been regarded as the most stubborn of Vietnamese. Tonkin became a protectorate, garrisoned with French troops. Internal matters were mostly left to handpicked Vietnamese lackeys, and hundreds of Jesuits came to convert my hardheaded countrymen to Catholicism. Many did become Christians, but most continued along the spiritual paths trod by their ancestors.

Annam, the central region, is small and poor, with too many people and few natural resources. Its major city, Hue, had once served as the seat of the imperial throne. Caring little about Annam, the French allowed it to become their puppet state under a succession of effete emperors.

Cochinchina, the great prize, was a colony. Like all colonies, its purpose was to enrich its colonizers. The southern weather is subtropical, and the Mekong River brings an enormous volume of plant nutrients; the delta in the southern part of the country is a vast granary that easily could have fed most of nineteenth-century Asia. In Cochinchina's cool uplands are expansive areas suitable for growing rubber, coffee, tea, and bananas; the French cut down forests and established plantations. Even as they were oppressed by native landlords and foreign colonists, the well-fed southerners led comparatively easy lives. To ensure the cooperation of landlords and other elites, many Cochinchinese were granted French citizenship. Within a few generations, the upper classes became thoroughly European in outlook. Their sons were educated in Paris; their daughters married Frenchmen. They considered themselves more French than Vietnamese.

When the Japanese took over, however, they eliminated geographic boundaries, reunified Vietnam, and installed Bao Dai, last monarch of the Nguyen dynasty, as emperor of their prize-of-war client state.

The French returned in 1946. The communists, though at first few in number, were secure in their mountain and jungle bases. Ho Chi Minh's guerrillas attacked French installations and troops and kept up the pressure for independence. Devastated financially by World War II, however, France was desperate to hang on to the colonial holdings that had yielded such immense profits. The French negotiated a settlement with Ho Chi Minh, and for a time the fighting ceased. Bao Dai returned to the throne, fostering the illusion of an autonomous Vietnam and buying the French time to deal with the guerrillas.

The emperor established a national government. Every government needs an army, and so, in 1950, Bao Dai declared a general mobilization: Every student between the ages of eighteen and twenty, virtually an entire generation of the national elite, was inducted for officer training. I was among them. To fill the ranks of this new Vietnamese army, young peasants were conscripted in great numbers. French officers and noncoms were employed as advisors and to lead larger units until Vietnamese could be trained to take their places. About the time Ho Chi Minh's accord with France dissolved over who would control Cochinchina, Vietnam's new army began to form. Its first mission: to fight the communists, known as the Vietminh.

My mother, naturally, did not fancy the idea that her only son was to become a soldier. She knew men in positions of influence and intended to have one of them get me an exemption from military training. I would not allow it. "Mother, no," I said. "Don't do that. My whole class is going into the army. All my friends. I also must go."

With my classmates, I spent ten months studying military fundamentals in a makeshift military academy near Hanoi. After I became a second lieutenant, my first assignment was a rifle platoon of the 20th Vietnamese Battalion. I want to emphasize that this unit was *never* part of the French army, though of course many of our Vietnamese noncoms were French army veterans. Years later, when I became a senior officer, communist propagandists were eager to make it seem that I had been a party to colonial oppression. They created the lie that I served in the French army, but that is not so.

My first command was a platoon of thirty-three infantrymen stationed near Hai Duong and Hung Yen, in the Red River delta,

North Vietnam's richest farming area, and therefore its most crowded and overpopulated. It was infested with communist guerrillas. My personal baptism of fire came on the very day that I reported to my company at My Trach. About eight that evening the Vietminh attacked. One of my soldiers—I had not yet even learned his name—was shot in front of me, the first time I had seen anyone die violently. When one becomes a soldier, he agrees to forfeit his life. I had already made this decision for myself, but it was sobering nonetheless to witness the premature end of this man's life and to realize that his mother would bear a pain that would never heal.

For my first few months my platoon patrolled every day, searching villages for guerrillas. We did not have enough troops to control every bit of territory, but we tried to keep the roads open and to provide security for the farmers. At night we set up ambushes, hoping to catch the enemy as they moved under cover of darkness. We made contact maybe five or six times, little skirmishes typical of the war at that time. The communists did not yet have the numbers to win a large-scale battle, so they attacked our outposts or ambushed our patrols. We tried to ambush them before they could attack, to disrupt their plans—but most of all, to protect the farmers. These encounters were usually brief. Often only a few shots were fired or a grenade or two was lobbed. Sometimes the guerrillas mined a road or blew up a bridge over a rural stream. In a firefight, where they were usually outnumbered, they would pop off a few rounds, then melt into the countryside.

Periodically the Vietminh would take over a village or small town. For a few days or weeks, they forced the villagers to sit through political indoctrination sessions, confiscated most of the rice crop, and conscripted young men into their army. These cadres said nothing about communism. They spoke of Ho Chi Minh and his struggle to restore Vietnamese nationhood and independence. The best-known man in the country, Ho drew people to his banner because he represented the resistance of the Vietnamese people to French colonialism. The communist cadre's main problem was overcoming political indifference and the inertia of traditional rural ways. Those farmers cared little about who sat in Hanoi or Hue, or if the French set the price of rice or if Ho Chi Minh did. They wanted only to plant and harvest in peace. They wanted only to feed their families.

As a very young second lieutenant, I didn't totally grasp the bigger issues. I knew that the communists were stupid, brutal men who couldn't be trusted, but I also held a low opinion of the French and their sycophants. What moved me were the very visible signs of famine and suffering in villages we visited: children with distended bellies, emaciated elders who resembled living scarecrows, dead babies, sickness everywhere. Thousands of innocent people died, most from lack of even basic medical care, many from malnutrition, and more than a few from the traumas of war. Peace-loving farmers, victimized by both sides, had nowhere to go.

It was a dirty war, but I much preferred being in the field with my troops to hanging around our headquarters. All the platoon leaders and soldiers in my unit were Vietnamese, but during this time of transition from French protectorate to independent state, we didn't have enough Vietnamese who were qualified to command battalions or even most companies. A few French officers and senior noncoms held those positions, their roles were less about leading us into combat and more about on-the-job training for this first cohort of Vietnamese officers, much like the American advisors who a decade later would come to South Vietnam.

But there was one big difference: The French army officers with whom I served behaved as if they believed themselves superior human beings and that French culture was mankind's supreme attainment. We young Vietnamese officers were not allowed to have minds of our own. We were obliged to follow the French customs.

One of these was taking dinner with the commanding officer. When in garrison, all officers were required to eat with this Frenchman. It was akin to dining with a king or demigod: After eating our meal, we junior officers were obliged to wait, usually in silence, until he excused us from the table. Our battalion officers included the French captain advising my company and two others who handled quartermaster and finance duties. At dinner they joined the commander to eat, to drink good French wine, and to discuss wives and families and life in France. There were few other diversions for these Frenchmen, and so every night they devoted four or five hours to such socializing. As they consumed more wine, they moved on to swapping the usual lies about women, fighting, and drinking.

During this time of transition, when these men were expecting to return to France, they were not eager to take chances with their lives. Once a week or so they would venture into the field, patrol for a few hours, then return to the safety of the fort. Things were different for me and my Vietnamese brethren. We were trying to put colonialism behind us and to establish our own country. The communists had very different ideas about what sort of place that would be and so we had to fight them. Individual French soldiers served only a year or two in our country and then returned to their homes. We Vietnamese conscripts were never told how long we would have to serve. I assumed that it might be many years, for as long as I was needed, until the communists were defeated.

To make that happen, we had to carry the fight to the enemy, and that meant leaving the comparative safety of our garrison. We patrolled from early morning until late afternoon, snatched a few hours of sleep in early evening, and after dark went out into the countryside to set up ambushes. Nevertheless, after each hard day in the field, I sat at the commander's table with my peers, listening in silence to the French conversations. Finally I said to one of the other Vietnamese officers, "We are finished eating. Why don't we leave and get some rest?"

"Oh, no," he replied. "We cannot go until the captain tells us to leave." I remained at the table for hours, saying nothing, until the commander, rising to leave, dismissed us. The next day I was so tired that even in daylight I found myself sleepwalking, awakening on the march and not knowing how long I had been out. It was a regimen that could lead to suicide, and since no one else was doing anything about it, I resolved to end it.

And so the next day, after I finished my meal, I stood and said, very politely, "Please excuse me, I must go on an ambush patrol." After I got a few hours' rest, I assembled my troops and we marched out of the cantonment.

The next night I did the same, and the next, and the next. Finally there came the evening when I stood to give my excuses and the captain said, "About these ambushes. You don't have to go yourself. Let your master sergeant do that."

"Captain," I said, "I cannot sleep here while my men are lying awake in rice paddies. And anyway, I always sleep better in a rice paddy. If you want to stay and talk, then please stay. But we patrol the whole day and then again at night. We need some rest."

Again I left the base with my men, but this time I passed the word that if the commander continued in his stupid way, some day, when he was out on an operation, one of us would have to shoot him. Apparently this Frenchman got the message, because after that he no longer bothered me or the other Vietnamese officers with French army barracks bullshit. I stayed out of his way and spent most of my time in the field.

Our infantry company had three rifle platoons, and although I commanded only one, the two other Vietnamese lieutenants, draftees like myself, did little more than go through the motions—truly, they were not interested in fighting. A few years later, after Vietnam was partitioned, both would go on to medical school and become doctors. But in 1951, when we took to the field in search of the enemy, the French captain remained back at the fort. One day my two peers took me aside to say "You are so much better at all this army stuff than we are—why don't you just run all three platoons?" So I did, while they stayed a few kilometers to the rear and manned the radios. Thus I became, de facto if not de jure, the company commander.

Along with my new responsibilities came a nickname: my peers dubbed me "Barouder," French slang for a tough, gung-ho soldier, the kind of guy Americans would now call "Rambo."

Despite our constant nocturnal patrolling and the ambushes we set up near bridges and trails, and despite the fact that the Red River delta was by 1950 a Vietminh stronghold, we encountered the enemy infrequently. When we made contact during daylight, it was often an unplanned encounter in a village or hamlet. With a minimum of training and little combat experience, such street fighting seemed just like the movies. It seems very odd and funny now, thinking back, but I was a young city boy from Hanoi, with little appreciation for war's grimmer realities, and when I found myself having to play the role of a soldier in a street fight, I took old French movies as my cue.

I do not boast when I recall that I was not distracted or inhibited by fear. I have only respect for those with dangerous jobs who feel great fear but nevertheless perform their duties. I did my job because I knew that I had to do it. I did not ask to be a leader, but it was my responsibility to accomplish our missions, to look after the welfare of my men.

When a bullet cracked by especially close to my ear, I thought, Hey, see that, that was very close. But I felt no fear. For example, one day while assaulting an enemy village, we came under intense rifle fire. We were in muddy paddies, thick with waist-high rice stalks, so no matter how hard we tried we could not move fast. When the Vietminh began firing, invisible behind a bamboo thicket, we were all as vulnerable as the silhouette targets on a rifle range. But I felt nothing. Five feet away the soldier carrying my radio went down with a bullet in his chest. I took the radio and went on toward the shooters. With each step I sank deeper into the mud; it was an effort to pull myself forward. Yet it never came to my mind that I might be shot, that I might be killed. Instead, I focused only on taking the next step and then the next. My men saw this and followed me. And then we were across the paddy and the enemy was before us, and there were too many things to do to worry about being hit.

Some people have trouble understanding my lack of fear. But my responsibility was to lead my men, not worry about myself. Buddha would look out for me, but I had to look out for my troops. If I let fear get in my way, I could not lead the platoon to the best of my ability. So I never paid attention to fear. I never made any efforts to be "courageous." I merely did my job as well as I could. This, too, was part of being Buddha's child: I was born to understand and accept responsibility.

I approached the gritty business of playing for keeps urban combat with the same enthusiasm that I had known as a boy playing cops-and-robbers. I directed house-to-house battles as if I were in a movie. With Buddha looking over my shoulder, I didn't get shot. I lost very few of my men. Usually the enemy surrendered, ran away, or died fighting. Soon even the French began calling me Barouder. I took a little pride in my nickname, but only a little. I knew that I was just doing my job.

One day on patrol my platoon entered a village where the Vietminh lay in ambush in a bamboo thicket. Suddenly they all started shooting at me. As I sprinted for cover, my men returned fire and deployed. We exchanged fire for several minutes. There were only ten or fifteen of the enemy, and when they saw that we wouldn't retreat and that we had them outgunned, they split up. Individuals began running in every direction, trying to slip into the countryside where they could hide. In pursuit, I rounded a street corner and literally ran into a Vietminh fighter. He wore a straw hat and black, loose-fitting cotton shirt and trousers—the everyday garb of the Vietnamese peasant farmer—but he was carrying a rifle. All I had to do was snatch his rifle away and take him prisoner.

Years later I saw that when the French, and especially their Legionnaires, caught enemy soldiers, they beat them or tortured them for information. This was the first Vietminh that I had met face to face since joining the army, but I couldn't see him as my enemy. He was on one side, I was on the other, and we both wanted the same thing: national independence. But we had different visions of how that would be accomplished and what our country would be like—and so we had to fight. There was no hatred in it for me, and I sensed none in my captive.

I marched this man back to our fort, took him to my office, told him to sit down. I offered him a Phillip Morris, and he took the cigarette gratefully. I lit up as well, and for a few minutes we just sat together, two soldiers taking a smoke break, chatting about the war. We talked about our different duties, and it struck me that we had much in common. After a little time, I sent him off to a POW camp. Now and again I wonder what became of him.

As time went on I began to notice that the French treated my civilian countrymen as if they were all communists. Almost every day some of the French noncoms would go to some village and round up fifty or a hundred adults at gunpoint as "suspected communists." Then the "suspects" would be forced to dig ditches or carry stones—whatever hard work needed to be done around our cantonment. They were rarely fed and never paid for their efforts. I became frustrated and angry with such behavior. When they were dragged away from their homes, few, if any, of those people had any love for communism. By the time they got back to their villages, however, most of them would be more than willing to listen to the Vietminh cadres. Why couldn't the French see this?

One day I encountered a group of people who had been brought in by a couple of French NCOs to do some work. "Why are you here?" I asked. "What happened?

"I don't know," replied an elder. "The French came with guns and told us that we must accompany them here."

"So you are not communists?"

"No, no."

"Then you are free. You may go home. I apologize for your inconvenience."

A little later one of the French noncoms came over. "Who gave you the order to free those suspects?" he asked.

"I gave my own orders," I retorted. "These are not communists, so I let them go."

The sergeant said nothing, because he knew that I was right. By then, of course, I had shown the French soldiers at our fort that I was not one with whom they wanted to tangle; the NCO knew that if he made any trouble for me, I would shoot him, and all of the Vietnamese troops, as well as the whole of the local population, would back me.

...

Over several months, as the size of the Vietminh formations grew and as more weapons and ammunition were smuggled in from Red China, our enemy grew bolder. One night my company got into a firefight, but instead of quickly breaking contact, the Vietminh brought in reinforcements. Soon we were surrounded, and the enemy was pressing us on all sides. We were rescued by a company of tough Foreign Legion paratroops, who attacked from the rear and battled their way down the road to save us.

My life settled into a blur of patrolling and maintaining our weapons and equipment. This routine was interrupted by the arrival of a circular asking for volunteers to become pilots in Vietnam's new air force. Anyone who qualified had to go to Hanoi for five days for a physical examination and to take tests.

I wasn't especially interested in airplanes or the air force, and I was certain that I would never be selected for such an elite assignment. But I had not enjoyed even as much as a whole day off in months. The testing couldn't take all day *and* all night, I reasoned. Over five days in Hanoi I could get home-cooked meals, spend time with my family and friends, and relax. So I told my company commander, the French captain who never left the fort, that I wished to apply for pilot training.

"Oh, never," he replied. "We can't spare you! You are the best platoon leader, and there is no one to take your place. Request denied."

Still, he had to forward my request to the battalion commander. I was very surprised when this Frenchman approved my request. "Ky is a fine officer," he said. "We have to give him his due, and the air force needs a good element." And so I went off to Hanoi, happy to take a few boring exams in return for five days of rest and relaxation.

4
PILOT

I began my career in aviation as a writer. After a physical examination, tests in mathematics, and a few other matters, each applicant was asked to write an essay describing why we wanted to join the air force. Because flight training was conducted by the French air force, this essay was to be written in French. I suppose now that those reading the essays cared much less about *what* we wrote than about the way we wrote it; one had to be near fluent in French to absorb preflight instruction, especially navigation and aviation engineering principles.

I no longer recall what I said in that essay, but months later, back at the 20th Battalion, long after I had given up all hope, I received a letter of acceptance. I had been so sure that this would never happen that I had not told my family about taking the tests. Now I had to prepare to leave for France, and since I had little cash—most of my pay was sent home—I asked my mother to buy me some luggage.

"Where are you going?" she said, very surprised.

"I must go to France," I replied.

"But why? What for?"

"To learn how to fly airplanes."

"Airplanes—they are too dangerous!" cried Mother. "France is too far, can't you learn to fly closer to home?" By then she was crying.

I explained that I had already passed the examination and was under orders to go. If I failed to report, the army would put me in jail. Mother was unhappy about her precious only son leaving Vietnam, but she bought me nice luggage anyway.

We flew Air France to Paris, my first time aloft. Of some forty students in my class, most were noncoms; I was one of about sixteen officers, all lieutenants. After a brief orientation in Paris, we flew to Marrakech, Morocco, for basic flight training.

Shortly after I arrived I was promoted to first lieutenant; with a bonus for flight pay, my salary came to almost 30,000 francs. My mother, whose only son was forced to live in Morocco, deprived of all civilized amenities and yet forced to maintain appearances, decided that I must be in desperate need of money. She sent another 30,000 francs every month! At this time, France was still struggling to get its devastated economy back on track and was very poor. Morocco, though beautiful, was even poorer. A good meal in a Paris café cost then less than 50 francs, and in Marrakech less. Sixty thousand francs a month was a fortune to almost any Frenchman. Suddenly I was rich!

Unlike the Frenchmen with whom I had served in Vietnam, the air force's ranks were filled with well-educated, open-minded, and thoroughly professional men. When you are in the air, you don't care if your wingman or flight leader or copilot is a three-star general or a sergeant, or if he is black or white or brown. You care only if he can fly the plane. So the air forces of the world are very different from the armies. I perceived friendship from a different angle, I felt tolerance, mutual esteem, and esprit de corps.

My first flight instructor was a sergeant, an excellent pilot who treated me with respect and deference. I spent most of my days and many of my nights learning how to fly in a World War II–era U.S. trainer, the North American T-6 Texan. It was a sturdy, simple, low-wing monoplane with tandem seating, and after a few hours in the air, the aircraft came to seem like an extension of my own body. I believe that most people can be taught to fly, but my instructors soon began saying that I was a natural, one of the few born to be an aviator. I could sense the distance between my wheels and the approaching runway; while practicing formation flying I felt precisely how far my wings extended, so that I could ease into a slot only inches from the next plane. I became one with the machine: Below the level of consciousness, my body was aware of the tiniest movements of rudder or aileron. I loved it! I wanted to spend as much time aloft as possible. When we finished training in Marrakech, I was first in my class.

Before I went to France, I considered myself a romantic. Although I had never had a girlfriend, I had great admiration for women. In high school I had pined over a beautiful classmate who had seemed the very epitome of young womanhood. Our relationship remained perfectly chaste; I imagined loving and being loved by her, but we never touched. In the infantry, patrolling nightly and sleeping rarely, there was neither time nor opportunity to pursue women; I arrived in Europe a romantic innocent, a twenty-one-year-old virgin man. But not for long. The French women were beautiful, available, willing, and uninhibited. And I had all that money.

I also enjoyed playing the tourist. Everything was new to me, and when I visited the souks of Casablanca and the Medina, or old city area, in Marrakech, I noted that Jews and Arabs lived happily and peacefully together.

After mastering the T-6, my class transferred to Avord, near Bourges in the south of France, for multiengine training. When our flying schedules permitted, we caught the train to enjoy weekends in Paris. After a few months, I accumulated the grand sum of 200,000 francs. I decided that I would like to have a car, which would have contributed greatly to my social life and those of my Vietnamese classmates. So I told everyone that when I went to Paris next time I would buy a new Citroën and we would all share its use.

One Friday night I entrained for Paris, and the next morning visited a Citroën dealer. But by the time I found the one that I wanted and had dickered over the price and options, it was late on Saturday afternoon. The owner wanted to close, so the sales manager told me to come back Monday to complete the paperwork.

Paris was very romantic in the early 1950s, with many underground cabarets, including La Cave and the Lucky. By this time I had visited these clubs so often, spent so freely, and become so familiar to management that the maître d'hôtel began calling me "Prince." After that I never bothered with reservations—I just showed up and was escorted to a good table near the stage. So that Saturday night, with 200,000 francs in my pocket, I found myself at a front-row table surrounded by off-duty performers. I bought everyone drinks, and they toasted my health. There was a new singer that night, so very beautiful, and she sang like an angel. I was captivated. I rushed to a jewelry store and bought a diamond necklace, then had it delivered backstage in a bouquet of ten dozen roses. When she came on stage wearing the necklace, I said "Champagne, *pour tout le monde*," buy everyone a drink on me. With the singer on my arm I went to classier and more expensive places in Montparnasse and Montmartre, and I bought more bouquets, drank more champagne, bought rounds of drinks. I got a few hours of sleep on Sunday and went out again, having a fabulous time, drinking, eating, buying bouquets, and treating total strangers to drinks. Monday, completely and utterly broke, I took the train south.

My comrades had gathered near my quarters, waiting to see the new car, and I had to explain to them how I drank up that Citroën. I must say that they took it very well. Looking back, that was a wonderful time, the most carefree years of my life, with nothing to worry me, plenty of flying time, and the most wonderful evenings and weekends a young officer could imagine.

I had many girlfriends, including a lovely *pied noir,* as the French call their countrymen who were born in Algeria—they consider them more Algerian than French. After multi-engine training but before learning to fly transport aircraft, our class was sent to Algeria for strafing and bombing training. Delighted, she decided to return to her home to Algiers and asked me to stay with her family. For the few months that I spent in Algeria, I lived under their roof and was treated as family. Every day we became closer and more intimate. Nevertheless, I was only twenty-four, and I was not expecting to marry anyone for some time. And I knew that my mother expected me to marry a Vietnamese. Nevertheless, one thing led to another, and when my training was completed and I was ordered to return to Vietnam, we were married.

If my mother was disappointed that I had not married a Vietnamese, she said nothing. And my new wife, to her great and everlasting credit, very quickly began to learn not only our customs but also our language. In only two years she was fluent in Vietnamese, and she went out of her way to please my mother, who, bless her heart, accepted my wife completely. As time went on, however, and our children were born, I began to regret having married so young. When we divorced several years later, my daughter and four sons remained with me, their father, as is customary in most of Asia. My former wife later married an American colonel, and today we are on good terms.

The Vietnam that I returned to in 1954 was very different from the country that I had left. After their demoralizing defeat at Dien Bien Phu by the communists, the French had agreed to leave. Vietnam was partitioned near the 17th Parallel; for a year the borders remained open and the citizens of the entire country were allowed to vote with their feet. Over a million Tonkinese, mostly Catholics, went to live in what was now called the Republic of South Vietnam. Among those who moved south, however, were northern communists, cadres who would soon start organizing yet another insurrection.

Emperor Bao Dai reigned over South Vietnam, but even he knew that it wouldn't be for long. A smart, tough, English-speaking anticolonialist named Ngo Dinh Diem, who had gone into exile and refused to serve in French puppet governments, formed a political party and began organizing to run for president.

All of that had taken place while I was in Europe and North Africa. By the time I got back to Vietnam, my own family had fled to Saigon, and it took me a while to find them. Hundreds of thousands of northerners fled in sampans, fishing boats, and small ships; more hundreds of thousands of political refugees walked or rode south on narrow, traffic-choked roads; on the last few days before the borders closed, the VNAF, South Vietnam's tiny, fledgling air force, evacuated thousands of people from Hanoi and Haiphong, which had the only two suitable airports. I flew many loads of refugees to the South.

On the day before the borders were sealed, I landed in Haiphong for one last evacuation flight. I caught a cab to downtown, where I wanted to have a last meal in my homeland and take a last look around. I sat at a restaurant table in my flight suit, eating slowly, savoring the moments before my exile. Suddenly a man about my age sat down at my table. He was a communist cadre, and for more than half an hour he tried his best to convince me to remain in the North. "Communism is the future," he said, but from my teen wanderings I knew more of the real face of communism than he did. I remained polite, even as he grew insistent. Finally I said, "No, thank you," and left.

Minutes later I was at the controls of a C-47, rolling down the Cat Bi Airport runway with the last group of refugees to leave the North. Packed into the cargo area were almost twice the number of people that the aircraft was designed to carry. I used every last foot of pavement before we had enough airspeed to stagger aloft. When I had about a thousand meters below me, I banked into a long spiral, watching the countryside roll away beneath my wings. It would be a long time before I saw my homeland again, even from the air. At this writing, I still look forward to again setting foot in the country of my birth.

5
WING COMMANDER

THE years immediately following the division of Vietnam into North and South, a relatively peaceful time, were for me the happiest and most tranquil period of my military career. In the South, the communist Vietcong kept a low profile. We know now that they were building an infrastructure, recruiting followers, and training a guerrilla army. There were incidents, of course—armed clashes, kidnappings, assassinations—but only enough to keep the pot boiling, and large North Vietnamese units had not yet crossed the border.

The North followed doctrinaire communist ideology, applying it to every sector of the nation. In the South we experimented with capitalist methods, with new forms of governance, with trying to turn an aggregation of religious cultures and competing political factions into a unified nation.

On paper, North and South Vietnam were twin countries born at the same moment. Compared to the sophisticated North, however, the government of South Vietnam was a very young and innocent sibling. Through participation in a series of international conferences and by pursuing a guerrilla war against a European power, Ho Chi Minh and the Hanoi leadership had demonstrated that they were a formidable political reality. The Hanoi regime took power with a record of resistance against colonialism and of struggle for national independence. By claiming to be liberators and disguising their communist design, they enjoyed from the outset the admiration and sympathy of the majority of the so-called nonaligned nations. That support was at least in part because these Third World countries often suffer from "oppressed people's complex." Their leaders reflexively oppose mighty and wealthy countries like France and the United States. Since South Vietnam had ties to both nations, it was easy to dismiss our nation as a mere puppet of "imperialists."

Moreover, in the South, political and military activities were at first heavily influenced by the French, who made most important decisions. France installed Bao Dai as the Republic of Vietnam's first head of state. A playboy with few intellectual pretensions and fewer attainments, he was a figurehead with no capacity to govern. But he was also the last ruler of the dynasty that had reigned for centuries, and that provided just enough of a fig leaf to spare the departing French the messy details of finding a more appropriate figure. All the men selected for the Bao Dai government were closely linked with the French colonial era. They enjoyed no support among those whom they governed, and consequently they soon gave way to Ngo Dinh Diem, a Catholic who brought to our newly independent nation an able and dignified leadership. I had never voted, but in 1955 I joined my friends and family and cast my ballot for Diem.

President Diem came from a noble family. In the seventeenth century his ancestors were among the first Vietnamese to embrace Roman Catholicism, and as a young man Diem became friendly with members of the Vietnamese imperial family. In 1933 he served as minister of the interior in Emperor Bao Dai's Annam, or Central Kingdom. Diem resigned after only a few months, however, frustrated because the French, who held the real power, would not permit any of the reforms that he proposed. Diem returned to private life until 1945, when he was captured in Hue by some of Ho Chi Minh's men. Hoping that Diem's presence would win Catholic support, Ho invited him to join the government that he had proclaimed in the North. Instead, Diem went into exile, spending nine years in France and the United States.

Shortly before the Geneva Accords and Vietnam's 1954 partition, Diem returned to honor Bao Dai's request to serve as prime minister, with the emperor reigning as chief of state. After the partition, however, Bao Dai was ousted in a referendum controlled by Diem's government, and Diem became the first president of the new South Vietnam. Splintered by dissident groups and competing factions, the South was so politically unsophisticated that Diem knew that the communists would exploit this weakness to gain control of the whole country. So he refused to allow participation in the 1956 nationwide election that the Geneva Accords had specified would establish a Vietnamese national government.

Instead, unable to trust Buddhists or leaders of competing factions, Diem appointed members of his own family to the top posts in his government. One of his government's most immediate problems was resettling nearly a million refugees from the North, a task accomplished with U.S. military and economic aid.

When he came to power, I believe that Diem had good intentions. South Vietnam was an unstable mess, with several military and paramilitary factions competing for power. Diem achieved unity by eliminating or suppressing these factions. But as time went on he became more and more isolated from the people, relying on reports from his brother and other close kin. His obvious preference for Roman Catholics invited criticism from the Buddhists, who were the overwhelming majority in South Vietnam. Even worse, however, was his family's insatiable greed. His brother Ngo Dinh Nhu created a Vietnamese gestapo that every South Vietnamese feared. Police informants were everywhere, and Nhu's goons terrorized anyone suspected of opposing the regime, driving countless peasants into the arms of the communists. Upon taking office, Diem launched a program of land reform, returning land to the peasants who had worked it for millennia. Nhu reversed this policy, and by 1960 three-fourths of all South Vietnam's land belonged to just 15 percent of the population.

We Vietnamese are fond of saying that "the emperor's power ends at the village gates." And indeed, for centuries each village was free to elect its own leaders and establish its own governing rules. In an effort to root out all opposition, however, Nhu repudiated that ancient bargain. In the name of security he replaced elected village chiefs and governing councils with hand-picked henchmen. These "professionals," many of whom had never lived in a farming community, quickly alienated villagers and not incidentally enriched themselves and their political superiors. Even the French colonizers had never dared this strategy. Ho Chi Minh could not have asked for more cooperation had he put Nhu on the communist payroll. Every disgusted villager became a prime candidate for communism.

Strangely, Nhu's activities, carried out in his brother's name, invited no criticism from the Americans, whose millions sent to stop the spread of communism instead lined Nhu's pockets. President Dwight Eisenhower praised Diem's patriotism and promised continued support for his programs. In the succeeding Kennedy administration, Vice President Lyndon Johnson declared that Ngo Dinh Diem was "the Winston Churchill of Asia."

I was one of the few command officers who made it a point to spend time with junior officers and noncoms, to stay in touch with the common people. As I earned their trust, they spoke openly in my presence of their frustration and anger with the ever-widening gap between rich and poor in Vietnam. But if I was aware of Diem's shortcomings, as a comparatively junior military man, my life in those years was devoted to flying and socializing. I had been invited to join Diem's Can Lao party, but I declined. Then and now, I did not think that military officers should engage in political activities. So I tried to avoid even thinking about politics. I had my hands full trying to build the VNAF into a capable, modern organization.

The VNAF was part of ARVN, the Army of the Republic of Vietnam, and then neither a large nor an important component. We had a few dozen helicopters, a squadron of North American T-28 trainers configured as short-range fighter-bombers, some L-19s—small, single-engine, high-wing monoplanes used mostly to adjust artillery fire—a few Bearcat naval fighters left over from World War II, and a lone squadron of Douglas C-47 transports.

All our aircraft, including the C-47s, the military version of the DC-3 that first flew in the 1930s, were castoffs from the U.S. and French forces. To Vietnamese airmen, however, the C-47 was important. It was the biggest and most modern aircraft we possessed at the time, and it was capable of international travel. To train me for C-47 operations, I spent several months attached to the French Squadron Senegal, which was based at Saigon.

A year or so after the partition of Vietnam, our French advisors departed; the VNAF became a totally Vietnamese organization. On his last day in Saigon, the French major who had called the shots for the First Transport Squadron, a thoroughly professional airman, asked me into his office. Without preamble he got down to business. "Captain Ky, you are now the squadron leader," he said.

"Thank you," I replied, trying not to show my astonishment. There were more than a dozen other VNAF officers of my same grade and length of military service. I had never asked for this or any promotion, never sought it, never maneuvered for favor with anyone so that I would be selected for the position. So I was surprised, but I knew that I could handle the job.

Two or three months later, about the time that I began to think that there was nothing much to being squadron leader, the VNAF acquired sixteen more C-47s and their related support equipment, enough for a second squadron. Again I had no advance warning; the colonels and generals of the army chief of staff's office never consulted me. Together these two squadrons comprised a wing, and a wing requires its own headquarters and commanding officer. Suddenly I was Major Ky, commander of First Transport Wing, the VNAF's unit with the most modern equipment. The United States Air Force also flew C-47s—the oldest aircraft in *their* inventory.

We were based at Tansonnhut, the sprawling civil and military airport outside Saigon, by far the most important VNAF base at a time when our installations at Bien Hoa, Soc Trang, and Da Nang were still quite small. Army brass decided that Tansonnhut needed a base commander, and since my wing was the biggest unit on the base, I was given that hat to wear as well. I was twenty-six, probably the youngest major in Vietnam, and certainly the youngest to command an air base of any size.

Until 1960, when the VNAF became a separate service, I reported directly to the army chief of staff's office. After that I reported to Lieutenant Colonel Nguyen Xuan Vinh, who had been among my classmates in France. Vinh was a brilliant scientist who would go on to a career of great achievements as a professor of aeronautics at the University of Michigan. He was not much of a leader or pilot—as an instructor on single-engine aircraft he was barely competent—but he was an avid supporter of President Diem and had become an early member of the Can Lao party. His promotion to lieutenant colonel and command of the VNAF was a reward for this political loyalty.

The VNAF had few pilots, not even enough to fly all the available aircraft, and we also supplied pilots for Air Vietnam, the new national airline that was a prideful component of our developing nationhood. For those reasons, although I had many administrative duties as base commander and wing commander, I was also obliged to fly many missions. I was in the air nearly every day, which suited me fine. Often I ferried top military or civilian officials from Saigon to another part of the country. Our C-47s also were used to deploy the ARVN's elite paratroop and ranger units, and I flew many of their training missions, hauling "sticks" of troopers over a drop zone about five minutes' flying time from Tansonnhut.

Aside from Saigon, Da Nang, and Nha Trang, most South Vietnamese landing fields were small. Many had extremely short runways and lacked air control towers, radios, and navigation beacons. At some fields there was nothing but a dirt runway—not even a wind sock. Untrained to operate under such primitive conditions, I had to teach myself how to make safe landings and takeoffs, and then I had to show my pilots how to do the same. After two or three years I became very familiar with these fields. I knew every runway pothole, every tricky crosscurrent, every hazardous approach obstruction, every fold in the surrounding terrain that might offer concealment to an enemy.

In memory these years of flying, between 1955 and 1963, seemed more exhilarating than dangerous. They were romantic times, reminiscent of the era of early flight personified by Charles Lindbergh, Wiley Post, and Antoine de Saint-Exupéry. We flew under all weather conditions, and because our aircraft were old and comparatively primitive, it was common for engines to quit, for radios to fail, for navigation devices to malfunction. But after those years of flying, for me handling a C-47 became as easy and natural as riding a bicycle.

I was one of the few Vietnamese qualified as an instructor pilot for multiengine aircraft, so I spent much time training and certifying command pilots. I also instituted an Air Transport Wing training program that included overseas flights. I was at the controls of the very first Vietnamese plane to land in Japan, the first to land in Australia, Taiwan, and Hong Kong and in several other nations.

On one navigation training mission, a long flight over water, we flew to Tokyo, with refueling stops in Hong Kong and Okinawa. On the first leg of the return flight, between Tokyo and Okinawa, we encountered an enormous cold front, miles high and over a thousand miles wide. It was snowing, and our C-47 had no deicing system to remove ice accumulating on our wings and fuselage. All we could do was blow hot air on the windscreen so that we could at least see out of the aircraft.

We couldn't climb over this storm because our engines lacked high-altitude superchargers, and even so, our crew oxygen was good up to only about 12,000 feet. So I descended, hoping that the snow would become rain at lower altitudes, that the sheath of ice growing on our wings would melt. But even at 1,000 feet all we could see was walls of falling snow. Our radio was working, but, because of the storm and our low altitude, reception was intermittent. Our radio compass, which depends on signals from known fixed points, could find no station and drifted idly. We flew on dead reckoning, noting airspeed and heading. Without knowing the exact bearing and strength of winds, however, I could not tell how far west the storm had blown us. Worried about intruding into Red China's airspace, I turned eastward into the Pacific. After a time we made contact with Kadena, a U.S. Air Force base on Okinawa. Kadena had us on radar, and since we were hundreds of miles west of our flight plan, apparently coming out of China, we were asked to identify ourselves. When I reported that we were a VNAF C-47 en route from Tokyo to Saigon, the USAF air controller didn't believe it. "Why are you headed that way?" he said.

I told them about the storm and the ice on our wings, about not being able to get above the front. I said, "Please, give me a heading and invite us to land."

As we taxied in, very low on fuel, the Kadena tower said, "Have your captain please report to the tower." I presented myself to the officer in charge, and explained what had happened, and invited him to inspect my plane, to see for himself that we were from South Vietnam, that we had no contraband. "I got lost, that's all," I said. That sort of thing happened often in those years.

...

My wing soon became well known throughout the military and also by top civilian leaders. Hardly a day went by without one or more of my aircraft flying a mission for some VIP. At that time President Diem's army chief of staff was the elderly General Le Van Ty, who had served in the French army as a master sergeant. Like many old generals, however, Ty found flying a fearful ordeal.

I don't know exactly why—maybe he heard that young Major Ky was the Air Transport Wing's best pilot—but every time General Ty had to fly he demanded me as his pilot. Knowing that even a little turbulence made him sick—and scared him silly—I tried to avoid unstable air, climbing over or detouring around stormy areas. Usually I made a very smooth flight, a very smooth landing, and thus I kept the old man happy.

Through his long service under the French, he had acquired some of the worst habits of French soldiers. He used a lot of bawdy slang, called everyone bad names, and cursed loudly at anything that annoyed him. He often behaved as if he were in the field. For example, one night while riding through Saigon in a small convoy from his office to his home, he suddenly told the driver to stop. He walked down the road to relieve himself in a gutter. A passing policeman saw a man urinating and began shouting at the general's back. When the old man swiveled around to face the officer and display his uniform, topped by a general's cap, the cop got a big surprise.

General Ty was Old Army, incapable of wartime leadership but a grand, patriarchal figure nonetheless. If some soldier had dirty boots or needed a haircut, Ty might give him ten or fifteen days in the brig—on the spot, no bother with a court-martial.

Despite his spit-and-polish emphasis, everyone knew that he had a good heart.

One day I had to fly old Ty somewhere, and as he was about to board the plane, he looked at me strangely. "Ky! Why are you wearing a mustache?" he bellowed. At that time, no one in the army was allowed facial hair unless he had obtained Ty's authorization. Because of his French army background, however, the general never approved such requests.

"I don't remember that you have my permission to wear a mustache," he said, sounding very irritated.

"No, sir," I replied. "I never asked you."

"Why do you want this mustache? What is this about?"

"General, the only reason I wear this mustache is that women like me with it. If I shave it off, then woman will not like me any more."

He laughed. "Okay!" he said. "You send me an application, and I will give you permission. We will make it official, otherwise you will appear undisciplined." I was not the only VNAF officer with a mustache, but from then on I was the only one with written permission.

Another time, Ty told me that I had to discipline one of my flight mechanics. "What has he done, sir?" I asked.

"He offered me a cigarette," said the old gentleman. "And I had never invited him to speak."

That was the French way. Contact was always initiated by the senior. Even a junior sergeant could not approach his platoon master sergeant except on urgent military business. Even then, he had to wait until the senior noncom told him to speak.

"This mechanic meant no disrespect," I explained. "He is a very poor guy. On payday he can barely afford to buy a pack of cigarettes. I can tell you that he has never offered *me* a cigarette! If he offered one to you, then it must mean that he has more respect for you than for me. That he loves you more than he loves me."

"Ah!" said the old general. "Now I understand."

In moving south, my family gave up their farm and left their businesses behind. My mother started over, but by then she was more than sixty years old, having problems with her health, and there was a lot of competition in the South because few businessmen had remained in the North. Mother made a living but was never able to attain the affluent lifestyle that we had enjoyed in the North. Sadly, I couldn't help her much, because VNAF officers, even pilots, were poorly paid, and I soon had three small children of my own to support.

Knowing this, General Ty took a fatherly interest in me. He knew that although I was poor, I did not steal from my troops or accept bribes for promotions or favors, as many army officers did. South Vietnam had no dairies, no fresh milk. Canned milk had to be imported and was so expensive that only the wealthy could afford it. Ty told his aide to send two cases of milk to my home every month. Beyond his kindness, I took his deed as a lesson about caring deeply about the welfare of my troops.

...

In 1958 I was promoted to lieutenant colonel and transferred from the Air Force Headquarters to serve as VNAF operations chief. Around the same time, American advisors began to arrive in large numbers, and they believed that all senior VNAF officers should undergo U.S. training to learn their ways. Perhaps because I had studied English as well as French at the lycée, and because I was working more and more with USAF officers, I was sent to the U.S. Air Force Command and Staff College at Maxwell Air Force Base, Alabama.

It was my first visit to America, but I did not particularly enjoy it. Then and now, I considered it a waste of time. And although I spent six or seven months in America, I saw little of the country; I could not afford to travel, even on weekends. More to the point, I was not flying, and the entire curriculum consisted of books and paperwork, which I find boring. My

American classmates were courteous enough, and we enjoyed each other's respect as airmen, but I made no lasting friendships. The only event that stands out in my mind was the first time that I tried Coca-Cola, which was not then available in Vietnam. Aside from a drinking fountain that dispensed harsh-tasting water, five-cent bottles of Coke were the only drinks available in the Bachelor Officers Quarters. I soon came to detest the taste, which was too sweet for my palate. But I got my ticket punched, and when I returned to Vietnam, I went back to my former position as air transport wing and base commander.

...

By 1960 there was an undeclared state of war between the two Vietnams. The communists regularly sent intelligence agents and other infiltrators into the South, and because we had a relatively free society, many escaped detection. But we were getting no intelligence from the North. One day I got a call from Colonel Vinh, the VNAF commander, who told me that the American Central Intelligence Agency had proposed a mission to send intelligence agents into North Vietnam using South Vietnamese airfields and aircraft. "Do you think you can do it?" he asked.

"Of course," I said. "Just tell me what you want done, and we'll do it."

Considering such a mission, I decided that the best way to insert people into the North from the air would be to come in at night from the sea, very low, under the enemy's naval radar, and follow a river upcountry to the mountainous and relatively unpopulated border area, where the agents could be parachuted to the ground. When Vinh asked for the names of the first crew to be trained for this mission, my own name topped the list. Vinh did not like this at all. "You are wing commander," he said. "You cannot go on such a mission."

"Tell me a reason why I can't go," I replied.

"Because you are the commander, and this is a very dangerous mission!"

"I must fly the first mission to prove that it can be done," I said. "Once we know that it works, then I can show other pilots the way to do it."

Vinh didn't like it, but finally he agreed. A few instructors, Americans in civilian clothes, flew in from the States, and we started our night training, flying C-47s from Saigon to the mountainous region near Da Lat, about a hundred miles northeast. We did so well that after a few days it was apparent that we didn't need American help. They went home, and after that, night after night, in any weather, we flew practice missions, following riverbeds through narrow mountain passes, learning to maneuver at low altitude in tight airspace at night.

Our objective was to drop small groups of agents with radios. After landing, they would disperse and take up residence in different towns. Once they were established, they could be used for almost any intelligence purpose or perhaps, eventually, as saboteurs. I didn't need to know much about that end of the mission; my job was merely to deliver the agents to the North and get back undetected and in one piece.

Several weeks before the first mission I was introduced to William Colby, who would later become chief of the U.S. Central Intelligence Agency; he was in charge of our mission. A compact, handsome fellow who spoke French but not Vietnamese, Colby was about forty, but with his thick eyeglasses and disarming demeanor, he might have passed for a student or an accountant. We became friends, often going out for dinner or a drink. As I came to know him better I realized that behind those inoffensive glasses was a brilliant mind—he didn't miss much. Colby was pleasant, good company, but unfailingly serious. In all the years that I knew him, I saw him smile only once.

For the North Vietnam infiltration mission, the CIA built a scale model of the entire flight profile, complete with every important terrain detail, including mountains, rivers, and bridges. We moved to the Bien Hoa Air Base north of Saigon to begin final training; once that began, we were confined to the field and could not leave for any reason. My job was to get the aircraft to the right spot at the right time. This was to be a night mission, and there would be few landmarks visible along our route. Once we were inland, we had to fly by dead reckoning. That meant dividing the flight plan into small segments of five minutes or so each, keeping very careful watch over airspeed, and making each preplanned course correction by the clock. With nothing to enhance the pilot's night vision, we didn't dare use lights in the cockpit, not even to read the map. I had to memorize every detail of the entire flight plan.

Upward of twelve hours a day we practiced the navigation and the rest of the mission. During this training, as during the mission, the copilot and the navigator stood behind me, calling out the time in one-minute intervals. "Three minutes, two minutes, coming up on the turn of the river, thirty degrees left, one more minute . . ." I had to keep every detail in my mind. To make sure I did not make a mistake, my copilot and navigator also memorized the flight plan.

We went over it again and again, by day and again by night, sitting in a C-47 cockpit inside a closed hangar. Even while I slept, the flight path was always in my mind, the map, the route, the elevation of surrounding terrain, how many minutes and how many seconds to fly at what speed for each leg of the flight, where the river turned, the locations of bridges, power lines, or other obstructions. Even now, I think, I could fly most of that route without looking at a map. Just give me a C-47.

On the day before the mission we flew to Da Nang, about three hundred miles north of Saigon. We tried to rest, but if everyone was as keyed up as I was, I doubt that anyone got much sleep. In early evening we went together, agents and aircrew, to a Chinese restaurant, for what might be our last meal. As we sat around the table my copilot pilot said, "Colonel, we are thirteen! It is unlucky! I should stay here."

I could tell that he was afraid. "Thirteen or thirteen and a half, you will go," I said.

After dark we went through a final check of our aircraft. As a full moon rose over the South China Sea, six or seven Vietnamese men in dark, nondescript farmer's clothing loaded equipment and parachutes into our ship, then climbed in. These were all volunteers, on the American CIA payroll and specially trained for this mission. It would be a long time before I knew much more than that about them.

Like our passengers, the aircrew wore the black cotton pajamas of the Vietnamese peasant farmer. In our pockets were small sums of North Vietnamese money, North Vietnamese cigarettes, even North Vietnamese matches. If our plane went down over enemy territory, we needed to be able to blend in with the locals. But each of us also carried a hundred U.S. dollars, in case we had to bribe someone. Even then it seemed funny: If we crashed in those mountains or over the sea, I could foresee no situation where we might have time enough to use our parachutes. If we went down, we would be very lucky to have any use for currency or cigarettes.

We took off from Da Nang, near the southern end of the Gulf of Tonkin, climbed to several thousand feet, then headed out to sea. Once we were out of sight of land, I eased the stick forward. We descended and when I could see white froth atop individual waves, I leveled off. We were two or three feet above the water at nearly 200 miles per hour, as fast as we could fly, and if enemy radar was pointed our way we hoped that our image would be lost in the clutter of the perpetually moving sea surface.

After heading east for several minutes, I brought the nose around to the left until it was pointed north by northwest, a bearing of about 330 degrees that took us straight for the mouth of the Red River. At Thanh Hoa we turned inland, crossing into North Vietnamese airspace.

The navigator standing behind me said, "This is my country!" We all felt it. Most of my crew, and all of the CIA agents, were northerners, and this was the first time that any of us had been this close to our homeland. It was a strange and humbling feeling, but I put it aside to think about later. I needed to focus every bit of my attention on the mission at hand.

Once inland, we followed the Red River. We might have flown within rifle shot of my former patrol area in the 20th Battalion a decade earlier. With the light of a full moon behind me to illuminate the landscape and no more worries about naval radar, I climbed just enough to avoid bridges and power lines. North and west of Hanoi we passed near my childhood home in Son Tay. The land rose, the river valley narrowed, and the dark bulk of mountains loomed all around. With my copilot and navigator calling out course changes, we found the drop zone without difficulty. As far as I could tell by moonlight, every parachute opened.

It was impossible that no one on the ground had heard us pass, but they had no time to react. If we returned the same way that we had come, however, we knew that the communists would be waiting. So with our cargo delivered, we continued west into Laos. Once out of North Vietnamese airspace I climbed to 12,000 feet, then flew south until we could turn east. Inside friendly airspace we were finally able to relax. I let the autopilot take over while we smoked a few cigarettes.

It was dawn when we landed in Saigon and taxied to an unmarked hanger. To my astonishment, Colby was waiting inside with a whole group of Americans and Vietnamese—and two cases of good French champagne. It never tasted better.

We trained five or six teams for these missions, and over the next few months I flew several others, each by a different route and to a different drop zone. We refined and made small adjustments to our standard operating procedures. For example, instead of spending hours in Da Nang on the day of the mission, we flew out of Saigon and stopped at Da Nang only for fuel and last-minute weather information.

After our second or third mission, Colby came to Tansonnhut with a delegation of Americans from Washington. They all wore civilian clothes; I assume that they were CIA officials out to observe how well my pilots performed. Colby asked me to fly them from Saigon to Hue, and I did so in routine fashion. For the return trip, however, I decided to give them a taste of what their agents encountered. I flew out to sea, then turned south and descended until our prop blast blew foam off the wavetops. Then I pushed the throttles forward and flew at maximum speed. At this point, my crew later told me, all the Americans became very pale.

An hour later, standing safely on the Tansonnhut tarmac, Colby smiled—his first, as far as I know. "Next time I go flying with you I'll bring my fishing rod," he said.

A few weeks later, about five on the afternoon of what was to be my third penetration mission, I left my office at the air transport wing and went home to prepare for an 8:00 P.M. departure. Driving through the base housing area, I spotted Lieutenant Phan Thanh Van, one of my best pilots, standing in front of his apartment unit. Contrary to regulations, he usually flew barechested to beat the heat and rarely bothered with a safety belt. He waved when he saw me, and I stopped. He invited me in for a drink, but I declined, explaining that I was flying that night. "I have a date to go dancing with a girl in Saigon tonight, but right now I am going to call her and break it," I said. "Maybe I'll stop by tomorrow, when I come home."

"If you have a date tonight, I'll go in your place," said Van, a handsome lady killer well known in Saigon nightclubs. "I'd like to fly that mission tonight."

"If you want to take it, then go," I replied. About 1:00 A.M. the duty officer called me to the phone at the nightclub to say that the plane was missing and presumed down over the North. It would be almost a decade before I learned that Van's plane was shot down. When the aircraft hit the ground he was thrown through the cockpit window—and thus survived the fire that killed almost everyone else aboard.

Van's face was sliced up by windshield fragments, but Hanoi plastic surgeons restored much of his handsome visage. After his operation, however, he was locked up in Hoa Lo Prison, the infamous "Hanoi Hilton." His flight engineer, the only other survivor of the mission, died there. Van was freed after several years and eked out a bare living doing menial work in Hanoi. Then a relative in France, working through the French ambassador, got North Vietnam to allow him to emigrate to France.

How easy it was to get lost or run out of fuel became clear to me on my next penetration mission. After an uneventful flight into North Vietnam, we arrived over the drop zone on a cloudless night with a good moon behind us to provide light. All our agents got out cleanly, all their chutes opened—a perfect drop. We climbed and turned south, heading inland through Laos again. Once we were at altitude and out of North Vietnamese airspace, everything was routine. So I told the copilot and navigator, "Take us home." I went back to the cargo area, rolled up in a blanket, and went to sleep.

About two hours later the navigator woke me up. "Captain," he said. "I don't know where we are. I think we've had a very strong side wind—maybe we are somewhere over Burma. Or China."

I looked out of the cabin window. We were at about 13,000 or 14,000 feet, and below us in every direction stretched an endless sea of white clouds. We tuned around the dial, but our radio compass could find no station from which to get a bearing. Strangely, our long-range radio had also failed. I thought for a few minutes. "Okay, we are too far northwest, so we'll head southeast. In about an hour and a half we should reach the coast of Vietnam near Da Nang." I was guessing, but I couldn't let the crew know. While the copilot had indicated that we might have been over Burma or China, in truth we might have been anywhere.

Central Vietnam has towering mountains, but after flying by the compass for ninety minutes and covering about 300 miles, we could still see nothing but clouds, as if the whole planet were mysteriously shrouded in cotton. If we were near where I thought we were when we turned southeast, then we should have been near Da Nang, perhaps even past the coast and over the sea.

Our fuel was almost gone. My only option was to descend, hoping that when we came down through the clouds we would find the ocean. If I guessed wrong, of course, we would probably slam into a mountain.

Still radiating confidence, I told my crew that I could smell Da Nang and the sea. I throttled back and very slowly we began to slide down through the clouds. It was like swimming in an ocean of cotton batting—for several minutes we could see nothing but clouds that got darker and darker as we lost altitude. At any moment I expected to hit a mountain. Passing 7,000 feet I began to breathe again. We were either totally lost or over the sea.

Both fuel gauges rested on empty; we might have ten minutes of flying time left—or only seconds. I gave the order to prepare to ditch at sea. If I saw the surface in time, I would try to keep the angle of our impact gentle enough to hope that the plane would hold together long enough to launch our life rafts.

Altimeters in those days were calibrated on the ground by adjusting to the air pressure. When we left Saigon it had been cloudless, a sign of high pressure. Now, clearly, the pressure was lower. I knew that we couldn't trust this instrument to give an exact reading. As the altimeter unwound past 2,000 feet, impenetrable clouds gave way to falling fountains. We were in the midst of a cloudburst! I switched on the landing lights but could see nothing but sparkling raindrops. It was about 3:00 A.M., and with the lights off, beyond the windshield it was black as a peasant's pajamas. We had no choice but to continue the descent.

When the altimeter read 300 feet, ocean waves appeared in our landing lights. I leveled off and reiterated the order to strap in and prepare for ditching. I wished that I could have sent an SOS, but our radio was still out. We might ditch safely only to drift for days or weeks, until thirst drove us mad.

At 200 feet, gripping the wheel hard and preparing to ease down into the waves, I glanced to my left through the window— and saw a tiny light. Even as I thought Wait a moment, that must be the coast of South Vietnam, I banked to the left and yanked the nose up. There was Da Nang, maybe five minutes away. Maybe we could still make it.

We roared over the city so low that I am sure people leaped from their beds and dogs howled. In those years the runway was closed at night. There was no one in the tower, no lights to aim for. But I had flown over this city and into this field dozens of times, and we were well trained in night operations. I turned on landing lights and followed the beach until the airport appeared, then banked sharply and landed. We had taxied about 300 meters when both engines hiccuped, then quit. We coasted to a stop in the middle of the runway. During over eight hours in the air we had burned every drop of gasoline in our tanks.

As we waited a few minutes for a reception committee, I suddenly realized that we were all wearing black pajamas, exactly like the farmers. Exactly like the Vietcong! We walked toward the fence, and a pair of armed sentries appeared.

"Stop, who is there!" called one.

"Cao Ky!" yelled my men, almost in unison.

"What is the password?" asked a man with a rifle.

"I don't know," I replied. "Call the base commander."

When he arrived, still sleepy, the base commander was not sure what to do. "What are you doing here?" he asked. "What happened?"

We were very lucky that night, because the commander came before one of the sentries got frightened and shot us, and most of all because we did not fall into the sea.

Such good fortune, however, was not what was in store for the brave men when we had delivered over the North. Every last one of them was picked up by the communists, most within a few days of arrival. A few were shot, the rest imprisoned. Some spent over thirty years in confinement before they were released. The CIA, which had invested a large effort in this operation, had failed to note that virtually all North Vietnamese wear sandals. All the men that we dropped in wore shoes. We also failed to realize that after only five years in power, the communists had so thoroughly indoctrinated the people that there were many subtle but telling disparities in the way northerners and southerners spoke and acted. There were differences in vocabulary— certain words that southerners used, for example—and in the way people tendered pleasantries. Northerners even ate differently, used different condiments to season their soup, and gripped their spoons with different fingers.

Furthermore, so completely had the communists organized their society that anyone not known to a particular small, insular community was immediately viewed with suspicion. When the men that we dropped in sparsely populated areas appeared in towns or villages, they were soon spotted as outsiders.

So we made mistakes, and these cost men their lives or their liberty. Nevertheless, we were fighting a war. We had to try to get intelligence, even at the sacrifice of dozens of men. I think the agents understood this. Most survived their captivity, and when they were finally released in 1995 the U.S. government gave each of them a cash settlement of $50,000. There could never be enough money to repay these men for their suffering, but their service was noted with appreciation, and besides the money they were welcomed to live in the United States if they so chose. I believe that every one of them left Vietnam.

By the end of 1961 the CIA knew that something had gone very wrong with their efforts to establish clandestine forces in the North, and the operation was discontinued. In the South, the communists, who now called themselves the Vietcong, or National Liberation Front (NLF), had begun to escalate their guerrilla attacks. There were more and bigger ambushes of ARVN troops; in response, the ARVN mounted more counter-insurgency operations and acquired more American advisors.

As the VNAF flew more missions in support of these operations, its role became more important to the war effort. We got more aircraft, including a squadron of Skyraiders, a big, powerful single-engine attack plane fitted with bombs, rockets, and cannon and used in support of ground operations.

When the richest and most powerful nation in the world opens its coffers, hardware is relatively easy to come by. Pilots were another matter. By 1962 the VNAF had only 225 qualified pilots but 271 cockpit or staff flight positions. To enhance VNAF capability, eighteen of my pilots were transferred to other combat squadrons, and a detachment of American pilots was assigned to the First Air Transport Wing, the first time that American pilots flew under a foreign commander—me.

The first group arrived in April 1962, thirty pilots, mostly captains, under Major Charles P. Barnett, USAF, who had previously flown with the VNAF while serving as a USAF advisor. Because Vietnamese consider billy goats as especially randy, perpetually seeking sex—in the same way as most military pilots— and because Americans think of goats as dirty, the detachment chose as their logo the head of a billy goat superimposed on a lightning bolt, and called themselves the Dirty Thirty. How this name actually came about remains in dispute. One story is that after days of flying, an American pilot was accosted by a senior

U.S. Army officer who berated him for hygienic failure. Another story is that some Vietnamese referred to Americans as goats because they ate out of tin cans. But I think the reason was that there was a popular Vietnamese lottery that used the goat as a symbol for the number thirty.

Although a Vietnamese officer was nominally in command of each aircraft, in practice the USAF pilots shared flying duties equally with their Vietnamese comrades. At the outset, some Americans doubted the abilities of their Vietnamese counterparts—including my own. This was not an unusual attitude, because every good military pilot considers himself the best to ever strap on a parachute. For example, several months before the Dirty Thirty arrived, I flew as copilot with Colonel Benjamin King, a World War II fighter ace who had made a daring escape from behind Japanese lines in China. Our mission that day was to drop propaganda leaflets, and when we had finished Colonel King headed back to base, one of sixty Vietnamese airfields where a C-47 could land—but not one of the thirteen that had paved runways. We came in too fast, used too much runway, so King pulled up, added power, and went around to try again.

His second attempt was no better. As we came around for a third time, he looked over at me. I was shaking my head. "Can you do any better?" he asked, and took his hands off the controls.

I had landed at this strip many times. This time I put down so short that I had to throttle up in order to reach the end of the field and turn around. Later I discovered that King had the impression that he was supposed to be teaching me to fly!

Most of the Dirty Thirty were over thirty years of age, and many had flown in World War II. Several, however, were not yet qualified as command pilots or even as copilots in the C-47. Few, if any, had as much flight time as the average Vietnamese C-47 pilot. My pilots flew every day, but they were younger, many still lieutenants, and generally so youthful in appearance that Americans might mistake them for schoolboys. But these baby-faced airmen dropped parachute flares to provide night illumination over the battlefield, ferried critical supplies, evacuated wounded, hauled troops into and out of battle—every conceivable type of mission—and until then had never lost a plane.

My pilots knew local flying conditions and the terrain so well that we relied on landmarks and ignored or even turned off our radio direction finders—to the consternation of the Americans, who had flown only in an environment that emphasized instrument flying and who were unfamiliar with local terrain. For the first few weeks the Americans thought that my pilots did not know how to use instruments, a fact seemingly confirmed because they often performed radical maneuvers to get below rain clouds in order to find landmarks. In fact, our pilots and navigators were much more familiar with fundamental cockpit techniques—including the nuances of low-frequency radio beacons and the vagaries of the magnetic compass—than the Americans, whose experiences were with more advanced equipment. Until experience taught the Dirty Thirty that our techniques had been proved and were the safest under the conditions, our apparently reckless flying scared hell out of many American pilots. Also, while my pilots spoke English, their thick accents were often hard to understand. None of the Americans spoke Vietnamese, and at first there were misunderstandings in the cockpit.

In July 1962 several American and Vietnamese pilots witnessed the crash of a C-47 on a strip at Kon Tum, in the Central Highlands. Engine failure was the probable cause of this mishap, and everyone aboard, including Captain William Bunker, was killed. He was the only member of the Dirty Thirty to die in Vietnam.

Soon after this tragedy, I called a meeting of all pilots, and we aired and discussed our grievances and problems. By the end of the meeting it was apparent that both groups of pilots were professionals who knew what they were doing. We just did things differently. From then on, we began to function as an integrated unit, perhaps because my style of leadership made the Americans feel at home, while the Vietnamese felt equal and appreciated.

My pilots lived on the base, while the Americans were billeted on one floor of Cholon's Dong Khanh Hotel. When we went to Da Nang for several weeks of duty, my pilots offered to share their tiny but clean BOQ rooms with their American comrades, who otherwise would have been billeted in leaky tents.

As in every flying unit, we competed daily for bragging rights, a friendly rivalry over who was the best pilot. I don't recall who started it, but one night we had a contest to see who could fly best while drunk! The Americans picked one pilot, a captain, as their representative, and my men chose me. We each drank a fifth of whiskey, then climbed into separate planes. With an instructor pilot sitting alongside, we took off. The IP's job was to judge our flight skills. Once we were aloft the IP said, "Okay, make a left turn and descend to 5,000 feet on a heading of 165 degrees," or some such order. As the alcohol worked its way into our systems, each of us became woozy, too drunk to stand. When we landed we called it a draw and went off to have another drink.

Often we went dancing in one or another of Saigon's many first-rate nightclubs. On one occasion, about one in the morning about twenty-five of us, Americans and Vietnamese together, piled into five or six Jeeps and drove to Saigon. The road to the nightclub passed the Presidential Palace. Mr. Diem was a bachelor; for all we knew he went to bed at nine every night. That isn't much fun, I thought—so we stopped at the palace to demonstrate our talents at singing American and Vietnamese songs.

The next day, Colonel Do Mau, chief of military security, telephoned my office. "Some drunken soldiers woke the president last night, singing and carrying on. It could only have been your bunch," he said. "Am I right?"

"Yes, it was us," I replied. "We were having a good time. So what?"

"Be more careful." He laughed and rang off.

After Barnett rotated back to the States, Major Raymond Nicholson took over as detachment commander. Not long after his arrival, all my pilots, American and Vietnamese, went to the firing range to qualify with .45-caliber service pistols. Frankly, most pilots, even military pilots, don't care about such things. To encourage wholehearted participation, the Americans challenged the Vietnamese to a one-on-one match, with several cases of American beer at stake. They selected one of their captains to shoot. Again, my men chose me to represent the squadron.

This was certainly because I was a member of the Vietnamese National Pistol Team, a fact not shared with our American friends. In partial compensation, we invited the Americans to help us drink the beer.

Probably because they got many more hours in the air flying with us than they would have had with the USAF, many of the Dirty Thirty went on to become airline pilots after they left the military. One tall, handsome fellow wrote me a few years later to say that he had named his first son after me. I wish I could recall his family name.

...

In war all soldiers need the kind of support that only a woman can give—the intimacy, the consolation that makes it possible to bear the loss of close friends and to ease the pain of being forced to witness terrible tragedy. I, too, required such tender support, and after I ended my relationship with my first wife, I began to seek it from other women.

I soon acquired a reputation as a playboy. This was not entirely accurate. By nature I am a very passionate man; I often fall in love very quickly. But once I am in love I must go all the way, like the old Sinatra song. After the end of my marriage, there were many ladies in my life, but only one at a time. Even if a man could afford a hundred women, and even if all were willing to be intimate, it is not wise to have multiple relationships simultaneously. To me, as well as to women, loyalty and fidelity are important. Speaking as a man, so is capability. If I cannot satisfy one woman, how can I make two or three or four or five happy? It is beyond my physical capability.

And so it is with other dimensions of my life. When I am engaged in some project, I put all of my energy, all of my thinking, my entire heart into it. Not until I have finished the one do I think about the next. With women, it is the same.

My first love, chaste and unrequited, was a seventeen-year-old Hanoi college student. Tuong Van, which means "peaceful cloud," lived on my street. Then I was drafted into the army, and when I returned from France the country was divided; her family stayed in the North, and I lost track of her until about 1995, when I heard that she was still living in Hanoi. I asked my present wife, Kim, who travels to Vietnam frequently, to look for her, to offer help, some money that might make her life easier. Kim found Tuong Van's house, but neighbors said that she had moved a few months before. I am still looking for her and hope one day to find her, to see her at least once before it is our time to die.

Not long after becoming wing commander, I met another student. Cam Van, "golden cloud," was related to one of my pilots. She lived in Nha Trang, a picturesque seaside city more than an hour's flight north of Saigon, and came to the capital on vacation. Travel by road was increasingly hazardous; the Vietcong often stopped buses or cars and robbed, kidnapped, or shot passengers. So after her vacation, my pilot asked me to arrange for her to fly back to Nha Trang. She was about nineteen and so reminded me of Tuong Van that I fell in love almost instantly.

I strapped her into the copilot's seat of my C-47 and flew her home. Along the way I showed her how to fly, let her handle the controls until it was time to land. All the way back to Saigon I could think of nothing but seeing her again.

Despite the difference in our ages—I was over thirty—I fell head over heels in love with her. I even had a mechanic paint her name on the nose of my aircraft. Her family was aghast at the mere idea of her being seen with me. It was not only her tender age, but my reputation as a flying playboy, a man who had been seen with so many women, a man who had divorced the mother of his children. She wrote me beautiful, poetic letters and for the first time in my life I spent the time to pen long, soulful replies.

Every time I went to Nha Trang—and I found a reason to fly there nearly every day—I had to see Cam Van. We could not use the telephone: If her parents even suspected that we were in communication, they would punish her, perhaps even lock her up. So every time I flew up, before landing I made a very low pass over her house. Fifteen or twenty minutes later she would make some excuse to leave home. The first time she waited for me at a beachside café, but because we could not chance sitting together in public, where some friend of her family would see us, she followed me to the graceful cathedral near the city's center. On weekdays, this ancient Catholic church was always deserted until evening; it became our regular rendezvous, a place where we sat and talked without touching.

On our first visit, the priest said nothing. The second time, he came into the high-ceilinged sanctuary and said, "This is a church! Not the place for this kind of stuff!"

I gave him a hard look and rested my hand on the revolver on my hip. "So what?" I said. "We are only talking. We have done nothing wrong. Is this place closed to the public?"

"Okay, okay," he said. "Just don't make noise."

Among the many women whom I met in South Vietnam,

Cam Van remained the only one with whom I maintained a pure and platonic love. We never kissed. I did not even touch her hand. In the end her parents forced her to marry a teacher. Before the wedding she came to Saigon and asked to see me for the last time. We acted like students; I took her to the movies. There, in the dark coolness, I ached to hold her close. But I didn't.

I never saw her again, but for years afterward, although she had married and had several children, she continued to send occasional letters. She might say that she saw me on television and that I was still handsome. About 1980 a Vietnamese lady, a stranger, came to an event that I attended in Washington, D.C. This woman told me that Cam Van was living in Germany, and gave me her address. I told myself that I had to write or call her, but for some reason I never did. One Christmas I told myself that I must send her and her children gifts—but I didn't. About 1997, the lady whom I had met in Washington telephoned to say that Cam Van had passed away. Before she died, however, my former sweetheart called her children together and told them about me for the first time. She said, "If for any reason you need anything, ask Cao Ky, and he will help you."

Whenever I find myself wishing that things had turned out differently between Cam Van and me, I take comfort in the fact that she was very young, a good daughter who obeyed her parents, and that if our romance was far too brief, we nevertheless shared a pure and noble love that was strong enough to survive a lifetime apart.

6

COUP D'ÉTAT

By 1960 peace had begun to give way to war in South Vietnam. The Vietcong were forming larger units, taking control over more areas of the countryside, and had begun to attack government troops and provincial cities in company and battalion strength. Thousands of Americans arrived in Vietnam and deployed to advise Vietnamese commanders at nearly every level of the ARVN and the VNAF. Millions of dollars of American aid money poured in, funds intended both to arm and equip South Vietnam's military and to build infrastructure and improve living conditions for the impoverished rural populace.

Sadly, many of those U.S. millions did nothing to help the poorest and neediest of my countrymen. Instead they went to Diem's greedy family, mostly into the pockets and purses of his brother, Ngo Dinh Nhu, and his brash wife, and into the coffers of "Mr. Chew Tobacco," Ngo Dinh Can.

Nhu was the power behind the throne, officially "counselor to the president" but a sort of shadow president. He led the Can Lao, or "Revolutionary Personalist Labor party," controlled the secret service, and commanded a palace guard of some 80,000 special troops. Nhu was substantially responsible for the regime's use of political terror, which he often employed for personal criminal purposes. Since Diem was a bachelor, Madame Nhu (born Chuong Xuan Le) took on the role of Vietnam's first lady.

Can was the youngest and the least educated, and as his older brothers entered public life it fell to him to care for their aged mother. Within a few years of Diem's ascent to power, Can was the uncrowned king of Annam, the supreme fixer. He held no office, answered to no one but his brother, and lived in a huge, ostentatious Hue home more suitable for royalty. Practically everyone in Vietnam had a Can story to share; his greed and stupidity became the fabric of folktales. An endless parade of odious favor-seekers passed through his palace to pay their respects to the family matriarch, and each enriched Can. Aside from money, his chief vice was an especially messy fondness for chewing tobacco, Vietnamese style, which meant winding a leaf into a tight roll and tucking it between gum and cheek. While Can was supreme in Vietnam's central region, throughout the rest of the country it was known that if you wanted something from Diem or Nhu but couldn't get past their gatekeepers, you went to Can. After relieving you of your cash, he would go whining to his brothers on your behalf.

As the ruling clan's rapaciousness became more obvious and its popular support dwindled, Diem's regime became more oppressive. Something had to give, and a few days after John F. Kennedy defeated Richard M. Nixon for the U.S. presidency, I witnessed the first overt challenge to Diem's mandate.

Unhappy with Diem's greedy cronyism and with the military's growing politicization, VNAF major Phan Phung Tien, my classmate in Hanoi for officer training and again in France and North Africa for pilot school, joined three Army field grade officers in a plot to remove Diem. I was not aware of this scheme until they went public.

This quartet enlisted the support of other officers and of civilian politicians. To oust the president, however, required troops. The Airborne Brigade, to which two of the officers belonged, had the toughest, best-trained men and was based only a few miles from Diem's residence. The quartet of plotters asked Captain Soan, who worked for the airborne commander, Colonel

Nguyen Chanh Thi, to support their coup. When he refused, they shot him.

Before Soan's body was cold the plotters went to Thi's house. A tough paratrooper, Thi had served as a noncom in the French colonial forces before Vietnam's partition, but he had no command experience. Yet Diem, who never married and fathered no children, regarded Thi almost as a son and appointed him brigade commander. Nevertheless, when Thi was offered an opportunity to avoid sharing Soan's fate, he quickly turned on his sponsor. However reluctantly Thi had joined the scheme, he was senior officer; when the plot went public, he alone held the spotlight.

Before dawn on the morning of November 11, 1960, Thi deployed three battalions of heavily armed paratroopers around Saigon to seize key government buildings and installations, including Tansonnhut Airbase. Thus I became his prisoner, though it was hours before I was aware of it. Thi and I were well acquainted. My C-47s carried his paratroopers on training missions and on combat operations, and his garrison was adjacent to Tansonnhut. He was six or seven years older than I, and we got along well.

With his men in position, Thi prepared to attack Diem's palace. Before he could launch this assault, however, the president sent word that he wished to parley. Instead of shooting his way into the palace, Thi walked in and sat down with Diem. Late that night, after much conversation, Diem promised that he would resign and allow Thi to form a new government of national unity. Thi's troops controlled the government radio station—Vietnam did not yet have television—and in the morning, tasting victory, he broadcast a message outlining his plans for a new administration.

Neither Diem nor Nhu had any intention of resigning. Talking with the unsophisticated Thi was merely a device to divert his attention while an overwhelming force of loyal troops quietly moved into the capital. Within hours these soldiers recaptured most of Saigon, and Diem was back in control.

I learned of this when Thi came roaring onto Tansonnhut, accompanied by about fifteen of the conspirators, and sped to my office to beg for a plane to take them to Cambodia. "Quickly, or Diem will have our heads," said Thi, terror in his voice.

I was inclined to help these friends and brother officers. Still, I hesitated. If *I* flew them to safety, I would be perceived as a conspirator and forced into exile. Even if I merely ordered one of my pilots to take Thi beyond Nhu's grasp, the president's brother would have my head. Buddha smiled. Among the conspirators was Major Tien, one of my pilot. I allowed the rebels to take a C-47, and it carried Thi and the others to safety in Cambodia.

Nhu was understandably curious about how this had happened, and I soon got a call from Colonel Do Mau, chief of Military Security. Our conversation was perfunctory. I explained that I had no interest in politics and that I had nothing to do with the attempted coup. I added that I had enjoyed Thi's friendship, that I had not thought about consequences of my actions but merely acted to help comrades who were fleeing for their lives.

Although helping the conspirators was a serious matter, I am sure that Nhu and especially Do Mau understood clearly what sort of person I was, that I was not political, that I just helped a friend. I remained in command of the Air Transport Wing, and a few months later my long-awaited promotion to lieutenant colonel came through.

Yet in hindsight this was a most peculiar episode. Most Vietnamese had good reason to be frightened of Do Mau and the government's security apparatus. I don't know why, but they never scared me. One might speculate that this was because my conscience was clear—but under such regimes the security forces have no interest in anyone's conscience. If they want to kill you, they never stop to inquire about such matters. Also, just because a man is not scared of them doesn't mean that they will leave him alone. To the contrary. Such people view anyone who is not afraid as a potential threat, and they will find a way to eliminate him. Yet they left me alone; I am still amazed. As wing and base commander, I was senior enough that any involvement in the attempted coup was a serious matter. Had a member of the Can Lao party made such a mistake, he was finished. It shows that even at that stage of my life, I enjoyed either extraordinary luck or remained under Buddha's protection.

It would be five more years, however, before I would learn why Buddha had smiled: Perhaps he was trying not to laugh at all the mischief that Nguyen Chanh Thi would one day cause his country and for the many difficulties that I would encounter trying to undo his foolishness.

Diem went on radio after the attempted coup and promised to make changes in the way he governed. Rather than getting more involved in day-to-day matters, however, Diem turned still more power over to the lean and hungry Nhu, who filtered what the president was allowed to hear and see. One day, by chance, I saw exactly how far Nhu would go to insulate his brother. Diem had decided to refute the critics who claimed that he was out of touch with the common people and scheduled a visit to Saigon's busy Central Market. By chance, I was there shopping a few hours before Diem's arrival. The usually busy but calm square buzzed with hyperactivity. Nhu's henchmen called on every merchant and instructed each that if the president inquired about what something cost, he was to cut the market price by half, by two-thirds, by even more, to whatever it had cost when Diem first came to power. The police did not say so, but it seems to me that this was to keep him from discovering the terrible inflation that had already impoverished millions of South Vietnam's farmers, workers, civil servants, and soldiers, and would soon get even worse. And so Diem strolled through the market, where everyone knew the cost of a kilo of rice except the man who thought he ran the country.

It was not the first time that Nhu had gone to extravagant lengths to fool his brother, and it was not even the most outrageous. One of Diem's better ideas, borrowed from the successful campaign against communist guerrillas in Malaya and in turn from the Israeli model, was to create kibbutz-style villages and protect them from the Vietcong by training an armed militia recruited from among the villagers. The idea was to free the farmers from day-to-day reliance on the ARVN and to give those with the greatest stake in maintaining their independence, the villagers, means to defend themselves.

An excellent idea that might have worked. The United States provided weapons and ammunition—and Nhu and his henchmen diverted them to the black market, pocketing millions. When Diem said that he wished to inspect one of these kibbutzlike villages, Nhu's men swooped in. They passed out new clothes, brought in tons of rice, and created the illusion of a bustling, prosperous rural community. As a charitable gesture to this Potemkin Village, they transplanted a grove of orange trees, boughs bent with ripening fruit, from a town several miles away. After Diem had gone, Nhu's men moved the trees back whence they came.

While Diem failed to make positive changes in his governance after Thi's attempted coup, Nhu's gestapo clamped down on dissidents, arresting or questioning over 50,000 people. Many innocent civilians were tortured. Dozens were executed.

Even though I spent most of those ugly times flying and attending to command duties, I became increasingly disenchanted with the way that one-party politics was diminishing the effectiveness of the armed forces. In the ARVN it became an article of faith that the fast track to promotion was joining Diem's Can Lao party. I saw the military becoming like the Red

Army, where the road to higher rank depended on membership in the Communist party, and where the officers with the greatest responsibilities were almost invariably not the best fighters, the ablest leaders, but those who had demonstrated party loyalty. I made no secret of my displeasure, and because at that time even to speak against the Diem regime was dangerous, my closest friends begged me to hold my tongue before Nhu put me in prison, had me demoted, or sent me to an out-of-the-way base.

In that era, VNAF commander Colonel Nguyen Xuan Vinh, a Can Lao stalwart, convened quarterly command meetings at his headquarters. At these gatherings wing, division, and base commanders, along with some of the general staff—a total of about forty officers—made individual presentations about their commands or their areas of responsibility. Usually we discussed what had happened since the last meeting, what progress had been made in resolving deficiencies, any new problems that had arisen, important personnel matters, and so forth. When it was my turn to speak at one of these gatherings in 1961, I abandoned my prepared presentation. With little advance thought to this sudden departure from the agenda, I raised the issue of fast-track promotions to Can Lao members in combat units. I pointed out that few of these officers had proven combat capability; they were merely active party members. "That is wrong!" I said. "Doing this will destroy the leadership and then our combat capability."

The room went utterly silent. For more than two minutes no one spoke, not even Vinh, a Can Lao officer with no combat record—as everyone knew. I began to think that maybe I had gone too far, but I did not care; when I feel something is wrong, I say so. That has always been my nature.

When the silence became painful and it was apparent that Vinh didn't know how to respond, Dr. Nguyên Tan Hong, the VNAF's respected flight surgeon, got to his feet. "I think the atmosphere is very heavy in here," he said. "It is too hard to breathe. But this afternoon there is a soccer match between Vietnam and Taipei." He turned to Vinh. "I suggest to you, sir, that we adjourn and let everyone go enjoy this match. And then we will meet again tomorrow."

"Okay!" said Vinh. In moments the room was empty.

The next morning, an hour before the conference was to resume, Vinh telephoned. We had been classmates in Hanoi, we had gone to Marrakech for basic flight school together, we were the same age. Even if he was VNAF commander, he couldn't expect me to swallow any bullshit.

"Ky, come here" was all he said. When I got to his office he said, "Hey, why don't you tell me those things first? Why bring them up in the big meeting, in public? You will get yourself in trouble—and you will get me in trouble too."

That was undoubtedly true. Nhu's informants were everywhere, and if a leader failed to control his men, or if an underling was considered disloyal, his boss also was held responsible. I was a little amused to see that Vinh was actually frightened. "If I merely discuss this with you in private," I replied, "it means nothing. And what I said has been the talk of all officers, and of most in the military, for a long time. It was time that someone said it aloud, so Nhu and Diem will hear."

"Maybe so," he said. "But now you just put yourself in trouble."

"I know," I replied. "You can tell them what I said, and whatever they want to do to me—just do it. Send me to Pleiku, I am ready to go." Pleiku was a dusty little frontier town in the highlands near the Cambodian border. The Vietcong harassed the surrounding roads, and there wasn't a cold drink or a decent meal for a hundred miles. I didn't care; we needed pilots in Pleiku, and I could fly from there as well as anywhere.

And indeed, that afternoon, minutes after the command meeting ended, I got another call from Do Mau in Military Security. "Hey, Ky, what happened? Big bomb! Big noise, everyone is talking!" he said. "Is it true what I heard that you said?"

"Yes. I said it. And I do not apologize. In the field of politics, I understand that you must organize the party, and this and that. And you know that I don't get involved in those matters—I am just a flier. But bringing politics into the army and basing promotions upon party membership—that is not the right way. It disrupts the chain of command. It undermines leadership. What will happen if *all* the military leaders are members of the Can Lao party? How can you expect that such a force will become a strong army to fight the enemy?

"I have no intention to get into politics or to be against the regime," I added. "But I think it is wrong, and you should correct it. That was my only intention in speaking out."

"Well, the president is not happy," he replied.

"You can tell Mr. Diem that I serve at his pleasure. I am ready to accept punishment. I am ready to move to Pleiku."

I was pretty sure that they could not put me in prison. Nhu's secret police kept a close watch on the top military leaders, but I was known as a good fighter. In the air force we had too few pilots, and even fewer good ones. Diem's VNAF commander could be a party loyalist because he didn't have to fight; he had only to assure Nhu of tight control over his organization. But even Nhu had to realize that he could not put a political paper pusher in charge of a combat unit, even if that man was ready to die for President Diem. And surely Nhu must have known that I was merely expressing a common opinion, one held even by many enlisted men. Finally, I reasoned, they must see that if I was planning to do something disloyal, I certainly would not draw attention to myself. Probably Nhu didn't see me as a threat; I heard nothing more about my speech.

The following year, however, on February 27, 1962, two VNAF pilots flying A-1 Skyraiders took off from Tansonnhut on what was supposed to be a ground-support mission against the Vietcong. Instead they turned back over Saigon and bombed Diem's official residence. Much of the Presidential Palace was destroyed, but Diem and his family escaped serious injury.

One of the pilots, Nguyên Van Cú, escaped by flying to Cambodia. The other, Pham Phu Quôc, one of the ablest and most courageous aviators that I have had the privilege of knowing, was shot down over the Saigon River by a gun crew on a Vietnamese navy ship, probably the only aircraft ever downed intentionally by our armed forces. Quôc survived his crash landing, and Nhu clapped him into prison.

These two rebel pilots had acted alone and told no one of their intentions to assassinate Diem and end his dictatorial family's rule; only luck saved the First Family.

Cú was an idealistic young patriot; his father had been among the founders of the Vietnamese Nationalist party, the Kuomintang, and had spent many years in China with Chiang Kai-Shek's followers. Quôc later returned to active duty and died when his Skyraider went down on a bombing mission over North Vietnam. When news of his death reached me, I cried a long time. I asked Pham Duy, Vietnam's leading singer-songwriter, to write a ballad about this brave man. It became a very popular tune, in part because Phu Quôc is not only a man's name but also means "first for his country." His death was a great loss and still saddens me.

Cú has a happier story. After returning from exile, he became active in politics; as a member of the Kuomintang slate, he was elected in 1966 to the constitutional assembly. He later became a congressman. He now lives in San Jose, California.

Even though Quôc and Cú had acted on their own, after the palace bombing, a furious Nhu fired Vinh as VNAF chief, replacing him with Colonel Huynh Huu Hiên, another of my former classmates—and, of course, a staunch member of the Can Lao.

Diem tightened his grip on power and ruthlessly suppressed

dissent, and the Vietcong continued to escalate their guerrilla activities. For the most part, our armed forces did not prove effective against them. I believe that with training, equipment, and good leadership, the Vietnamese fighting man was equal to any challenge. Most of our top leaders, unfortunately, had neither the mettle nor the experience for protracted, low-intensity combat. Far from Saigon, in the regions where the communists were strongest, some ARVN generals made accommodations with Vietcong. Often they made a show of providing security, but these old generals, without exception holdovers from the colonial era, were more interested in the possibilities for money and power than risking the hazards of fighting a guerrilla war.

And so more and more American military advisors arrived, and more and more U.S. money poured into the national economy. Anxious about their growing stake in Vietnam, senior U.S. diplomats tried to reason with Diem. Many attempted to get him to broaden his political base by introducing more democratic methods and fostering democratic institutions instead of merely tightening already strict security.

In January 1961, ten days after John Kennedy became president of the United States, Edward Lansdale, a former U.S. Air Force officer who had served several years as the CIA's South Vietnam station chief and was then deputy assistant for special operations to the U.S. secretary of defense, sent a letter to President Diem following a visit to Saigon. Lansdale reported that the new Kennedy administration remained staunchly behind Diem and that JFK had expressed a strong interest in Vietnam:

"I am sure that you can count upon him as an understanding friend and that you will be hearing further about this. It would have 'warmed your heart' to have heard this conversation. So, you see, you do have some sincere friends in Washington," he wrote.

After more assurances, Lansdale got to the point:

However, there will be some here who will point out that much of the danger of your present situation comes about from your own actions. They say that you try to do too many things yourself, that you refuse to give real responsibility to others and keep interfering with what they do, that you feel you are infallible personally, and that too many of your organizations like the Republican Youth Corps and the Can Lao Party are actually formed by coercion—that is, people join because they are afraid not to—rather than being genuine organizations rooted in the hearts of the Vietnamese people. I believe there will be many of these criticisms voiced in private talks here as word gets around about favorable reactions to my report.

The best answer to these criticisms would be actions by you in Vietnam. The critics would then have to close their mouths in the face of your actions. One action would be for you to announce your reorganization of the government very soon. Also, you could make your Security Council become alive and dynamic. Please remember my suggestion: Call the military commanders and province chiefs in from the 1st and 5th Military Regions—to meet with the Security Council. You could make a talk to this group, and broadcast it all over Vietnam to all of the people of Vietnam. Your country needs you to rouse spirits right now, the way Winston Churchill did for Britain at a dark hour. Your countrymen need to be told that Vietnam is in grave danger from the Communists, that the help of every citizen is welcomed by the government, and that Vietnam must and will be kept free and independent.

I have no inkling why Lansdale would write such a letter. An intelligence officer of his long experience should have known that even if Diem ever saw the letter, he would ignore any such pointed suggestions from his American allies. A better approach, one far more worthy of Lansdale's skills, would have been to pay a visit to Nhu. Lansdale could have attempted to persuade this counselor to the president to find a way to get his brother's attention. That would have been difficult; at this point in Diem's career, he seemed to think that he took instructions only from God, although he did sometimes listen to Nhu's advice.

While such independence may have earned Diem the admiration of South Vietnam's ruling circle—which is to say, his own family—it did not persuade anyone else. With the wisdom of hindsight, I can say that had I been in his shoes, before I ignored the Americans, I would have consolidated my position within Vietnam. Without the support of the people, how could anyone stand against U.S. power? Even worse, despite Nhu's heavy-handed efforts, Diem no longer held the ARVN's trust or loyalty. It is likely that given Nhu's efforts to insulate and isolate him, however, Diem never fully understood how widely he was feared and hated. In his mind, he had progressed from viewing himself as a divine instrument to becoming a god himself. He expected every loyal Vietnamese to love him, to obey and even worship him. It was a fatal mistake.

About eleven on a warm, sticky autumn morning in 1963, Do Mau telephoned my office. He said, "Do you have time for soup?" Slight, swarthy, and poorly educated, Mau was Can Lao Number One, Diem's strongest supporter, Nhu's right-hand man in the army. I would have been foolish not to accept his invitation.

Since childhood, I have been fond of pho, a hearty soup of rice noodles, thinly sliced beef, and fresh vegetables seasoned with lime juice, chili sauce, the traditional fish sauce known as nuoc mam, and other spices. It is a Tonkinese dish, but so many northerners had moved to the South that within a few years after the partition it was widely available. Mau and I ate in a modest restaurant just outside the air base, making small talk. Afterward we stepped outside into the din, heat, and exhaust fumes of midday Saigon.

"Come with me," Mau said, beckoning to his driver. Mindful of his role as Nhu's hatchet man, I climbed into his car. The driver seemed to know where we were going, and after ten or fifteen minutes we turned into a potholed, unpaved street lined with sagging building and dusty shops. We stopped before a small, nondescript house, and a servant led us to a room lined with books, scrolls, old maps, and astrological charts. Waiting was the sightless Minh Loc, widely known as a fortune-teller. Among his clientele were some of Saigon's most powerful and important people.

It was common knowledge that Mau was a devotee of the occult. He was said to keep a security dossier on every key officer in the armed forces. Each file included an extensive horoscope based on that officer's particulars. Mau was also known to consult with a phalanx of seers and astrologers. In this he was far from unique. Many of my countrymen, as well as many other Asians and many Americans—including at least one former American first lady—believe in astrology and fortune-tellers. Even today, Americans buy more books dealing with the occult than scientific matters.

I have never believed in such things. While I firmly believe that Buddha guides my destiny, I don't think that anyone alive has the knowledge or ability to predict the events of another's life with any certainty. Even if I had known where he was taking me, I would have gone with Mau; he was not one to confront over such matters. He provided Minh Loc with my birth information, including the hour of my entry into this world. Then he asked, "Is this a loyal man?"

Without touching me or even asking my name, Minh Loc sat still and silent, evidently calculating my horoscope. Seconds and minutes ticked away. Finally, he spoke. "This man has a good heart," he declared. "He is very loyal. You can trust him."

Mau's only other question: "Is there a chance that he will some day be in prison?"

"Never," replied the soothsayer. "According to his horo-scope, his destiny is that he will never go to jail!"

With that out of the way, we returned to Mau's office, where he got to the point. "Well, you know the situation with Diem, and especially Nhu—we cannot work with them any more. So I am among a group that is planning to overthrow them."

Mau's voice was calm and unaffected, as if he were describing an errand that he had to run instead of revealing a plan that could put him behind bars, or worse. "Will you support us or oppose us?" he asked.

Neither the announcement nor the question surprised me. Mau had spies everywhere, and no cabal of military conspirators could have hoped to succeed without his participation. At the same time, having seen the year before what just two Skyraiders could do to the Presidential Palace, no move against Diem would have much hope of success if the VNAF opposed it. I did not command the VNAF, but by this time it was apparent to Do Mau, if not to most of the generals, that the pilots, at least, would follow me if I chose to fight.

With Diem as a living example of how not to lead, I had long made it a point to stay in touch with the common people, including both my own troops and the peasants, shopkeepers, and laborers whom I encountered in my daily life. Because it was known that I avoided graft and corruption, many NCOs and junior officers confided in me. When we went for a beer after a mission, they shared what was on their minds. Many were unhappy about the widening gap between the rich and the poor. These young officers and soldiers could see colonels and generals getting rich and themselves becoming desperately deprived. Corrupt officers stole army rations and equipment, and inflation robbed the troops of the purchasing power even for essentials.

At this time there was also a rising tide of political unrest in South Vietnam and in particular among the Buddhists, who had grown steadily more militant under Diem's rule. In 1963 about

11 million of South Vietnam's 15 million people described themselves as Buddhists, but of these, only about a fourth, less than 4 million, engaged in Buddhist activities.

I must emphasize that the Vietnamese Buddhist leadership was chosen not by the laity but by the monks in private councils. Unlike most Western religions, Vietnamese Buddhists obeyed no central authority; the pagodas competed with each other for influence, followers, and funds to the degree that before 1963, even the most fervent Buddhists of Saigon could rarely be roused to support coreligionists in Da Nang or Can Tho or even Hue. Perhaps because of this power vacuum at the top, many Buddhist leaders harbored political ambitions extending well beyond their pagodas. The most extreme example of this was Thich (Venerable) Tri Quang. Quang aspired to become a sort of Buddhist pope; that is, he sought absolute temporal power over Vietnam's Buddhists, which would have made him Vietnam's king. While the ruling cliques of most pagodas had far less ambition and generally pursued what they felt was best for their pagoda, in no sense were any of these monks democratically chosen representatives of their group, a fact usually lost on outsiders, especially Americans.

Hue was Vietnam's seat of Buddhist power, a fact symbolic of ancient times when Buddhism was not merely Vietnam's favored religion but the moral authority behind the dynasties that ruled from Annam's capital in central Vietnam. According to many historians, when in the seventeenth century the French became Indochina's rulers, Hue, the imperial capital, emerged as the locus of church power. In my time this lovely old city was the see of Archbishop Ngo Dinh Thuc, brother of Diem, Nhu, and Can. Some Vietnamese, including many in power, associated Roman Catholicism with Diem's government.

On May 8, 1963, Hue's Buddhists celebrated Buddha's birthday, thronging the streets with banners and flags. Nhu's security forces called this an antigovernment demonstration and ruthlessly suppressed it. When an angry crowd gathered at the government radio station, the deputy province chief, Major Dang Sy, used first fire hoses and then tear gas on the outraged Buddhists. When the crowd refused to disperse, he issued live ammunition and grenades to his troops. By the time the carnage was over, nine people were dead.

Despite hundreds of eyewitnesses to the contrary, Nhu claimed that Vietcong bombs had caused these deaths. Buddhists all over Vietnam demonstrated their anger in the streets. Perhaps if Diem had quickly accepted responsibility for the incident and paid reparations, the issue might have evaporated. If Diem had gone to a pagoda, uttered friendly words for the victims' families, or made some dramatic gesture of conciliation, he would have been seen as a statesman and emerged stronger than ever.

It never happened. Perhaps influenced by Nhu, the government continued to insist that the Vietcong alone were responsible for the deaths. Within a few weeks the Buddhist protest began to spread to other cities along the central coastal and to Saigon. Vietnamese newspapers controlled by Diem loyalists ignored the protests, so Buddhists tipped off Western correspondents about planned demonstrations. They made mimeographed copies of stories printed in the United States and Europe and distributed them from pagodas.

Unrest spread to Saigon with a sit-down hunger strike in front of the National Assembly. By June the Buddhist resistance had begun to worry Nhu; all over South Vietnam, people were becoming aware of a new force that was standing up to the Diem government as none had before. Nhu and Diem worried that Vietnam's many other religions and interest groups would unite behind a Buddhist spearhead. On June 8 an organization run by Nhu's wife, the so-called Women's Solidarity Movement, announced that the Buddhists had been infiltrated by communists. To the Americans, already spending $1.5 million a day in South Vietnam and weary of Nhu's despotic ways, this statement seemed to suggest that more drastic measures were imminent.

They were. Three days later, Thich Quang Duc, a seventy-three-year-old monk, sat down in a busy downtown Saigon intersection. As Quang Duc assumed the cross-legged lotus position usually assumed for meditation, two other monks doused him in gasoline. Quang Duc struck a match, burst into flame, and burned to death without moving or uttering a word. A story circulated afterward that although his body was reduced to ashes, his heart was miraculously unburned, a sign of the Buddha's supernatural influence. The story might be true, or some other creature might have been sacrificed to sharpen the point. It did not matter. Pictures of Quang Duc's horrifying sacrifice were shown on television and printed in newspapers all over the world. They had the desired effect: Few any longer believed Diem's assertions that Vietnam's Buddhists were not being persecuted.

In the weeks that followed Quang Duc's self-immolation, six more monks died in the same manner. Madame Nhu, never one to show delicacy, described the protest as "monk barbecues" with "imported gasoline."

Under pressure from the United States, Diem's government negotiated with the Buddhist leaders. While still refusing to acknowledge responsibility for the Hue killings, the resulting communiqué restated the divergent views of both sides and called for a government committee to investigate the Hue incident.

Diem's family, especially Madame Nhu, was unhappy with this small gesture because they felt it displayed Diem's weakness. At the same time, many monks began to worry that ordinary Buddhists would be angry at leaders who settled for the hollow language and empty measures of the communiqué. It was widely rumored that Diem had no intention of honoring the accord and that Nhu would arrest the leading monks.

In July Vice President Nguyen Ngoc Tho announced preliminary results of the "investigation": The Vietcong alone were responsible for the Hue deaths. As newspapers controlled by Nhu continued to attack the Buddhist leadership, the younger monks, men in their thirties and early forties, began to ignore their more conservative elders. Perhaps they saw themselves as too deeply involved to turn back. Whatever their thoughts, younger and more militant monks took over the protest movement.

By August the Buddhist protests seemed perpetual, with no end in sight. The attacks on Diem and Nhu became direct; there could be no doubt that the monks were trying to bring down the government. Not only did demonstrations disrupt Saigon and the major cities of the central coast, dissension began to seep into the countryside and finally into the army. While the Americans told the press that this crisis was not hurting the war effort, everyone in the ARVN knew that the opposite was true. The seemingly endless unrest had already eroded both morale and combat efficiency.

America's dwindling support for Diem was conveyed by U.S. ambassador Frederick Nolting, who was due to be replaced. Since the Buddhists were obviously hoping to provoke the government into foolish or imprudent acts, Nolting counseled restraint. For a few weeks, Diem seemed a bit less repressive. To the Can Lao generals who had long supported his regime, however, it looked like he had gone on the defensive. As the generals assessed the situation, Nhu laid plans to resolve the crisis by crushing the Buddhists. On August 21 he made his move.

President Diem may not have been aware of what was about to happen, but the Buddhist leaders certainly were. Alerted by friends, they tipped off American reporters that Nhu was planning to raid Xa Loi Temple. Instead of dispersing, however, most of the leading monks decided to stay, to allow Nhu to do what he would. The notable exception was Thich Tri Quang, who found refuge in the U.S. Embassy. A junior embassy official, John Negroponte, was assigned to keep an eye on him.

Although telephone lines to the embassy had been cut by Nhu's police to forestall U.S. intervention, foreign reporters began to appear on the streets near Xa Loi just before midnight. About thirty minutes later the so-called combat police, Nhu's specially trained gestapo, reinforced with elite ARVN units, smashed their way into Xa Loi and other important Buddhist strongholds throughout the country. More than two thousand monks and nuns were arrested. Hundreds of ordinary Buddhists were taken from their homes. Xa Loi Temple and An Quang Pagoda, among others in Saigon, were ransacked. A monk at Xa Loi was mistaken for Thay Giac Duc, among the most eloquent of the Buddhist protest speakers, and was beaten to death on the spot.

The Buddhist movement had some strong leaders and an excellent sense of how to manipulate the Western news media, but few weapons, no national organization, and limited logistical assets. Buddhists alone could never have toppled the Diem government. Even if their protests had succeeded in forcing Diem and Nhu from office, the Buddhists did not possess the power to replace them or the capability of running the country.

The army, however, had everything needed to oust Diem and take control. Only two things stood in the generals' way: fear of antagonizing the Americans and their own ineptitude. In fact, by the time of the Buddhist crisis, Diem had lost all popular support. He was finished. Even if the generals had not acted, his government would have fallen as an overripe pear drops from a tree. It was only a matter of time. The coup happened because, after Nhu's crackdown, the American CIA gave the generals permission to act.

My trip to the fortune-teller with Do Mau came several weeks after the Night of the Pagodas. "Personally, I am very unhappy with the Diem regime," I told Mau that afternoon in his office. "We are against the communist one-party dictatorship in the North, but we in the South have a one-family dictatorship that is worse than any party.

"I don't like any kind of dictatorship," I continued. "When you have only one party, one family, one group—they serve their own interests, not the people."

I was not part of the coup's inner circle, so I had no way of knowing then that Nhu's assault on the pagodas had been the last straw for President Kennedy. Unable to grasp that the so-called Buddhist crisis had little to do with religious issues but was instead a struggle for political power orchestrated by a handful of ambitious monks, Kennedy decided that Diem had to go. While the new U.S. ambassador, Henry Cabot Lodge, Jr., continued to try to persuade Diem that he should replace Nhu with a more moderate figure, Kennedy authorized a top-secret telegram to a cabal of ARVN generals indicating that the United States would not intervene if they took action against Diem.

Even as Ambassador Lodge begged Diem to release the monks Nhu had imprisoned and tortured, Colonel Lucien Conein, a CIA agent, began supplying the generals with information they would need to overthrow Diem.

The plotters were all among Diem's inner circle; the president considered each an adopted son. Most ARVN and VNAF officers, while fearing their power, considered these generals little more than Diem's servants, men in their early forties who had served the French as noncoms or junior officers.

The high-minded Diem, who had come to office with good intentions, demanded total loyalty from his generals and expected love and support from the common people of his country, but as time went on, he gave both the generals and the people less and less in return for this loyalty.

Dictators often start as patriots with noble goals, but when they become tyrants, it is usually their entourage who determine their fate. What happened to Julius Caesar would happen to Park Chung Hee and Ferdinand Marcos—they would be betrayed by those closest to them. Years later I would have a long chat with Marcos about the problems of politics. "If you have only five officers who are loyal for you, ready to die for you, nobody can stage a coup d'état," he said. In the end, Marcos did not have five.

Neither did Diem.

Duong Van Minh, Big Minh, served as Diem's military advisor. Despite a good combat record, Minh had fallen victim to Nhu's suspicions and had been passed over by less able men for a top command. The others at the apex of the plot were General Tran Van Don, acting chief of the joint general staff and one of the few ARVN officers who had graduated from St. Cyr, the French military academy, and the shrewd Le Van Kim, who served as Don's executive officer, a post with few responsibilities. One needs troops to seize power, and thus General Nguyen Van Thieu, commander of the Fifth Division, became part of the scheme.

The plotters moved very cautiously, bringing in other key officers over a period of weeks. Early on they gained the consent of General Nguyen Khanh, the II Corps commander whose forces controlled the Central Highlands from Pleiku, and General Do Cao Tri, whose I Corps command was headquartered in Da Nang and encompassed the South Vietnam's northernmost provinces.

Of course, I knew nothing of such details at the time. When I sat down with Do Mau, my feelings that political change must come to Vietnam were mostly in my heart, the product of years of frustration with Diem and the Can Lao; I did not think much about the actual plot except to wonder how it would unfurl. While I knew that many generals were ready for change at the top, others commanding troops in Saigon and in the Mekong Delta would remain loyal to Diem. How would the plotters overcome them without launching a bloody, protracted civil war that would make all South Vietnam vulnerable to a communist offensive?

September dragged on, and then it was October, and by then even the pho sellers in Saigon's markets knew that something was in the wind. With every day that passed, I expected to hear something about the coup.

An officer whose name I do not recall stopped me on the street one afternoon and whispered that the coup was set for noon on the next day, October 24. So I invented an event, the anniversary of the founding of the First Transport Wing, and scheduled a ceremony at my headquarters. I invited Colonel Huynh Huu Hiên, the new VNAF commander, and his staff, to attend the ceremony and a lavish lunch afterward. On the morning of the ceremony I told the crew chief and flight mechanic of my aircrew that there would be a coup. They were to arm themselves; when I gave the word they were to arrest Hiên and the general staff.

A few minutes before the ceremony, however, another officer came to my office and said, "No, no coup today, there is a delay." I heard nothing more until midday on November 1. I was at the home of a friend, enjoying lunch with my family, when an officer of the Transport Wing telephoned. He said only that "something has happened" and that I should return to the base.

Waiting outside the main gate was Major Do Khac Mai, VNAF chief of staff. A short, slender, swarthy man with the blunt features of a peasant, he always seemed to me to be a less-than-average Vietnamese in every aspect, from education and intelligence to integrity and looks. Most of his few flying hours were in the tiny, single-engine L-19 used for observation and artillery spotting. As wing commander I had taught many basic pilots to make the transition from trainers to transports, and I am sure he would never have qualified. But Mai was a Can Lao member and Do Mau's protégé. "It is the coup," he said. "We start now." I waited for more, but that was all he had to say; I received no instructions. Nobody said what was expected of me.

Mai went to the coup headquarters to report, as I later learned, that VNAF Headquarters would soon be secure. I went directly to my wing, where it was apparent that everyone knew that a coup was in progress. I assembled my troops in a hangar, about three hundred men, including pilots, mechanics, and ground support personnel, and told them that the army had moved against President Diem. "I agree with this action," I said. "But as for you guys—you must each decide for yourself. If you think that what I am doing is right, stay on this side of the hangar and be prepared to follow my orders.

"But if you don't want to be involved, for any reason at all, then you are free to go home and wait until the situation has resolved itself. I will not force anyone to stay, and if you leave you will not be punished. I am not giving any order that you must take part in the coup. I am only telling you what has happened. Support the army or go home—it's up to you."

Every last one of my men remained in ranks. "We follow you, whatever you do," they yelled. I was proud of them, but they had behaved exactly as I had expected. That was why I had not planned for the coup, had not prepared my troops in any way. I knew that they would follow me.

Now that the coup had begun, however, I knew that I must take action immediately. The first thing I did was secure my wing. I strapped on a pistol and had weapons issued, then gave orders that no one was to enter our part of the base.

Then I told one of my sergeants, a burly mechanic, to get a Browning Automatic Rifle and a few magazines and come with me. We walked the block or so to VNAF Headquarters, where we went to the offices of Colonel Hiên. As was the case with his predecessor, Hiên was a classmate with whom I had gone through training in Morocco and France. Hiên was loyal to Diem, and a good pilot.

Since becoming head of VNAF, Hiên had somehow developed an active dislike for me. Perhaps he was jealous. Whatever the reason, when my semiannual performance reviews came up, his reports were always peppered with criticism. I was a womanizer, I frequented nightclubs, I was accused of all sorts of bad behavior. But I had friends in Diem's palace who liked and respected me, and they told me that every time Nhu got these reports he said, "Maybe he is all these things you say, but I understand that Ky is a very good fighter, a good commander—so leave him alone."

When I walked into headquarters, Hiên's secretary jumped up and saluted. "Where is the commander?" I asked, and he pointed to the office. I left my sergeant outside and entered Hiên's office without knocking. I found him at his desk talking on the telephone, perhaps to someone at Diem's palace. Hiên saw me but didn't react; he continued to talk. "Stop talking," I said. "Come with me."

"Yes" was all he said. He put the phone down.

I told my sergeant to place him under arrest, accompany him to ARVN HQ, and hand him over to General Minh or one of the other coup leaders.

Then I walked over to Operations, the nerve center of the air force, where all aircraft missions were planned, scheduled, assigned, and tracked. The operations center occupied a large room filled with telephones and wall charts used as status boards. As I entered, someone called "Attention!" and everyone jumped up and saluted. I looked directly at Major Tran Van Minh, VNAF operations officer.

"From now on you will take orders only from me," I said. There was a chorus of "Yes, sir!"

I looked at my wristwatch. An hour had elapsed since I had

been notified that the coup had begun. I controlled the HQ and the biggest airbase. Just then a telephone rang: It was Lieutenant General Tran Thien Khiem, calling for me.

The generals leading the coup did not control the whole army. Between a third and a half of the division commanders were still loyal to Diem, and if they moved their troops into Saigon there would be a bloody battle. And maybe Diem would win.

I was asked to deliver a message to the commander of the Twenty-first Division, based near Can Tho, several hours' drive south of Saigon. The division was preparing to move north and come to Diem's assistance. I dispatched an L-19 to drop a pouch addressed to the division commander. In it was a message from me: "Don't move your division, or I will bomb it." I added that I would send a helicopter for him. In an hour this Diem loyalist was back in Saigon, where he surrendered to Minh.

The army also needed air force help to deal with the palace guard. A regiment loyal to Diem held the Presidential Palace; Khiem wanted me to encourage them to surrender.

The VNAF's only Skyraider squadron was then Bien Hoa, north of Saigon, so I told Major Minh to scramble two T-28 Texans, short-range, single-engine trainers that we had converted to the attack role. Before they took off, I went to the flight line and met with the pilots. "I need you go up and fire one or two rockets at the palace guard's base," I said. "For now, try not to kill anyone."

After the second rocket exploded, the officer commanding the guard radioed that he understood the situation, and his men put down their weapons and surrendered. For the first time I realized that I had power. The coup was over, and the junta that now ruled began the difficult job of running the country.

I was in VNAF headquarters about 2:00 A.M. on the morning following the coup when a message arrived from army headquarters promoting Major Do Khac Mai to colonel and giving him command of the VNAF. Mai's part in the coup had been to stand next to the Tansonnhut gate and wait for the army to arrive, as he put it. Even so, I was not surprised, because while Mai had not shown any leadership skills, he had certainly cemented his connections to Do Mau and the generals. I recall no other reaction; I have never thought about promotion, never sought it, and I was content to remain as commander of the Transport Wing.

I was shocked and angry, however, the next day when I learned that Diem and Nhu had been shot to death. The generals must have feared that as long as Diem was alive, he remained a threat to their own power. But killing him was not necessary, and if I had known that murder had been on the conspirators' agenda, I might have reconsidered my participation. It was too late to go back, but with these killings I lost what little respect I once had for the generals. It showed how fearful they were of maintaining power.

The day after that, just two days after the coup, Colonel Mai called me from VNAF HQ. After a few preliminaries, he said, "I want you to be my deputy commander."

"Bullshit," I said. To me, Mai was nothing. Maybe he wanted me as deputy so that he could turn the day-to-day details over to someone who would make him look good. Or maybe he wanted me close so that he could keep an eye on me. Or because he thought I expected some kind of plum for my role in the coup. No matter. I would not play that game, I would not accept anything from an air force commander who could barely fly.

"Forget about it," I said, and hung up.

The junta that had deposed Diem, along with several other top ARVN generals, called themselves the National Leadership Committee, or something like that. Just one week after I turned down the deputy commander's job, the committee scheduled a conference in Da Lat to discuss their new government. Under the old regime I had often flown such VIP missions, and so when the request for an aircraft came in I took the mission. Since I was only a wing commander, I did not attend any of the meetings, but I stayed close in case my aircraft was needed.

A day or two later the conference adjourned and I went to the airport. I approached my C-47 to find four or five of the generals waiting. Big Minh beckoned me over. "At the meeting we talked about the air force," he said. "And we all realized that the guy we named chief is not a good man and that he is not popular. And everyone agreed that *you* are the right man for this job. So, from now you are the air force commander," he said.

I said, "Thank you, General." Then I flew the generals back to Saigon, my last mission as a VIP pilot. Perhaps because of my role in the coup, I was promoted to colonel. A few months later I pinned on the silver star of a brigadier general.

As for Colonel Mai, my well-connected predecessor, he came to see me a few days later to ask for assignment to Germany as military attaché. It was a post requiring little in the way of brains or courage, and Germany was a place where he could enjoy a good life and not worry about coups or the Vietcong, so I gave him the job.

Big Minh, who took the title of chairman of the Military Committee, dismissed Colonel Hiên from the service. About six months later his wife, whom I did not know well, came to see me. "My husband is without a job and cannot support his family," she said, sobbing. "Can you help him?"

"What would you like me to do?" I asked, and she said that wanted her husband to join Air Vietnam. At that time the national airline had no pilots of its own, probably because airmen were in very short supply nationwide and anyone who could have been trained to fly had first to complete military service. Therefore, pilots from First Transport Wing, either on short furloughs or during their off-duty hours, flew all Air Vietnam flights. Because civilian flying paid far better than military wages, and destinations included such desirable ports of call as Hong Kong and Tokyo, Air Vietnam assignments were prestigious and much sought after—and I was the one who decided who got this privilege. I had reason enough to send Mrs. Hiên away empty-handed, but I never considered that. I felt sorry for her, so I wrote a note to the chief of Air Vietnam, and former Colonel Hiên got his job. The Hiêns now live quite comfortably in Houston, Texas, and I suppose that one of these days they will remember their manners and get around to sending me a little thank-you note.

7

YOUNG TURKS

THE generals who deposed Diem were no better equipped to manage South Vietnam's affairs than were those whom they replaced, so the coup that ended Diem's corrupt and oligarchic regime brought neither peace nor prosperity. Nor did it bring social justice to the millions of ordinary Vietnamese whose sweat and toil had for so long enriched the wealthy and powerful. The coup did not even result in the generals focusing their efforts on fighting the communists. Like Diem and his family, the men who overthrew him had grown to maturity under French colonial rule, and their values and perceptions were so tainted by this experience that they had few ideas to offer. They understood wealth and power only in terms of their own enrichment. They did not know how to lead, how to legitimize the power they had seized at gunpoint by giving those whom they ruled a stake in their government's success, by giving ordinary people the hope of better lives.

Even worse, many of the older generals did not truly understand the danger that the Vietcong posed. Venal and unprincipled generals believed that they could do business with the communists, come to some accommodation, buy them off as their own fathers had been co-opted by the French. Unlike those of my generation, who came of age during and just after World War II, they had never had their noses rubbed in ideological communism. Most of these old generals would grasp the full peril of the threat only when it was too late, and some would never understand.

If the ARVN was big and bristling with guns, its power was diluted by divisiveness. The older generals jostled and maneuvered and intrigued in quest of personal power, possessions, and position. Fortunately, the military also included a small cadre of younger leaders not mired by ties to corruption and colonialism. Like the air force that I led, South Vietnam's marine corps, navy, and paratroops were commanded by men in their thirties or early forties. After supporting the coup that toppled Diem, Chung Tan Cang, head of the navy, became a commodore; and Marine Corps Commander Khang and I became one-star generals. We were soon joined by Brigadier Generals Nguyen Bao Tri, Nguyen Duc Thang, Cao Van Vien, and Nguyen Chanh Thi, who with Diem's fall had returned from exile to resume leadership of the Airborne Brigade. Regardless of our rank, however, we shared a style of leadership that demonstrated the potential of the our military to fight well and to avoid the self-defeating temptations of corruption. Where the ARVN simmered with political intrigue, we presented a united front. When we began to speak out against inept leaders and bungling politicians, the newspapers dubbed us "Young Turks."

We met infrequently and almost never socialized with each other, but as events unfolded we often conferred by telephone. When action was required, we moved while the older generals considered options and argued over details. We sought nothing for ourselves: Our only agenda was to crush the communists and achieve the peace that our country required for economic and social development. Backed by elite and loyal troops, our growing power was recognized by the older Vietnamese generals no less than by American advisors and diplomats. The Young Turks was an informal group with neither dues nor dogma; for several reasons, including my ability to speak clear English, I emerged as the group spokesman, as the first among equals.

So when General Nguyen Khanh telephoned in February 1964, less than three months after Big Minh took power, I was not surprised. Khanh commanded I Corps, the northernmost of Vietnam's four military regions. He had something on his mind, but all he said was "Why don't you come up and have a drink?"

Khanh was headquartered in Da Nang, only two hours by air, and I had plenty of transportation, so I paid a visit to this wiry, compact man who sported a goatee and wore the jaunty red paratrooper's beret. When cocktails had been poured and we were alone in his office, Khanh started ranting about Big Minh. "I have begun to think that Minh and [Prime Minister Nguyen Ngoc] Tho are not truly anti-Communists," he said. "Maybe they want to set up their own political party, make a deal with the Vietcong."

This was a very strong accusation. Even if Khanh didn't mean his words to be taken literally, he was saying that Minh and Tho were not patriots. We were making conversation, and I was a guest, and I had never had much respect for Minh, so I didn't dispute the charge. "Maybe so," I said. "It is possible."

I didn't think too much about of this conversation; the old generals were always jockeying and scheming. So I put it out of my mind until a few weeks later. At 7:00 A.M. on January 30, 1964, the phone rang and there was Khanh. "Last night I staged a coup," he said. "I put those generals in prison. But someone told me that you air force guys are against this. Is that so?"

"No," I replied. "I'm not against you."

I was not *against* Khanh, but mostly I was not *for* Big Minh and his supporters. My view was that I should stay out of it, that the disagreement was among the ARVN and its generals, and I preferred not to be involved in this family squabble. I was not one of the army brothers, I was only their air force cousin, and I thought it best to stick to flying and fighting the war. I had plenty to do: Thanks to America, the VNAF was getting new aircraft and U.S.-trained pilots, our base facilities were being enlarged and upgraded, and South Vietnam was getting a modern air traffic control system. I was proud to lead the way, happy that the VNAF could at last begin to take the offensive against the communists.

Khanh's government lasted nine days. Then Big Minh's supporters forced him out. Khanh escaped Saigon, regrouped, made new alliances; five weeks later he was back in power.

Despite my desire to stay out of politics, the generals recognized the power and the influence of the VNAF and the role that I, based near the seat of power, could play in supporting or stopping a coup. If Diem had appointed an able and loyal officer to head the VNAF, instead of weak paper-shufflers, he could not have been deposed so easily. Thus when powerful men whose troops were far from the political center began to covet the Presidential Palace, the generals came to me.

After Khanh took power a second time and had begun to consolidate his position, General Duong Van Duc, the IV Corps commander, invited me to his headquarters in the steamy Mekong River town of Can Tho. Duc typified the old-guard, a French-speaking political hack with a reputation as a heavy drinker. He put a glass in my hand and immediately launched in on what bothered him about those Saigon rascals: practically everything.

Ever the polite visitor and still a little naive about such matters, I raised no objection. I should have known that he was planning another coup—but they all talked, those old generals. Talked and talked and talked. Several days later, while lunching at home with a few of my pilots, Marine Corps commander Le Nguyen Khang telephoned.

"I think there is a coup!" he said. "I see tanks moving around the city." I told my pilots to return to their units, stand by their planes, and watch to see what happened. Two seconds later they came running back.

"General, tanks are all around Tansonnhut—they now occupy the base."

I got ready to go to the First Transport Wing, but before I

could leave, General Khanh, the prime minister, burst into my house shouting "They staged a coup!"

"Follow me," I said. Trailing my Jeep in his black Mercedes sedan, the prime minister drove to the First Transport Wing. Flanking the compound gate were a pair of big tanks. The tank commanders saw me, saw Khanh—and watched us drive around them through the gate. Perhaps they had no orders to stop anyone going *in*.

It was lunchtime, and everybody was in the dining room, including mechanics. I put Khanh aboard a C-47 and prepared for takeoff. As I had done many times under combat conditions, I topped off the fuel, did a preflight check, made the engines ready. To avoid wasting time looking for an auxiliary power unit, I turned one massive propeller until it moved freely, then jerked it down hard several times, until the engine coughed to life. I used its electrical power to start the other engine. We taxied out onto the concrete apron and down the runway; at the end I turned around and prepared for takeoff.

And saw a dozen tanks rumbling toward us, spreading out across the tarmac. Very clever, I thought. Put tanks on the runway and no one can take off or land. I thought that they might be about one second late as I kicked off the toe brakes and punched the throttles to maximum power. We roared straight toward the tanks. Each had a cannon and two machine guns; a burst or two would have crippled my thin-skinned C-47. The tanks did not fire, however, and as we reached airspeed I pulled back the yoke and the nose rose. We cleared their turrets by inches; if the tankers had elevated their cannons, they would have torn off the bottom of my plane. Even if we survived the crash, the history of my country would have been quite different.

Once aloft I called the commander at Bien Hoa, Vietnam's second-biggest air base and only twelve miles from Saigon. This was Pham Phu Quoc, one of the Skyraider pilots who had bombed Diem's palace in 1960. When Diem fell, I got him out of jail, made him a colonel, and put him in charge of the base and its air division. When I told him of the coup, he said that nothing had happened in Bien Hoa. We remained in control.

"Put everyone on alert, and don't allow anyone to occupy your base," I said. Then I asked General Khanh about his plans. Where did he want to go?

"Take me to Vung Tau," he said. "The troops there are loyal to me." When I dropped him at the pleasant, seaside resort south of Saigon, I asked about the mess in the capital. "Go back to Saigon and do whatever you think necessary," he replied.

Instead I flew to Bien Hoa, established myself in Colonel Quoc's headquarters, and acted as if Bien Khanh had put me in charge of the whole country. I called the commanders of the marines, the airborne, the navy, the Saigon military district—all the Young Turks—and I called General Duong Van Duc, the IV Corps commander. "You must return to Can Tho, and take your tanks and troops with you," I said. "I don't appreciate what you are doing. It is not good for the country."

Duc still thought that he could take power and turned a deaf ear to my request. So I asked Quoc to send a few Skyraiders south toward Can Tho. They found Duc's armored columns rolling north on the highway and fired off a few rockets, destroying one or two U.S.-made Pattons. The column clanked to a halt. It was on a narrow road surrounded by miles of flooded rice paddies interlaced with canals—soggy terrain through which no tank could maneuver. The armor commanders did not require a Patton to explain their situation: If a few rockets could kill a tank, block the road, stop the column, a few more could cut off all retreat. Then my planes could destroy the whole unit at leisure. The next day the tanks turned around and returned to Can Tho.

Unfortunately, it was not the last coup.

...

The war became even more complicated after August 2, 1964, when three North Vietnamese patrol boats attacked the U.S. destroyer *Maddox* in the Gulf of Tonkin ten miles off the coast of North Vietnam. The patrol boats fired torpedoes and machine guns, but only a single bullet actually struck the ship. The communists were driven off by aircraft from the U.S. carrier *Ticonderoga*, which sank one boat and damaged the other two.

Much has been written about this and a second incident in the Gulf of Tonkin, and I will not add to that body of literature except to recall that it was a turning point in my nation's struggle against North Vietnam's invasion. Armed with war powers from the U.S. Congress, President Johnson sent combat troops to South Vietnam and began pouring what would be billions of dollars into helping to defend my country.

On August 21, 1964, responding in part to student and Buddhist protests in the streets of Saigon but also to incessant pressure from the U.S. Embassy, Khanh restructured his government to share power with two of the generals who had brought down Diem: Big Minh and Tran Thien Khiem. This did not end the violence or bring stability, and less than a month later, on September 13, former minister of the interior General Lam Van Phat tried to oust the Khanh government. He did not succeed.

Here is what U. Alexis Johnson, a senior embassy official, said about the attempted coup in a secret, high-priority telegram sent to the White House:

> spent one and one-half hours with Phat and another hour and one-half with "Big" Minh . . . Phat very confused with vague ideas of big committee of 100 or so with an executive committee to run govt in place of PriMin for four month period end of which general elections would be held. Claims support from most military elements except I Corps, admits that Ky,

Air Force, is sitting on fence. I was tough with him, made it
clear thought his ideas were harebrained, and we were still
supporting Khanh as PriMin of recognized govt. Talked hard
about necessity avoiding clashes between ARVN forces, leaving areas in 4th [Corps] uncovered for VC, etc. . . . He promised that he would do all possible avoid clashes and would not
initiate any attacks . . . Minh was in low sprite [*sic*] but made
it emphatically clear that as much as he disliked Khanh, he
felt Khanh was not at fault for much of what had happened.
He thought Duc, Phat and company were mad in what they
were attempting to do, had no support from population or
anyone else . . .

In response, U.S. Secretary of State Dean Rusk's office cabled U.S. ambassador Maxwell D. Taylor:

it is imperative that there not be internecine war within South
Vietnamese armed forces, whose energies and resources are
needed for victory over a common enemy, the Viet Cong . . .
the picture of petty bickering among Vietnamese leaders has
created an appalling impression abroad and causes friends of
South Vietnamese freedom all over the world to wonder how
serious South Vietnamese are about their freedom and security and what there is for others to support; Communist capitals are already expressing their glee over most recent news
from Saigon . . .

The US has not provided massive assistance to South Vietnam, in military equipment, economic resources and personnel, in order to subsidize continuing quarrels among South
Vietnamese leaders. The use of US equipment and resources
to pursue quarrels is an outrageous abuse of such assistance
and raises the gravest issues for the USG and people . . . The
US has pledged its full commitment to the security and in-

dependence of South Viet Nam . . . It is we who stand between the free peoples of Southeast Asia and that potential
tide sweeping down from the north. But what can be the purpose of this commitment and the massive US force in position
to meet it if South Vietnamese leaders themselves cannot declare a moratorium on personal rivalries and secondary differences about the details of government until such time as
their country is secure . . . South Vietnamese leaders need not
look among themselves for enemies; they all have a common
enemy in the Viet Cong. Remind them of Viet Cong plans for
their liquidation and of Benjamin Franklin's remark that if
they do not hang together they will surely hang separately . . .
emphasize that Vietnamese leaders must not take the US for
granted. We have tried to exercise the greatest patience because of difficulties which have been bravely faced by the
Vietnamese people but patience and understanding are being
drained away by disputes which seem to us to be intolerable
in the face of our common dangers and tasks. The American
people are already beginning to ask what are we supporting
and why when they hear of these repeated internal differences
among comrades in arms.

America has had many generals but few authentic military
heroes. Among these was General Taylor, who distinguished
himself during World War II, again in Korea a few years later,
and capped a brilliant military career by serving as chairman of
the Joint Chiefs of Staff. Taylor became U.S. ambassador to
South Vietnam in July 1964 and had hardly settled in when he
received the telegram just quoted. I wonder how he felt about
this State Department missive, which might be taken to imply
that Taylor, no less than we Vietnamese generals, needed lessons
in history, civics, and diplomacy.

Even if he ignored the schoolmarmish tone of that telegram,

Taylor the warrior was not by temperament a diplomat. He tried very hard but never meshed with any of the five South Vietnamese governments that he confronted during this politically unstable period. He was a fine old soldier who would have done a superb job running the U.S. military presence in Vietnam—but what we needed from America just then was a diplomat. Despite his comparative youth, General William Westmoreland, who had recently assumed leadership of the military side of the U.S. team, would have been a better choice as U.S. ambassador.

...

By December 1964 Khanh, still head of the armed forces, had bowed to U.S. pressure for a civilian government and allowed the so-called High National Council, a nine-man junta chaired by Dr. Phan Khac Suu, to appoint Tran Van Huong as prime minister. A former Saigon mayor and schoolteacher, Huong was old and in poor health, and had about as much chance of succeeding as a toddler riding a racehorse. He vacillated on important decisions and did not stand up for the people. Soon the streets of Saigon were again filled with demonstrators protesting his rule.

One night in December, General Westmoreland invited the Young Turks to his villa for dinner with himself and General Taylor. Westmoreland was cordial and fed us very good steaks accompanied by an excellent wine. Taylor took the occasion to lecture us on the importance of political stability in Vietnam. He repeated and amplified the thoughts quoted in the telegram from Rusk and strongly implied that stability was a condition of continuing American help. Unlike Big Minh and his cronies, the young generals at the table did not require such a lesson from Taylor or anyone else. But of course we did not say so; the ambassador was right about the need for stability. He concluded his performance by saying, quite clearly: "Stop the coups. No more coups."

Only a few days after that dinner, Khanh asked the Young Turks to come to his office at the headquarters of the ARVN General Staff, where he told us that Minh and four members of the High National Council were planning to depose Suu and Huong and take power. We discussed this among ourselves and after a time decided that we had no choice but to stop this plot before it happened. We sent officers accompanied by military police to the conspirators' quarters, and in a few hours all were in custody. I had them flown to Pleiku, where they were placed under house arrest in a comfortable villa.

An angry Taylor immediately called Khanh and demanded that he come to the embassy. Khanh knew exactly what Taylor had in mind and was not about to accept a trip to the woodshed from any foreigner. He asked me to represent him at the meeting, and when I reluctantly agreed, Admiral Chung Cang Tan and Generals Thi and Nguyen Van Thieu decided to accompany me.

When we were ushered into Taylor's office, he barked "Sit down!" not "Good morning," or "Thank you for coming." Just "Sit down," as if we were schoolboys summoned to the headmaster. His face white with anger, Taylor began to berate us. Ambassador Taylor was fluent in French, but General Taylor chose to speak in English. "I told you this, I told you that, and still you did this," he ranted. On and on he went. "Don't you remember at dinner I explained it to you? I wasted my dinner," he growled.

I think Taylor was angry because he identified closely with us as military officers, and he was as shocked and disappointed as if he had actually been our senior in the Vietnamese armed forces instead of the representative of an allied nation. In fact, using a contemptuous tone of voice, Taylor reminded us that he had been a general while Khanh was still a cadet! I bit back my anger and just listened.

When Taylor had finished his diatribe, I waited for Thieu,

the senior officer, to respond. Instead he sat silent, as if he did not know how to reply. The others also held their tongues, but I think it was because their English was so poor. The silence grew oppressive, so I took the liberty of answering.

"Mr. Ambassador, you said you wasted your dinner," I began. "I don't agree. In all my life I have never enjoyed such a beautiful steak, such a fine wine. As a poor man, it is very rare for me to have such a dinner. So you didn't waste it; I really appreciate the meal you gave me. Now, if you want to talk about what we are doing, that is a different matter."

Taylor was still angry, but he had cooled down a bit. "Why did you do it?" he said. "Why another coup?"

"Maybe we are wrong, but we thought that we acted in the best interest of our country," I replied. Where he was angry, I was calm. Where he scowled, I smiled. "So what *you* think is different than what *we* think—and that is that."

I half expected Taylor to become even angrier, but once the ambassador saw that I spoke English well enough to challenge him, he calmed himself, changed to a more conversational tone, and again explained why Vietnam needed stability, and so forth. And at great length. In his report to the U.S. State Department about this meeting, Taylor wrote:

I pointed out that they had in fact usurped power which had been transferred to HNC [High National Council] and government last August 27 and all the world would interpret action simply as military coup. They had destroyed charter and whole basis for orderly development of government started last August 27 and which had so greatly encouraged US and rest of world. If Huong and Suu remained in office under these conditions it would make a mockery of civilian government, it being obvious they remaining only at sufferance of military and at best were military puppets subject to removal any time military displeased with them.

That message was of course highly classified and not intended for Vietnamese eyes; I first read these words more than thirty-six years later. What is astonishing, even now, is that on the one hand the Americans recognized that the only group in Vietnam with unity and strength was the military—and on the other hand, because in the U.S. system, the military *must* be under civilian control, the Americans expended enormous diplomatic efforts to insist that the Vietnamese military abandon the leadership role in favor of a civilian government!

According to other recently declassified documents, George Ball, then undersecretary of state, affirmed this peculiar dichotomy, and on more than one occasion. Ball was the only one of President Johnson's top advisors to conclude that civilian government in Vietnam was an illusion, that realistically the United States must choose between embracing a military government or withdrawing its support. In 1964 we Young Turks were well aware that the military was the only institution capable of leading the country. Our challenge was to do so in the face of continuing U.S. pressure to bring in civilian leadership.

Yet even Taylor seemed to understand that South Vietnam's civilian leaders were not capable of governing. "Suu certainly not capable of resisting the military; Huong is capable only with strong U.S. encouragement," he cabled the U.S. secretary of state, Dean Rusk, only the day before our meeting with him. How could the chief of state, an old man in poor health, give orders to the military and expect that they would be obeyed?

So when at the end of his tirade Taylor suggested, very firmly, that we attempt to undo that which we had accomplished in the preceding days, we could not even discuss such a move. "What is done is done," I replied. "We cannot return to the past." We said good-bye politely, but when we reported Taylor's rudeness, anger, and paternalistic attitude toward not only Khanh but the entire Vietnamese military, Khanh became as angry we were. We decided to call a press conference and declare Taylor persona non grata.

As it turned out, however, the CIA had either a listening device or an informer in our headquarters. Within ten minutes someone at the U.S. Embassy called Khanh and begged him not to expel Taylor. Soon after that several senior American officers arrived to talk with us, all very concerned about what we planned to do. Khanh and some of the other Young Turks wanted to use Taylor's conduct as a way to discredit not only the U.S. ambassador but also the civilian leaders whom Taylor wanted to remain in power. I was inclined to support Khanh, but finally one of the Americans cleverly raised the issue of military solidarity and espirit de corps. To destroy such a heroic former general as Maxwell Taylor was not good, he said. "You are all military, he is one of your own," he argued. Declaring him persona non grata would be an ignominious end to a long and distinguished career. It would forever tarnish his reputation, damage Vietnamese relations with the U.S. military, and make it very difficult for Taylor's successor.

That made sense, and I changed my mind. In private, I asked Khanh not to expel Taylor. The others still wanted Taylor gone, but Khanh had to listen to me, because he knew that he could not remain in power without my support. When the Americans departed we discussed the matter again. In the end we decided that a press conference describing why we had ousted the civilian government and arrested Big Minh would be enough. Khanh, however, took the opportunity at the conference to tell the press that Taylor's attitude was indicative of America's colonialist attitude toward South Vietnam. This was not true, but it generated headlines. After a year in Saigon, Taylor was replaced by Henry Cabot Lodge, Jr.

...

One of the more memorable attempts to oust Khanh came in February 1965, masterminded by ARVN Colonel Pham Ngoc

Thao and General Lam Van Phat, former minister of the interior. Once again General Duc's troops occupied Saigon. Thao had been one of Nhu's favorites; brother Diem made him chief of Ben Tre Province. A bon vivant with a glass eye, he was a fabulous character, well liked by Americans because they fancied him a plain-speaking man. He was also secretly working for the communists. Many Vietnamese suspected this about Thao, but confirmation did not come until after the war.

A few hours after Phat's tanks rolled, the senior U.S. advisor to the VNAF, Brigadier General Robert Rowland, called me at Bien Hoa to inquire, on behalf of his government, if I supported Phat. I said, "Hell, no."

I mentioned that Thao had been involved in the coup that overthrew and murdered Diem and that his loyalties were suspect. Phat was a different story. He had a poor combat record, and when he lost his temper, a common event, he reputedly kicked and beat his troops, conduct that has no place in any army. Even more important, I told the general, I did not support the coup because I was against this kind of infighting.

I told Rowland that I had sent a message to Phat giving him until 7:00 P.M. to remove his troops from Tansonnhut and go fight the communists. If the troops had not left Tansonnhut by this deadline, I would bomb the air base.

"I'm right here, don't kill me!" said Rowland.

"It is better that you leave before seven," I replied. Make no mistake: I was not bluffing.

At 6:00 P.M. Rowland called to say that Thao wanted to see me. I agreed—but launched two flights of Skyraiders, eight aircraft carrying thirty-two tons of rockets—to fly over Saigon. Those planes could remain aloft for four or five hours. With this move I both controlled the air over the capital and would be able to quash further hostile troop movements into the city.

Thao arrived after dark in a U.S. aircraft accompanied by

Colonel Samuel Vaughan Wilson. Wilson was CIA; he would go on to become a specialist on Soviet communism and a three-star army general who served as U.S. military attaché to Moscow. The day that we met, however, he was trying to protect Thao, who later proved to be a communist agent. Wilson carried a submachine gun, and when he got out of the plane my men told him that he couldn't bring it into the meeting. There was a shouting match, with Wilson yelling and threatening to bring the wrath of the United States of America down on anyone who tried to take his gun away.

Eventually someone asked me for a decision: Let Wilson and his gun in the room, or keep both out. "Don't worry," I said. "Let him keep his gun."

Thao came in and after the preliminaries spent several minutes earnestly tried to persuade me that the coup was in the best interests of the country, that he merely sought to replace a government that was not working.

"Maybe you are right about Khanh, but replacing him with Phat is even worse," I replied. "What sense is there in replacing one who is not good with one who is really bad? What is the benefit to the country?

"I think that considering all the general officers who might take Khanh's place, I would make the best prime minister—but I would never consider a coup. Right now only the communists benefit from our infighting. So don't talk nonsense to me. If you want to do something for your country, ask Phat to send his troops back to their bases and fight the communists!"

I paused for a moment and looked right at Thao. "Otherwise, tomorrow I will destroy all of you."

Finally he understood. The next morning at eight, Thao told me that Phat's troops were heading back to their garrisons.

Thao came to an unhappy end. After this abortive putsch, he went underground, but was nabbed by civilian police in Saigon. He died in jail a few weeks later, probably from a beating.

Between coups and flying combat missions, I somehow found time to fall in love again. At the beginning of my romance with an Air Vietnam stewardess, I asked her to dinner in Saigon. She was scheduled for a flight to Da Lat, however. Without thinking, I said, "Then I will accompany your plane from Saigon to Da Lat."

Then I learned that the venerable C-47, with its two recip-rocating engines, could not keep up with Air Vietnam's four-engine DC-6. In fact, the only VNAF aircraft capable of holding formation with that prop jet was the Douglas A-1 Skyraider. Contrary to what the oft-honored writer Frances FitzGerald has written, it is not a "tiny" aircraft. It is the biggest single-engine, propeller-driven attack plane ever built. A Skyraider carried more ordnance than the four-engine B-17 Flying Fortress.

As VNAF commander I thought that I should know how to fly every kind of aircraft in our inventory, but the Skyraider was still a fairly recent addition, and I had not yet gotten around to flying it. Normally, making the transition to a new aircraft type requires at least two or three days, starting with ground instruc-tion to learn the characteristics of the airplane. If you are an experienced pilot—and by that time I had logged over nine thousand hours—after ground instruction and a couple of hours flying with an instructor pilot, you are ready to take the new aircraft for a solo flight.

But the VNAF had only one dual-control Skyraider, and it was in use that morning. And I didn't have two days. I had an hour, and I had a promise to keep. I went down to the A-1 squadron and explained my problem to the squadron leader. "Let me borrow one Skyraider," I said.

"You ever fly this airplane?" he said.

I shook my head. "Never."

"I cannot let you fly," he said.

I studied his face for a minute. "Are you the commander of

the air force, or is it me?" I said. "Now give me your best and newest parachute, and come down to the flight line with me."

I strapped on the parachute and climbed into the cockpit. "The preflight checklist," I said, and took a few minutes to study the paper. "Okay, now show me how to start the engine," I ordered, and the squadron leader set the throttle and the fuel mix and pressed the starter button. As the engine warmed up I got him to show me how to put the wheels down and a few other essentials. Then I taxied out to the flight line and did some preflight tests, running the engine to maximum rpm, looking over my shoulder to see that the rudder and ailerons worked.

Never had I flown such a powerful aircraft! It was designed to carry four tons of bombs and rockets, but of course the racks under the wings were empty, so as I raced down the runway the Skyraider was a tiger leaping into the sky. As I climbed, the plane tugged left, then right; it took all the strength of both arms and both legs to establish control. By the time I had stabilized aircraft attitude, I was at 12,000 feet. I didn't know where I was, nor where to find the DC-6. I radioed Saigon tower and asked for a heading and an altitude that would bring me to the Air Vietnam plane.

The tower gave me a vector and I went to full power, using the engine's full 2,800 horsepower to reach a speed of about 350 mph. Soon I had the Air Vietnam ship in sight, and as I came alongside I sideslipped until only a few inches separated our wingtips. The DC-6 captain and his copilot, both assigned to the First Transport Wing, knew exactly who was flying the Skyraider—and that it was my first time. But they also knew me well enough to say nothing until a certain pretty face appeared in the cockpit window and maybe ten minutes had elapsed.

"Uh, General, I think maybe that is enough," said the Air Vietnam pilot over the radio. "Maybe you should go back to Tansonnhut now." I didn't want to scare them and their passengers any more, so I waved good-bye and edged away until I could safely bank and head back to Saigon.

Now came the biggest problem: landing safely, and without looking like a fool. As I approached the field, most of the Skyraider squadron's pilots, plus other VNAF aviators and civilian and military traffic controllers, gathered in the tower to watch.

I made the worst landing of my life. I bounced up and down and almost killed myself getting that plane under control and stopped. I knew they all up there in the tower looking at me, but I was angry with myself. I called the tower and said, "I'm going to do this more time, one more takeoff, one more landing."

"No, no, General, that's enough," said the squadron leader's voice in my headphones. That was all I needed to hear. I gunned the engine and roared off into the sky, this time looking very professional, and when I came back through the air traffic pattern for my second landing I set down lightly, as if I had been piloting Skyraiders for years. The next time I took off in an A-1, I would carry a full load of bombs to drop on the enemy.

Despite my reputation as a ladies' man and a womanizer, when I began to pursue this air hostess I was unsure of myself. I discovered that she was also a northerner; her father, a staunch anticommunist, had become involved in politics. He was shot to death by guerrillas in Hanoi. In 1954 his widow and children came south. They lived for a time in Nha Trang.

Two or three weeks after I taught myself to fly a Skyraider, I made a date to take the air hostess to dinner. That morning I flew a helicopter over two hundred miles to the Mekong River on an operation, and by the time I returned to Saigon there was not time enough to go to Tansonnhut, shower, change clothes, then drive to her house. If I did that, I realized, I would be at least half an hour late.

I should have telephoned from the base, but instead I decided on a grand gesture. My new girlfriend lived on Le Loi, Saigon's principal boulevard, and when I hovered my Huey helicopter just above the trees near her house, the late-afternoon streets were jammed with cars, pedicabs, taxis, and pedestrians. My rotor wash kicked up an enormous whirlwind of dust, trash, and tree leaves that stopped traffic in all directions. I hovered until she came outside, then shouted, "Please wait for me, I will be a little late!" Then I flew off in a cloud of debris.

I enjoyed a very pleasant evening, but the next morning at seven Prime Minister Khanh, called my office. "Hey, Ky!" he bellowed. "One of your pilots landed right in the center of Saigon yesterday! What was he doing down there? Find out who that fool is and kick him out of the air force! Send him to prison!"

I waited a few beats. "Well, General, it was me," I said. His voice changed. "Oh, you again. What were you doing down there?"

I told him about being in love. "I was late for our rendezvous, I was afraid she would go out with someone else. So I stopped by to tell her to wait for me. That's it."

Khanh understood. He really liked me, and I had supported him through tough times. And, with the Young Turks behind him, he felt very secure. I heard nothing more about my near landing on Le Loi Boulevard.

When the air force attacks, we move very quickly. Don't give the enemy time to think! So I approached this romance as I would a military campaign. First I ended my affair with my previous girlfriend and arranged to support the child she was carrying. A few years later, she, like my first wife, married a U.S. Air Force colonel and left Vietnam.

Then I proposed marriage to the air hostess. Her mother was against me, and I could not really blame her. I had a very bad reputation, she said. "But that depends who is talking," I replied. "I was good and polite enough to ask your permission— but I can tell you that with or without your agreement, I will marry your daughter. You can do nothing." After that, she gave up, because she knew that she could not prevail against my determination. We were married in April 1964.

About that time General Khanh gave me a check for a million dong, the equivalent then of nearly U.S. $10,000 and in today's currency worth about U.S. $50,000. My monthly salary as head of the air force was between 4,000 or 5,000 dong. The prime minister, who had many expenses, got only 50,000 dong.

I supposed that this extraordinary sum was intended to buy my allegiance, so of course I knew that I couldn't keep it. When I returned to my office I showed all my officers the check. "I will donate this to Air Force Welfare," I said, referring to a fund used to help airmen with family emergencies, for survivors' death benefits, and for funeral expenses. There was no life insurance in Vietnam at that time, and without this fund the burden on the families of airmen killed or wounded in the line of duty would have been intolerable. There was never enough in the fund to cover all the demands on it, so there was no way that I could keep such a sum when my men were so poor.

But I was not quite ready to part with the money. "Please let me keep this for a little while, because this is the first time I am a millionaire," I said. I carried the check in my shirt pocket and showed it to people wherever I went. I was a millionaire just that once, and I savored the thought. But after two or three days, I gave the money to Air Force Welfare.

My joy at marriage was tempered by the death of my mother, who a few weeks earlier had passed away from the complications of diabetes. I still regret that Mother did not live to see my elevation to prime minister.

...

Despite some success in defeating Vietcong units in our countryside, the political instability that wracked Saigon encouraged the communists to take bolder and bolder actions. After the Gulf of Tonkin Resolution enabled President Johnson to take a more active role in our defense, Americans became prime targets for the Vietcong. On November 1, 1964, they attacked the U.S.

compound at Bien Hoa Air Base with mortar fire, killing five Americans and wounding almost a hundred other men. In the next few weeks, about 10,000 soldiers of the North Vietnamese Army—regulars, not guerrillas—invaded the Central Highlands region, bringing sophisticated weapons provided by China and the Soviet Union. These troops reinforced understrength and worn-out Vietcong battalions with weapons and provided experienced leaders. With this action, however, the communists dropped the mask they had worn in trying to pretend that they were engaged in a civil war. Now the world could see that this was an invasion. A few months later, in February 1965, the communists attacked the U.S. military compound at Pleiku, killing eight Americans, wounding 126, and destroying ten aircraft.

Finally, President Johnson had had enough. After a few days he approved the bombing of a North Vietnamese training base near Dong Hoi by U.S. Navy aircraft. I thought that it was important for both civilian and troop morale in South Vietnam that the VNAF have a role in this operation, and the Americans agreed. That month we prepared the first VNAF strike on North Vietnam. I created an elite unit, the Thanh Phong Squadron, for the first mission. In the ancient Chinese characters used by my ancestors, *thanh phong* means "divine wind." Japanese, whose kanji writing system is based on older Chinese ideographs, pronounce these characters *kamikaze*, but I think the Vietnamese is rather more elegant. Every pilot in the squadron volunteered for this raid; we held a lottery to determine who would go. Just as I had flown the first infiltration missions over the North, I decided that I must set the example by leading this first strike against the communist homeland.

On the day before the raid we flew to Da Nang, where I took a call from the I Corps commander. "The people of Hue want to see you and your men before the attack tomorrow," he said. If our mission had ever been secret, I realized, it was no longer.

When we landed at the ancient city on the Perfume River, we were taken to a huge auditorium packed with upward of a thousand students from the lycées and the university. So many beautiful girls in their flowing *ao dai*! So many earnest young boys! Clad in our flight suits, we took the stage to thunderous applause.

I had not expected such a huge throng. Nor had I prepared remarks. I spoke from my heart: "Tomorrow we cross the border, and perhaps none of us will return. But we are here to show that we will carry the fight to the enemy. Remember us if we don't come home, remember that we came today, remember that we said good-bye." We filed out of the building, surrounded by tearful students who reached out to touch us as we went by.

In that moment I recalled the warrior Kinh Kha, who lived in the time of the Tan dynasty, when northern Vietnam was ruled by China. Kinh Kha was asked to assassinate Emperor Tan Thuy Hoang, the tyrant who began construction of the Great Wall. This mighty king was very well protected; even though Kinh Kha's feats were already legendary and he was the most famous swordsman of his time, this was an obvious suicide mission. Because even an unsuccessful attempt would send a vital message, however, Kinh Kha accepted the task. As he set out from his homeland, thousands of people lined the roads, weeping and reaching out to touch him as he passed.

In the morning, before heading for the target, we flew over Hue, twenty-four Skyraiders roaring low over the city in single file. I looked down from the lead plane and saw every street filled with waving people. It seemed like the entire population had turned out to cheer us on.

An hour later, still in single file, we approached Dong Hoi, where I had selected my squadron's target. Still at cruising altitude I saw dozens of U.S. Navy planes bombing and strafing our target. Later I would learn that the Americans, fearing for

my safety, had decided to try to knock out some of the antiaircraft guns first and make it easier for us to bomb.

But I wouldn't learn that until my return. Closing on Dong
Hoi at 350 miles per hour, watching the sky fill with dark puffs
from exploding flak, I thought that perhaps the Americans had
made some mistake. Because the original target was under attack, I looked around for something else. Suddenly I saw a huge
building bristling with dozens of antiaircraft guns. This must be
a very important place, I thought. Attack it! Later I learned that
it was headquarters for an antiaircraft division.

I pushed the stick forward and dived at maximum power. At
about 2,000 feet a swarm of glowing tracers come arcing upward
to envelop my plane. The Skyraider shook and shuddered from
one impact after another. A big tracer flew directly at me—I
threw up my left hand to protect my eyes just as the windshield
shattered.

My first reaction was to climb and turn toward the Gulf of
Tonkin, because I did not know how badly my aircraft was damaged or if I was wounded. If I had to ditch or bail out, I knew
that I would have a better chance of seeing home again where
the Americans controlled sea and sky.

So I banked eastward. Although a typhoon of air rushed
through what was left of the windshield, in a moment I could
tell that I was unhurt, that my aircraft was operational. I tried
to tell my pilots to continue the attack, but our air-to-air frequency was jammed with their chatter—no one heard me. Then
I glanced back and saw that when I turned away from the target,
everyone had followed: In the air strike business it is customary
to follow the leader. And so we stupidly flew away from the
target, Mother Goose and twenty-three bomb-laden goslings.

After a minute the others could see that I was still in control
of my aircraft. Their chatter quieted. On the radio I told them
to concentrate on the target, follow me back, and get on with

the bombing. Someone said there was too much flak, the target was too well defended, we should find another target.

"No," I said. "Come on." When I turned again toward the target, they all followed. I came in low this time, but we needed more altitude to drop bombs. The communists were waiting: As I made a climbing approach more tracers greeted me and I took two or three more hits in the wings. Time seemed to crawl by in slow motion, flak exploding all around, the sky filled with tracers zipping by at every angle. Then I released my bombs, pulled back on the stick, jammed the rudder to the left, and clawed my way toward the safety of the clouds. Behind me, one by one, my pilots did the same.

When we formed up I counted all twenty-four aircraft. Every plane was hit. Two pilots reported that their A-1s were so damaged that they could not land, and they could steer only with difficulty. We flew together until Da Nang appeared ahead of us, and I called for a rescue helicopter. I told the pilots who could not land to bail out over the sea. By the time the rest of the squadron had set down in Da Nang, both had been rescued.

Before flying again, I asked the mechanics to look for the bullet that smashed my windshield. They found a 12.7 mm slug buried behind my seat; when I sat down again, the hole in the seat was near the center of my back. Then I raised my left arm and saw that my black flight suit was burned white beneath my biceps and along my side. I peeled off the suit to find purple bruises beneath the burned areas. Apparently, just as I threw up my hand to protect my eyes, a copper-jacketed steel bullet weighing about half a pound and traveling 2,500 feet per second traversed the arc of four propeller blades revolving over 1,000 times a minute and then threaded the slight gap between my arm and my chest.

How did the bullet miss smashing my propeller? How did I avoid losing an arm, then bleeding to death?

I can never know for sure. What I do know is when I took

off from Da Nang, around my neck was a copper amulet with a likeness of the Buddha, a gift of Savang Vatthana, King of Laos. Upon my return to Tansonnhut, my office was inundated with hundreds of letters and calls from army officers expressing admiration for my feat and confirming a great surge in the morale of their troops. I felt proud and humbled by my good fortune.

A few months later I became prime minister.

8
PRIME MINISTER

A few hours after accepting the assignment of prime minister from the Armed Forces Council, I returned to my office to find visitors waiting: a small Buddhist delegation led by Thien Minh, an influential monk in his fifties whom I knew well. "It would be better if you did not serve as prime minister," he said. "It's a trap. By giving you such heavy responsibilities, your enemies seek to destroy you. We don't want that to happen—you are a son of Buddha, a good Buddhist."

"Listen, I did not ask for this position," I replied, and explained how the civilians had turned power back to the military, and the military chose me. Thien Minh replied that the monks had opposed Diem, a Catholic who discriminated against Buddhism. Diem was gone, but Catholics still held most of the power in government. With a Buddhist premier, it would be very difficult for them to continue their struggle for religious freedom.

I listened politely as the monks tried to convince me. Finally I said, "I didn't make the decision that I should be premier, but once I accepted it from the military, I must carry out my responsibilities: bring back stability and unite our efforts in the fight against the communist invasion. Just as in the past, when I received orders, I will do my duty."

There was much truth in Thien Minh's message; the monks considered me sympathetic to their cause, and if, as prime minister, I appeared to side with the Buddhists, some powerful generals might use this against me. But after my visitors had departed and I had a chance to reflect on what actually troubled the Buddhist leaders, I realized that while they perhaps regarded me as a more able foe than those who preceded me, there was more to it. It would be almost impossible to continue cloaking the Buddhist political agenda behind claims of religious oppression with a prime minister known to be sympathetic toward religious concerns.

I believed that in the long run, the interests of Buddhists, Catholics, and all other religious, regional, and political factions would best be served by fostering unity among all in order to defeat the communists. The Buddhists, I now saw even more clearly, were concerned only with the present situation, with influencing events to satisfy their own narrow concerns. In this they were no different from any other political entity. None seemed to understand that unless South Vietnam remained united, the communists could win. But I knew that the communists were very determined and that if we lacked the strengths of unity, they *would* win—a disaster for all who loved freedom. After meeting with Thien Minh, I knew that I must deal swiftly and harshly with all who sought to undermine political stability, be they religious, military, or civilian.

Several months after I became premier, Tri Quang told officials at the U.S. Embassy that he could not support my government. Attempting to head off new demonstrations, Ambassador Henry Cabot Lodge called on Tri Quang and asked him what he wanted, what would make the Buddhists happy. "General Ky must step down," replied Quang.

"And if that were to happen, who would you want to replace him as prime minister?" asked the diplomat.

Tri Quang thought for a second. "I would put Ky back in," he answered.

In other words, Tri Quang, who could not hold power and wear a monk's saffron robes, wanted me to be *his* prime minister instead of the nation's prime minister. If I agreed, Tri Quang would become a sort of Buddhist pope, the power behind the throne.

Among those who guided the pagodas, Tri Quang was not the only one who harbored political ambitions. I was on good terms with leading monks from every region of Vietnam and from every major Buddhist sect. They had called on me even before I became head of the VNAF and had come to know me as someone who would listen to their concerns and respond from the heart. Many other monks felt some degree of sympathy for me. But as premier I represented the government, and most felt that they had to oppose *any* secular authority. Before they could move against my government, however, they had to unify their many factions, including pagodas led by men who still regarded me as a friend.

...

With a little breathing room from the Buddhist crisis, I began to consider the composition of my cabinet. Because of the way that I took office, I felt no pressure to satisfy any group by bringing its people into it. It made my choices easier: All I needed was technocrats to handle the economic, finance, education, and social dimensions of government.

As in America, where one cannot say that the Democrats represent Catholics or that the Republicans represent Methodists or Episcopalians, Vietnam's religions were not represented by any particular political party. Accordingly, I decided *not* to treat any religious group as a political entity. I picked the individual best qualified for each job and never considered their religious affiliation.

I chose General Nguyen Huu Co, the II Corps commander, to fill the sensitive post of defense minister, and General Linh Quang Vien as minister of the interior. My cabinet included five southerners: An Truong Thanh (Finance), Truong Van Thuan (Communications), Nguyen Van Truong (Education), Truong Thai Ton (Economy), and Vo Long Trieu (Youth). I gave little importance to the Foreign Ministry; in dealing with our most important allies, the Americans, I would serve as my own foreign minister. I therefore retained Dr. Tran Van Don, who had headed the ministry for years, and told him that when I had more time to review the field of candidates, I might select someone new. While far from perfect, I felt that this group was the best I could then assemble.

U.S. Ambassador Maxwell Taylor described my new cabinet in a June 21 telegram to the Department of State:

On the whole, the new Cabinet seems a very good one by Vietnamese standards and potentiality. There are seven holdovers from Quat's team and a better regional balance of Ministers than Quat had, particularly in relation to the number of southerners. There is no particular religious complexion to the Cabinet which is outstanding for its number of young, competent technicians, many of whom in the past have hesitated to serve in a Cabinet. The main question mark remains General Ky himself, who thus far has been very cooperative and approachable in the limited dealings which I have had with him in the past few days. He has a rather disarming way of alluding to his inexperience and need for assistance in an unfamiliar role.

As Taylor reported, I was acutely aware of my shortcomings: I was a flier with no political background and little patience for administrative minutia, and I had never prepared myself to lead a nation. But we were at war, the enemy was growing stronger, and once I accepted the job I knew that I did not have the luxury of a leisurely transition.

The technocrats of what I termed my War Cabinet, however, would never accomplish anything unless they could operate within the framework of a stable political system. When cabinet ministers come and go every few months, their organizations have little opportunity to attack even the most urgent problems. Worse, when there is constant turmoil at the top, quality people will not serve in the government. The great tasks of nation-building are left to underpaid, midlevel bureaucrats and second-rate minds—and if anything of merit is ever accomplished, then it is a sort of miracle.

So, along with unity of purpose, my country needed to end the game of musical chairs that had preceded me. When Thien Minh warned me that accepting the post of prime minister from the Armed Forces Council was a trap, he only confirmed what I had already perceived. From the moment that I accepted the job, I began grappling with ways to avoid the kind of mistakes that had already cost my country so dearly.

By overthrowing Diem, the military had demonstrated that they held the power in South Vietnam. At that time, however, military leadership lay in the hands of older officers, generals lacking not merely idealism but also ideas. Supported and prod-ded by American officials, they carried out a coup—and did not know what to do next. These conspirators were an ad hoc group brought together by a mixture of low motives. None trusted the others completely, and once Diem was gone, they no longer felt any unity of purpose. It was every man for himself, the great curse of Vietnamese politics.

The series of coups and anticoups that followed Diem's de-parture were symptoms of internal struggles between the rank-ing generals. Their divisiveness opened the door to all sorts of troublemakers: the Buddhists, the Catholics, and assorted political groups. But between November 1963, when Diem fell, and June 1965, when I came to power, as inept as the generals often seemed, only the armed forces were capable of governing the country. Mao was right: Political power grows out of the barrel of a gun, and the army held the most guns. When the last civilian government threw up its hands and quit, it showed that there was no alternative to the military except handing things over to the communists.

By that time, however, most of the generals who had overthrown Diem were no longer in uniform. More than half of the top leadership were comparatively junior officers like myself; the others had either been exiled or been forced to retire after one coup or another. And the military was fed up with politics. Even the most ambitious positioned themselves to watch and wait, to avoid risk. I was appointed prime minister because none of the senior officers dared to fail. My sense, even then, was that those who put me in office thought, "Let that youngster take care of all that political stuff so we can get back to fighting the enemy, or making money, or whatever. If he succeeds, fine. If not, we'll get somebody new."

If I had been like most of the senior officers, a "normal" general, I would have tried to run things all by myself or with a few close cronies, never asking the others what they thought about anything. After I had stumbled around for a few weeks or a few months, the others would have gotten together and kicked me out. One might have moved tanks around, another sent paratroops or marines—and there would have been a new backside warming the chair behind the prime minister's desk.

And Vietnam's many problems would have continued to fester. The nation would have spun still further toward anarchy and the communists would have been closer to seizing control. I decided that if I was to have any chance of succeeding, I had to get the military to share the responsibilities of governing. I wanted not just the generals but the entire officer corps involved. If I could find a way to bring them into the equation by sharing responsibility, it would not be Nguyen Cao Ky who succeeded or failed. We would all succeed, or we would all go down together.

I believed that if I could get the military leadership to sit down with me and discuss ideas and problems face to face, something that had never happened before, if I could rule less by decree and govern more by consensus, I could keep their support. I had faith in my fellow officers. I believed that with good leadership I could guide them, convince them to go my way.

So I began with a council of ten, the senior generals, including the four corps commanders, the defense minister, the chief of the Joint General Staff, and so forth. The National Leadership Committee was informally known as the Directorate. As a member of this armed forces politburo, I sat down with the others to discuss a new set of national laws to serve in lieu of the constitution that would come later. I took what we had agreed to and drafted a formal document, a national charter that spelled out the organization of the new government.

With that, the Armed Forces Council was dissolved and replaced by the Directorate. The charter, however, also created a new Armed Forces Council, comprised of officers down to regimental commanders and their air force and navy equivalents—about 1,600 colonels and generals. In this way the whole military leadership was involved in governance. When the Directorate needed input, or had matters of broad significance to discuss, we convened the council to solicit its opinions.

This organization was in some ways similar to that of the Communist party, a structure that had proven remarkably durable. The council, which met infrequently, served the same purpose as a party congress: to permit ideas to flow upward as well as downward and to involve the entire military in national affairs. Council resolutions expressed ideas and feelings that the Directorate could approve, modify, or veto. Because the council collectively chose the members of the Directorate, it had the power to force change by removing any of its members.

Within the Directorate was a smaller group, a sort of executive committee or politburo comprised of General Thieu as chief of state, General Cao Van Vien, chief of the Joint General Staff, General Pham Xuan Chieu, secretary general of the Directorate, and myself, prime minister. I chaired this group and ran the government through my cabinet.

General Taylor noted the creation of my politburo and decided, erroneously, that I had been put on a short leash:

> The charter which has been promulgated is an imperfect, hastily written document obviously designed to keep Ky under the control of his military peers. There is nothing of importance which he can do as Prime Minister without the approval of the directory [*sic*] of ten officers (of which he is a member) presided over by General Thieu. It looks as if this new government will be far more of an oligarchy than an autocracy.

Taylor was correct about the charter being imperfect and hastily written. But in any organization, and especially within a small group, a strong leader can impose his policies through deep convictions and the force of his personality. This is what I intended to do for my country. Few American officials ever grasped this, at least not until after I stepped down.

The Americans also did not understand that I had asked Thieu to serve as chief of state, or why. Ambitious but cautious, he relished the grand title, office perquisites, and high visibility that came with the public bowings and scrapings of foreign diplomats and generals. But Thieu held no power. I answered to the Directorate, which he chaired, but as prime minister, the politburo and the cabinet, including the minister of defense, reported to me. By sharing *responsibility* with the entire Directorate, however, everyone, and especially Thieu, had an incentive to help me succeed.

I was careful to establish the atmosphere of the Directorate immediately. We did not meet daily, but whenever an important decision came up, I called it together. I emphasized that the

Directorate was a team of equals, that although my duty was to run the day-to-day affairs of government, they also had important responsibilities and that I did not consider myself their superior but rather their teammate and comrade in arms. This made everyone happy. At these meetings I spoke openly, sharing my feelings and thoughts and encouraging the others to do the same. As I had hoped, as weeks melted into months, the others gradually became more open. They began to defer to my judgment, to support my decisions without reservation.

This was in marked contrast with previous "armed forces councils." Speaking of my immediate predecessors, once a general had succeeded in his coup and was in power, he began to think only of himself or a small group of his closest friends. He forgot about the force that had put him in power—the army— and began to forge political alliances with various coalitions and factions and with the religious groups. Soon those who had put him in power became frustrated and plotted another coup.

As prime minister, however, I had legitimate means to reward members of the Directorate with things that were important to them, to their careers, and to their commands. I did not buy them the way politicians buy votes, with money or lucrative government contracts. I appealed instead to their sense of patriotism, to their better nature. I told them how important they were, how we were a nation at war, how much the people depended on them, that they had the power to make a difference in the lives of millions. When you speak passionately of the good and the right thing, who can openly oppose you?

After six months, we were a team. They believed in me, and it became plain that the Directorate would do pretty much anything that I asked. Had I cared to, I am certain that I could have gotten the votes to exercise full control.

I took the same approach with the Armed Forces Council, calling meetings every few months, appealing to their patriotism, letting the officers know how vital each of them was to our nation. Looking back, I am surprised to discover that even at such a young age, I had a very political mind.

In September 1965, after the first meeting of the Armed Forces Council, *Newsweek* made me the subject of its cover story. Soon afterward I received a gift from a man whom I had yet to meet, one of my childhood heroes, John Wayne. He sent a pair of ivory-handled John Wayne Commemorative Colt .45 revolvers. I am told that only 150 of this particular model were manufactured, and so I kept one in its original box and wore the other proudly whenever I armed myself. For some reason, however, American newspapers mistakenly reported that my sidearm was "pearl-handled." Only a bordello pimp would be seen packing a pearl-handled gun! Nevertheless, the myth that I wore such a firearm was accepted as fact and repeatedly published.

...

While my elevation to premier certainly affected my daily life in many ways, it did not alter my basic personality or my view of my place the world. I did not believe that I was suddenly on a more exalted plane, or that God or Buddha now spoke to me. I took no pleasure in my greater powers. Certainly I had far heavier responsibilities, and while I appreciated these, my values were as ever. I knew that inevitably I would make mistakes, and because their consequences would likely be borne by my countrymen, I felt humbled by my fallibility even as I vowed to do the best job I could.

The two worst mistakes that I could have made, I knew from air force experience, was to appear indecisive and to let those whom I charged with the day-to-day business of government avoid shouldering responsibility for their actions. For example, one day I received a complaint that Vietnam still did not have enough classrooms for college students, and especially medical students. Because we had very few doctors trained in Western medicine, one of the first big American aid projects had been to help us build Vietnam's first medical school, a large facility patterned after modern American institutions. It was part of Saigon National University.

During a cabinet meeting I asked the minister of education why we still had a shortage of medical training. He explained that the medical school had been completed but was not yet open for students. The reason: disagreement between the minister of education and the dean of Saigon National University, who was among the very brightest people in all Vietnam. Educated in France, where he earned some sort of super-Ph.D., he was known by every Vietnamese intellectual. Because most of our leading educators had been his students, including the minister of education, the dean was very influential. The dean had decided that the new medical school should be administered as a French institution, from the titles of administrators to the language used for instruction. Nearly everyone else concerned with the medical school, including the minister of education, preferred to start fresh and to do things the American way.

Because of the dean's reputation, however, they declined to force the issue. The school would stand empty and unused until the minister of education agreed to let the dean do things his way, the French way. It might still be empty, had I not asked the minister to explain the problem.

"I don't care whether our doctors are educated in the French way or in the American way," I said. "I owe much of my formal education to France, while today our most important allies are Americans. Either way is good. But I want the school open to train new doctors! In three days I will come down and cut the ribbon and officially open this medical school to receive new students. I want you to plan a big ceremony. When I come there, if the school is not open and ready to accept students, I will send both you and the dean to the army, and I will make sure that both of you have the privilege and the occasion to fight in the front lines. Do you understand?"

The minister nodded. He looked unhappy. Three days later, all smiles, he handed me a big scissors to cut the ribbon, and Vietnam's first medical students began their studies.

Unfortunately, I had to deal with many such situations. Although I am not expert in education, in finance, in transportation or communications, I discovered that all too often, when so-called specialists encountered a problem that they thought they could not solve, they either did nothing or came to me. Most of the time I solved the problem very simply: I gave them a short deadline and good reason not to miss it.

On other occasions I was unpleasantly surprised to learn that I was the first to confront what seemed like an obvious problem. I would have thought, for example, that the Ministry of Defense would have plans to help improve the lot of the ordinary soldier. Most were conscripts, poor peasants who became even poorer when they put on the uniform of their country—we paid them very little. The Ministry of Defense, however, had no such plans, so among the first things I did after becoming premier was to tell the minister that we must improve living conditions for the troops and especially for their families. A small increase in salary would have been meaningless: Inflation would soon have devoured it. And instead of sending a few hundred dong home to their wives, many soldiers would have downed a couple of beers and bought a pack of cigarettes—and God knows, they deserved it. Because a big raise would have cost more money than we could afford, nothing was done. My solution was to provide each soldier's family with basic commodities, including rice, sugar, and canned milk. With the government's purchasing power, we could buy goods very cheaply, and we could be sure, at least, that military families had enough to eat.

Another urgent concern was housing. My minister of youth, Vo Long Trieu, a young, idealistic Catholic, suggested a way to help the poorest people, those who lived in festering city slums. I had already launched a program to build military housing for noncoms and junior officers on or near military bases, but we did not yet have enough funds for a nationwide housing program. Trieu asked me to help improve conditions in District Eight, one of nine in Saigon, and requested that the government provide construction materials and equipment. "We will mobilize the people of this district for public work," he said. I put Trieu in charge, and with his neighbors he formed a kibbutzlike cooperative for housing.

I brought his success to the attention of the other cabinet ministers and told them that I expected them to come up with similar programs in their areas. I wanted them to understand that our government was committed to social justice, and to make that point, over the months that followed, I fired ministers who failed to create and implement programs to help the poor.

I ran the government somewhat differently from my predecessors. We drafted an action plan for each ministry that included every project that the cabinet considered necessary or desirable. For each project I asked the responsible cabinet member to prepare a feasibility study and a plan and, at the next meeting, brief the whole cabinet on it. At these meetings, everyone was allowed to participate in the discussion and to offer ideas and suggestions. Once the entire cabinet agreed on a plan, I gave each minister a deadline, five or six months for a short project, a year or two for more ambitious undertakings. I gave them total authority over their projects and backed them with the full power of my office. I held follow-up meetings with every ministry at two- to three-month intervals to check on progress. And I put every minister on public notice that when the time for his project had elapsed, if it was not completed or goals were not met they would be fired. I would not hear excuses; since the ministers had sufficient resources, authority, and time, if they failed to achieve their goal, it would only be because of their own shortcomings.

Even though my cabinet was composed of very capable men, supervising them, along with the other demands of my position, required me to work nearly all the time. The frenetic pace of my new life left little time to think about anything except the responsibilities, problems, and difficulties that besieged me every hour of every day.

One of these responsibilities was that I remained VNAF commander. Pham Phu Quôc, among the VNAF's best pilots, would have been my choice to succeed me as head of the air force. Alas, he had been shot down over the North several months earlier. There were two or three officers with whom I had flown that I would have liked to promote, but they were still too young for the top job. So I chose Colonel Tran Van Minh, who as VNAF operations officer had surrendered to me during the coup that toppled Diem. I picked him in part because he was *not* a close friend. He was a southerner, and he had a good heart, but Minh's flying had been mostly in observation aircraft and he did not yet command the full respect and admiration of many combat pilots. While not the ideal man, I thought that he could do the job. To give him an opportunity to mature, I made him deputy commander until he was ready to handle solo command.

To discourage the growth of rivalries and encourage cooperation from the military, I delegated broad powers to the four corps commanders—I gave them almost total authority over local decisions, much like state or provincial governors. I called frequent meetings of the council at which I discussed the most urgent problems, explaining how I intended to solve them.

My first Armed Forces Convention met for a daylong session in a Saigon movie theater on September 11. More than 1,600 officers, lieutenant colonels and up, from every service, came from every part of the country. I talked to them about the problem of desertion, which was the shame of our armed forces. Few soldiers would desert, I said, if they knew that their superiors shared their hardships and dangers. This had long been ARVN official policy; now the policy needed to become the reality. I also stressed the need to end corruption, especially among senior officers, and of improving troop education. Men who understand why they fight and the importance of their mission, I said, rarely desert their comrades.

The group voted to adopt several resolutions. One rejected any negotiations or coalition with North Vietnam. Another denounced activities tending to create disorder and division. But the most important purpose of the meeting was to give those who attended a sense that their voices could be heard, that loyalty in the military was a two-way street. I hoped that the very fact of the meeting would put those who would foment dissension and unrest on notice that the armed forces was unified in its commitment to defeating the communists.

These military officers collectively represented every region and every political faction, except, of course, the communists. In this and future meetings I sought to bring everyone into the tent, removing the element of surprise that had created so many jealousies and rivalries. Within several weeks there were few heated discussions, and fewer arguments. The possibility of a coup d'état, while still present, faded with each passing day.

For the first several months, however, the Americans seemed to expect the cycle of coup and countercoup to continue. U.S. Secretary of Defense Robert McNamara, privately described my selection as prime minister to his comrades as "the bottom of the barrel." French premier Charles de Gaulle issued an audaciously sanctimonious statement calling for the neutralization of South Vietnam and the immediate and permanent withdrawal of all American troops. Instead, I arranged for the immediate (but temporary) withdrawal of all French diplomats from Saigon and Vietnamese diplomats from Paris. Doubtless I rid myself of at least a few communist sympathizers.

As time went on some senior American officials in Vietnam began to have second thoughts about my chances for remaining in office. On June 30 Taylor reported to President Johnson:

> Whatever one may think of General Ky, he seems to be se- rious about fulfilling his campaign promises [?] to stir up the country and get it on a war footing. Impetuous as some of his actions have been, they seem to have the honest intent of energizing an apathetic people and creating an atmosphere of urgency where day-to-day routine has been the rule. With his hip-shooting tendencies, Ky is likely to continue to take ill- advised actions from time to time such as his breach of rela- tions with France, but it is just possible that he will be able to create a new outlook favorable to getting things done.

I had no time to worry about what anyone thought of me. Every day brought something new, some problem that I had never anticipated. Often this was a good thing; I had no precon- ceptions. With no political ax to grind, I was free to focus on finding workable solutions to urgent problems. There might have been better ways to resolve some of the issues that came before me, but I did what I could; found something that worked well enough and moved on to the next matter.

One urgent issue was the vitriolic and avaricious Saigon press. At that time Saigon had more than thirty newspapers, far too many for most to make an honest profit. With no tradition of dignified discourse, Saigon publishing was like the frontier days in America's Wild West. Various political and business fac- tions used newspapers to attack each other in the most vicious terms. Some publishers, including many affiliated with political parties, were no better than extortionists. They accepted bribes to print scurrilous rumors and practiced blackmail. They would target a prominent or wealthy man and tell him, "Pay us or we will publish a story that you are doing such-and-such." It did not matter if this was the truth; for these scandal sheets it was all about making money any way they could. The people were fed up but could do nothing about them.

I could.

A week after I became premier I invited the Saigon press to a meeting. I began by announcing that I would close all newspapers. One old man, a well-known figure who wrote stinging editorials criticizing the government, stood up and shouted, "Down with dictatorship! We will go home, we will all leave!"

"Sit down," I said. When he started to reply, I told him, "Don't start. I flew through the Vietcong fire many times and they didn't hit me. Compared to an anti-aircraft gun, your mouth is not big enough—so don't think that you will shoot me with it. You don't leave this room until I say that you may. Otherwise, you all go to jail. Or I will send you to the army, to the front lines. There you may talk as much as you like."

Everyone sat down. I told the publishers, "You must reorganize and reform yourselves. There are too many papers. Eliminate the bad people, keep the good ones. Starting tomorrow, we will look at the situation at every newspaper. You are to suspend publication of gossip and rumors immediately. Until you are ready to act responsibly, you are allowed to publish only information provided by the government.

"Then, if you behave like gentlemen, and you want to have a good newspaper, I will encourage and help you. Conduct yourself in a clean and honest manner, and if you need money or equipment, my government will give them to you. But you must tell the truth. You must behave with dignity. Instead of fighting each other, promote national unity. Promote the ideals of freedom, and fight communism. That is all that I want. I want your help to fight communism and not to fight each other."

I had made my point. The next day most of these men came to the information secretary to plead their causes. Of course, they all claimed to be honest businessmen and patriots. Over the next few months there was a wave of newspaper consolidations and mergers. Some ceased publication; others, following another suggestion that I made, turned themselves into newsmagazines patterned after *Time* and *Newsweek*. In the end fewer dailies remained, but each was stronger and more profitable. Nor did the publishers hesitate to criticize my government. One called it "a government of the poor"; and even though this phrase was flung as an insult, I accepted it with pride.

Another urgent issue was inflation. A delegation from the World Bank came to Saigon to discuss this with my finance minister, Truong Thai Ton, and after several meetings recommended that the dong, our national currency, be severely devalued. Ton expressed grave reservations over such a move. The country was still unstable, and any devaluation, in his view, was bound to have serious consequences. He feared that there would be riots and demonstrations and that it would bring down my government.

Nevertheless, the World Bank representatives urged devaluation. When Minister Ton turned them away, they met with Ambassador Lodge, who suggested that they make an appointment with me. The delegation's spokesman was a staunch anticommunist who had escaped Eastern Europe in his youth, and after listening to him I said, "You know, I'm almost ignorant about economics. But I trust your goodwill. If your recommendation is devaluation, then let's do it." I issued the order—and the subsequent announcement made scarcely a ripple in Vietnam's political stream.

Another time William Colby asked General Nguyen Ngoc Loan, the chief of National Police, to free the wife of Tran Buu Kiem, who served the Vietcong as secretary of foreign affairs. The police had imprisoned her for espionage activities. Naturally Loan was reluctant to let her out, and he said no to the CIA's request. So Colby came to me. "Give me a reason," I said, and he explained, as he had not done for Loan, that this woman had volunteered to become a double agent, ostensibly working for the Vietcong but secretly feeding them disinformation while reporting to one of Colby's controllers. Under those circumstances I was willing to take a chance, so I ordered the woman freed.

The lesson I took from these sorts of incidents, and there were many, was that even with many good men in my government, in the end I must make the tough calls.

...

As VNAF commander I was always well briefed on the overall military situation, but my focus was, of course, on my own service. Within two or three weeks of taking office I had acquired a more detailed picture of the war against the communists. Things were going poorly, especially in the Central Highlands, the II Corps area where it was only a little over a hundred miles from the sea to the western border. At least one regular North Vietnamese Army division had moved down the so-called Ho Chi Minh Trail through Laos and Cambodia, then invaded this region. More troops had reinforced Vietcong units throughout the highlands with thousands of well-trained North Vietnamese regulars, including many leaders. In past years the monsoon season, which begins in autumn, had signaled the start of a new communist offensive. It was still months before the monsoons, however, and the number and intensity of Vietcong incidents had increased dramatically. The enemy controlled all major highways leading into II Corps: Essential military and civilian supplies could be delivered only by air. In short, the enemy was on the verge of cutting South Vietnam into two parts. If that happened, the communists could hammer the northernmost part of the country, the I Corps region, from both north and south to swallow half our country.

The ARVN was deployed primarily to protect the most pop-

ulated areas of the countryside. Most of its operations were directed at pacification, which meant hunting down or driving
away the Vietcong in populated areas or defending cities and
towns from attack. The ARVN could not perform that mission
and also field enough combat-ready units to cope with the monsoon offensive. I intended to order a national mobilization to
build up our forces, but we needed help until the ARVN was
able to meet the threat on its own. I knew also that no army
could win the war on its own. To help the ARVN, I wanted to
energize public opinion, establish better local security measures
against Vietcong terrorists, bring more of the countryside under
government control, and end the corruption that left veterans
and the widows and orphans of ARVN soldiers without any
means of support. That would take time. Nevertheless, I was
confident that with public support, fair compensation for veterans and their families, better military leadership, and more
weapons and logistical support, in the long run we could repel
the invasion, deal with the Vietcong, and win the war.

In the short term, however, I decided that there were few
alternatives to asking for more U.S. combat troops. When Ambassador Taylor visited my office on the afternoon of June 28,
he found me discussing the II Corps situation with Generals
Thieu, Chieu, and Co, the defense minister. I went straight to
my main point, the need for additional combat forces.

Taylor responded that his people had long been aware of
our growing shortage of trained military manpower and had already announced intentions to add six U.S. infantry battalions
over the next month or so. Also, American diplomats had asked
the leaders of other free nations in and near Southeast Asia to
contribute combat and support troops to a multinational force.

"What we might consider doing thereafter would depend
upon requirements of situation as we might evaluate them," read
Taylor's report to the U.S. State Department.

It appeared timely to me for General Co and General West-moreland to undertake comprehensive review of military man-power requirements between now and end of calendar year, to establish goals for period in terms of year-end position to be sought and of means, particularly of personnel, required to reach it. In general terms, it seemed to me that our objective for period should be to hold population and territory presently under government control, to blunt and bloody VC monsoon offensive and to make preparations for passage to offensive in early 1966.

We agreed that Co would confer with Westmoreland and together they would decide what additional combat forces were required. Several days later, President Johnson announced the dispatch of the First Air Cavalry Division to South Vietnam. This new and elite unit would reinforce II Corps, as would the Tiger Division soon to be sent by South Korea.

About a month after our meeting, Taylor returned to Washington, where he continued to serve President Johnson as an advisor. Although we had experienced difficulties between us, notably when Khanh was prime minister and Taylor had treated him and the Young Turks as if we were children, he bore no grudges. On August 5 this old soldier told President Johnson's National Security Council that "General Ky is a young man, but he is better than one would imagine. He may mature . . . The present Saigon Government framework is solid but the members of the new government are not yet well-known to us. General Ky is no administrator but he has a strong social conscience."

The new U.S. ambassador, Henry Cabot Lodge, Jr., paid me a courtesy visit the first week of August. Tall, large-boned, ruddy-faced, and with a full head of gray hair, he impressed me as an aristocrat, a well-mannered intellectual. Tea was served, and we made small talk in French and English. Suddenly he

said, "Can you tell me, Mr. Prime Minister, about your government's policies and plans?"

His question took me by surprise. After a moment I said,
"Our policy is justice for the poor—social justice," a reply that
surprised me quite as much as Lodge. I was well aware that
most Americans thought of me as a young, flamboyant pilot, a
playboy partial to purple scarves, a bon vivant who wore his hair
too long. Perhaps Lodge expected me to say something about
fighting the war or to make some noncommittal and inoffensive
declarations. Social justice is what rose to my lips, a reply that I
had never considered to a question that I did not anticipate.
Now, so many years later, thinking back about all that happened
to shape that reflexive response, I know that this notion of bringing justice to the poor, justice to every strata of Vietnamese society, had entered my consciousness since I was a boy of
fourteen or fifteen, when my father had left to work for national
freedom and independence, and had been in my heart all those
years. When Lodge asked me to articulate my policy, I suddenly
realized that I was in a position to make things happen, to carry
out a program that would begin to heal the social wounds of
nearly two centuries of colonialism. And from that moment, that
was my policy: social justice. Once it became a reality, it would
revolutionize the face of our society.

Corruption permeated every corner of the Vietnamese social
order; the rich got richer, the masses of poor, who saw little
hope for improvement, were increasingly vulnerable to Vietcong
propaganda. Previous governments had attracted what little popular support they had by making promises to religious sects and
groups of politicians representing privileged splinters of society.
I intended to seek the support of the masses, particularly the
poorest people, to give them a sense of hope and confidence in
the future. My government would need to ask them for still
more sacrifices; therefore, we in the government must also make

sacrifices. I mentioned none of this to Lodge at the time, however. "Social justice" was all that I said.

"That is more than enough," he replied, and I know now that what I said impressed him very much. When we said our farewells after that first meeting, each of us felt as if we had made a good friend. Over the next two years we became very close to each other. This is what Lodge wrote to President Johnson about our first encounter:

I had a meeting yesterday afternoon alone with General Ky which lasted almost an hour, with him doing almost all the talking in deliberate, grammatical English, sometimes interspersed with French. I began by saying that I wished to help in every possible way and that he could count on me to respect a confidence.

Ky covered many subjects, but his chief contention was that the people insisted on a revolution, that it was impossible to compete with the Communists without treating the peasant, the poor man, the laborer, and the soldier properly. Neither Minh, Khanh nor Quat had really understood what a revolution is all about. It was impossible for a civilian government to carry out a revolution with the military standing on the sidelines complaining. The military had the power in Vietnam and they had to meet their responsibility.

For the future, he wanted the Americans to hold the "strategic points" so that the Vietnamese could concentrate on pacification operations . . .

I agreed that a Communist offer of a revolution, even though it was in brutality and slavery, could only be beaten by an offer of a revolution for a new life in freedom. We Americans agreed completely and stood ready to help. There were some things which we could not do, but there were many which we could do. If he and his associates could stay in power for a reasonable period of time, then it could be done. But another coup would really be bad. Could we be helpful in this regard.

Ky smiled at this, and it seemed to me that he didn't take the possibility of a coup very seriously. He said he had been at Dalat for the last two days and had met with all division and corps commanders, and that they had all been in agreement. He said there had been discussion about my arrival signifying that something new was being brought into the Vietnamese problems. They did not know whether this was true, but they all agreed that I was against Communism.

Comment: If this is true, it is good that I am not taken for granted. My main hope at the meeting with Ky was not to settle any specific problem, but to develop a good atmosphere. I feel that this was done to some extent. He was rather tense when I arrived but he had a big smile on his face and was much more relaxed when I left.

Other remarks by KY . . . :

The Communists gave the peasant what in effect is a license to kill the landlord and then take the land themselves. "We can do better than that," said Ky. I assured him of our desire to help, having in mind the report that landlords are heavily represented among generals . . .

Social justice! Unity! I began with Vietnam's poorest and most oppressed minorities, the so-called Montagnards. These are about forty ethnically distinct peoples who live mainly in the Central Highlands, tribes that over many centuries had been pushed out of their original lowland territories in China, Cambodia, and coastal Vietnam. Physically they resemble Polynesians and Malays more than Chinese or Vietnamese, and in some ways they were like the American Indians of the eighteenth and nineteenth century. They believed in a pantheon of spirits, practiced primitive slash-and-burn agriculture, were not yet acquainted with written language, had only recently been introduced to the uses of metal, and had yet to grasp more modern concepts such as sanitation. They lived in remote, malaria-ridden jungle regions, and previous governments had treated them contemptuously. We Vietnamese often called them *moi,* savages.

Yet they are human beings, worthy of respect, and they were part of my country no less than any of the other minorities or the Catholics and Buddhists. The communists had infiltrated Montagnard villages and turned them into safe havens from which to launch attacks on the rest of South Vietnam. By playing on legitimate grievances and promising a better life under communism, the Vietcong recruited Montagnard fighters to attack ARVN outposts. Other resistance units fought both the Vietcong and the Saigon government.

But I wanted to bring these people into our tent as well. Their leader, Ibraham, was well known as a resistance fighter. I sent word that I wanted to meet him and end the fighting. "Name the place and time," I said, and "I will come to meet you."

In July 1965 we sat down to talk in the provincial capital of Ban Me Thuot. I said, "Anything you ask, I will give you—except don't ask for the whole country because this I cannot give you." We resolved our problems in one meeting. Ibraham stopped fighting us and through General Vinh Loc, the II Corps commander, I gave his people schools, medical supplies, building materials for housing, agricultural implements—simple things that made their lives easier. Vinh Loc, impressively tall and beefy, was a cousin of Bao Dai, the former emperor, and among the most honest and earnest of all ARVN generals. He understood what I wanted for the Montagnards and was so enthusiastic that he described himself as their "big brother of the Highlands."

I also created a new cabinet post, secretary for minorities, and put one of Ibrahim's lieutenants in it, the first Montagnard to serve in a Saigon government.

There were other Vietnamese minorities that had been ignored or abused by previous governments, and I decided early that I must bring them, too, into the tent. In Central Vietnam's Tay Ninh Province live most of the Cao Dai, Vietnamese whose relatively young faith integrates the basic principles of Buddhism, Taoism, and Confucianism. The center of their worship is an ornate temple sited on several dozen acres. Diem collected government rents on that land, which was leased to the sect. When I become premier, Cao Dai monks came to see me. They said, "The Catholics have built many churches and own the land under them. The Buddhists have many pagodas and they own their land. For all the Cao Dai there is only one temple, and that land is leased from the government. Can you give it or sell it to us?"

No problem. I flew up to Tay Ninh and at a big ceremony signed a paper officially transferring ownership of the land to the Cao Dai, without payment. Later I did the same for the Hoa Hoa, a Buddhist sect that has millions of followers in the western part of the Mekong River Delta. And why not? It cost the government almost nothing, and it meant so much to those people. I still wonder why Diem and those who followed him didn't see such an obvious move. With such small things, significant numbers of Vietnamese began to think of themselves, for the first time, as part of a nation that cared about their welfare.

Perhaps it was because everyone who served as prime minister before me had fought for the job; once they had attained it they tried to hold on to their position, to preserve the fruits of personal advancement. Giving away even a little government land felt like squandering their own property. When I found myself in the position, however, I was acutely aware that my responsibilities were to do what benefited the country, not what brought me personal advantage.

Although I am a Buddhist and I participated in many public and private ceremonies, I never prayed to Buddha for guidance. By this time in my life I knew that I might make mistakes but in my thoughts I always sought to do what was right. I felt no inclination to seek divine guidance; once you realize that you have a good heart, you don't need to ask anyone what is right and what is wrong. Therefore, when I met with kings and queens, chiefs of state, prime ministers and powerful military leaders, I faced them all just as I faced the lowly and the poor and the wretched: with my heart, not with my face or my name or my position.

Another large minority in Vietnam was the Chinese community. Perhaps because they have lived as outsiders and exiles for many generations, they stuck together and seemed to have an almost innate ability to succeed. As a group they were more affluent and successful than most Vietnamese, especially in business. Such success breeds envy. Diem and his family imposed a series of harsh and discriminatory laws against Vietnamese of Chinese ancestry. Like the Nazi decrees against Jews, Diem sought to strip the Chinese of their wealth and to restrict most of their business activities. He justified this by claiming that they were in league with the communists. There was a grain of truth in this: Chinese Vietnamese controlled much of the export and distribution of rice, and in order to move grain from the fields to the cities, they were forced to pay taxes to the Vietcong in areas under their control. But were the Chinese communists, or sympathizers? I think not, or at least very few.

Many Vietnamese, especially those whose businesses competed with Chinese-owned establishments, agreed with Diem's suppression of the Chinese. Although most are descended from immigrants who arrived centuries ago, Diem labeled them foreigners. I never agreed with this. I believe, then and now, that Chinese Vietnamese are among South Vietnam's most patriotic and loyal citizens. I am certain that nearly all consider themselves far more Vietnamese than Chinese and perhaps even more Vietnamese than others because they are citizens by choice.. They have prospered in Vietnam far more than they could have had their ancestors remained in China.

Of course, the Chinese are as capable of corruption as any Vietnamese. Why should they be different? In my opinion, however, a Chinese is more likely to keep an illicit bargain, and he will offer more generous terms.

As premier I rescinded anti-Chinese laws and treated the Chinese as equals both in public and in private. I made frequent visits to Cholon, Saigon's Chinese quarter, and gave money for schools, temples, and fraternal welfare associations. To this day, many Vietnamese Chinese regard me with affection.

What I had done for the minorities and for the religions in the name of national unity I did also for the Catholics. I freed several prominent Catholics who had been arrested after Diem was driven from office and returned church properties that had been confiscated. I also gave $10 million to Saigon's Buddhists, funds used to renovate a pagoda that had been devastated by police during Diem's regime. They turned the temple into a showpiece and tourist attraction. Along with money, however, I issued a warning: Don't make trouble for the country. I am here to preserve unity, and I will destroy all troublemakers. For a while, even the worst offenders seemed to believe me.

...

Since the communists had begun their invasion, our war had been entirely defensive. Even the bombing of the North, which had begun as retaliation for Vietcong atrocities, was defensive in nature. As prime minister I felt that limiting our efforts to the defensive was a mistake, and with the wisdom of hindsight I am now certain of it. I was not the only one who wanted to carry the fight to the enemy; soon after I took office, several thousand people demonstrated in Saigon to encourage us to take the fight north.

Every competent combat commander knows that troop morale reaches its zenith by going on the offensive, yet such ideas were anathema to most of the ARVN's so-called top leaders—their fighting spirit translated into something like, "Leave me alone, I'm happy with this situation. Go off and fight in the north? No thanks."

Our U.S. friends also opposed striking north, in part because of their superpower geopolitical concerns. The Americans took their cues from their experiences in Korea fifteen years earlier: U.S. forces repelled the North Korean invasion, and China had continued to support its communist allies but had stayed out of the fight. When American troops crossed into North Korea and battered the communist armies as they drove north, however, the Chinese intervened. It had cost tens of thousands of American casualties, and the Johnson administration did not want to make this mistake again. They cited the 1954 Geneva Accords as prohibiting a ground attack on North Vietnam.

Perhaps. But the United States had not signed the accords, which also prohibited the French and the Hanoi regime from introducing new troops into the country, from building new bases, from violating each other's airspace. The accords had not stopped tens of thousands of North Vietnamese troops from invading South Vietnam.

The Americans feared widening the war. If we invaded the North, they believed that the Chinese would respond with millions of troops. What neither President Johnson nor any of his top advisors seemed to appreciate was that Vietnam and China had a historical relationship quite unlike that of China and Korea.

Korea had been an obedient Chinese vassal for thousands of years, relying on Beijing to defend it from Japanese invasion. But when China colonized Vietnam, we resisted. Vietnamese patriots fought Chinese emperors for more than a thousand years, and the greatest heroes and heroines of our folk literature were those who opposed the Chinese.

Furthermore, there were already thousands, and soon to be

hundreds of thousands, of Chinese soldiers in the North. Chinese operated the North Vietnamese surface-to-air missile systems and performed many duties that the North Vietnamese Army could not because most of its troops were fighting in the South. Ideologically, however, Hanoi remained closer to Moscow than Beijing. The proof was the nasty little war that communist Vietnam fought with communist China in 1979.

All of that notwithstanding, one day I told Lodge that I wanted to put a battalion of paratroopers into North Vietnam in the mountains near the western part of the country near the 19th Parallel. According to intelligence sources, this was a region where many people were fed up with the communists. There were so many U.S. and VNAF aircraft flying over this area night and day that I believed we could drop a few dozen men at a time over a period of several days without attracting any attention. The ARVN paratroop brigade had many tough and able fighters who could encourage local uprisings, raid enemy outposts, and sabotage Hanoi's war efforts in many ways. Resupplied by air drops, they could operate with less hazard than most Vietcong encountered while fighting us in the South.

Ever the diplomat, Lodge passed the suggestion along to the U.S. State Department, but the Americans were not at all sympathetic. I wonder now what would have happened if I had quietly ordered it done. Once we had a few hundred men on the ground, I feel sure that the Americans would have felt obliged to support them. Then, at the very least, we could have forced Hanoi to pull some of its troops back from the South.

...

One of my government's biggest challenges was to drive the Vietcong out of the countryside. Aside from military activities we had a program called Chieu Hoi ("Open Arms"), which encouraged and rewarded Vietcong deserters. We put those who rallied to our side through a brief counter indoctrination program, gave them money to buy clothes and start a new life, and tried in many ways to integrate them into South Vietnamese society. When I looked into it, however, I quickly became disgusted. Most Chieu Hoi funding came from the Americans, and as far as I could see, we had wasted their money. Provincial officials responsible for the program inflated their reports. Often the Vietcong used the program to get medical attention, decent food, and a few weeks' vacation from the war. Once they were rested, they redefected to the communists and continued to fight us.

I knew that General Lansdale of the CIA had been closely involved in the defeat of the Filipino communist guerrillas, so I invited him to lunch and he shared recollections and ideas. After World War II, Malaysia, then a British colony, also squelched a communist-led guerrilla war. Accordingly, a few weeks later I made a trip to Malaysia for my first meeting with Tengku Abdul Rahman, prime minister and the father of Malaysian independence, an able and remarkable man already well into old age.

Before our staff visit, however, I was entertained at dinner by the King of Malaysia. I was seated next to his queen, a very young but well-educated lady. At that time I was a heavy smoker, and after our meal I signaled my aide to bring a cigarette. The chief of protocol whispered to me, "General, you may not smoke until after the king makes his after-dinner toast." Apparently they still followed the British custom.

The queen overheard. "Do you wish to smoke?" she asked.

"You gave me the best wine, the best food, the best companionship—all that is lacking is a good cigarette."

She turned to her husband, the king, and with no reluctance said, "Please, let's have a toast, so that our guest can smoke." I thanked her very much. Later the prime minister and his advisors were equally generous with their time, and I learned much about how these brave people had defeated the communist guerrillas.

All of this input was useful, but in the end, designing an effective program to support pacification remained a Vietnamese problem. Near the end of September I appointed General Co to serve as deputy prime minister for "War and Peace" and put him in charge of pacification. After much thought, I asked Le Van Tien to serve as minister of pacification. Although he is a Catholic, he also kept the Buddha in his heart, and I felt that would be important to a program that is designed to turn enemies into friends. A very able and brilliant man, Tien had a reputation for coming up with excellent new ideas. Finally, I instructed Co and Tien to reorganize and retrain the 25,000 Chieu Hoi cadres, then form them into teams that would be tailored to the special needs of the location where they served. Wherever possible, I wanted these cadres to be longtime residents of the communities they served. I also gave orders that serving as a Chieu Hoi cadre would be accepted in lieu of military service, hoping that this would attract younger and more energetic cadres.

We did not have enough people or money to make a maximum effort in every district of every province, so we identified three or four areas that were especially vulnerable to communist recruiting and gave them the most resources.

I shared my Chieu Hoi ideas, as part of a larger program dealing with all aspects of pacification, with Lodge. He offered good advice: Instead of allowing this package to become known as the Ky Plan, I should give credit to others, and to the degree that it met with successes, I should try to involve and then reward as many top leaders as possible. In this way, explained Lodge, those who might otherwise work to sabotage the plan will work to make it succeed. I took this excellent advice.

Ultimately, however, no government plan, no matter how brilliantly innovative or richly funded, could succeed without the support of the people—and that brought me back to social justice. In order to energize the populace, I would have to give them real hope. My biggest and most important job, I realized, was to curb corruption.

9
CORRUPTION

THEY were young and they were old, they were thin or heavy, handsome or homely, smooth-shaven or mustachioed, and dressed, like most Cholon merchants, in loose trousers and vests, with open-toed sandals. Two or three wore rings; here and there a gold tooth glinted from between parted lips. On the whole, however, the seven men who filed into my office on that spring day in 1966 were so ordinary in appearance that few would have noticed them on the street. Yet they held the power of life and death over millions of Vietnamese.

In Vietnam, rice is life, not merely a staple but the primary source of nutrition, and these men controlled virtually every sack of it that the land produced. For generations nearly every tenant farmer in South Vietnam had borrowed cash to cover seed, fertilizer, implements, and operating expenses, including land rental, from one of these Chinese Vietnamese families. In return they pledged their harvests as security. The lenders charged interest on these transactions—as much as they could—and at harvest the farmers had little choice except to turn over their entire crop, at whatever price the lenders set. For the merchants, this arrangement was tremendously profitable. For the farmers, and especially for the majority who leased their land but didn't own it, it meant merely surviving long enough to plant their next crop. And that was in a good year.

Vietnam was the world's third largest rice producer. Before the war, when much of the Mekong Delta's enormous yield—

three crops, in most years—was exported, these rice monopolists became rich and powerful. When North Vietnam's disguised invasion began, the invaders and their Vietcong allies subsisted on the rice that they confiscated from farmers. The fighting devastated farm villages, drove people off the land, and interrupted planting cycles, so as the war grew in scale and intensity, we were no longer able to export rice. But these same merchants maintained control of the harvests, paying huge bribes to the Vietcong for the privilege of transporting rice to market. Collectively, the seven men settling into a row of chairs in front of my desk still held the power to feed the nation.

Or starve it.

A few days earlier Truong Thai Ton, the minister in charge of the economy, came to me and said, "In Saigon, rice now costs about 3,000 dong per kilo, about triple the official price. I think that in a few days, prices may go to 9,000. Even worse," he continued, "there is almost no rice in the markets. There are rumors that Saigon warehouses are empty and that no more rice is coming in from the countryside."

Vietnam is densely populated. Everyone knows his neighbors' business, and I had already heard odd reports of rice dumped in rivers near Saigon. When Truong mentioned that the price of rice had soared, I knew immediately what had caused the dumping: to create the illusion of scarcity, to raise prices, to increase the merchants' profits. Somewhere near Saigon, I felt sure, were many warehouses bulging with grain. When prices had risen to astronomical levels, the men who owned the rice would sell some. And they could always sell it to the Vietcong.

I was quite sure that if rice remained scarce, agitators would soon incite thousands of hungry rioters to seize Saigon's streets and vent their anger by smashing, looting, and burning. Starving people would not blame the war or the rice merchants. They would blame the government that allowed them to starve, and especially the man who headed it. They would blame *me*.

And that was precisely what these men wanted. I had declared myself against profiteering. The rice merchants wanted me gone, so that they could continue the monopolistic methods that had made them rich. How blind and arrogant they were! How shortsighted! I still wonder if they had ever paused to consider for even a moment that dissension and divisiveness hindered the war effort, that it hastened the day when the North triumphed. Did they actually believe that they would be allowed to retain their fortunes under the communists? How could they not recall that in 1956, the North Vietnamese executed over 2,000 landlords in Nghe An Province, those who had oppressed their tenant farmers but also those who were fair? How could these merchants, who exploited peasants as much as any landlord, expect that Hanoi would allow them to control the rice market? Perhaps they believed that the communists would win inevitably but hoped to increase their profits until it was time to flee Vietnam.

I said nothing of this to the men sitting before me. I looked carefully at each, memorizing their faces, then told Captain Tri, my aide, to get a pad of paper and give each man a sheet. "Write your names," I said. It was summer in the tropics, and before my visitors arrived I had turned off the ceiling fans and closed the windows. Tiny beads of perspiration appeared on the merchants' faces.

Tri, a young air force officer, collected the pages. I looked at the men again, then folded the first paper in half, then in half again, and in half again. I placed it in my cap, which lay before me, upside down. Then I took the next paper and folded it. Minutes passed. Only the faint sounds of Saigon traffic broke the silence. When all the papers lay folded in my cap, I spoke.

"We have a problem with rice," I said. "You know what I mean. You know what is causing this problem. And *I* know why we are having this problem. I also know that *you* can solve it. I have full confidence in you. I have no time to talk now, so, gentlemen, I give you one week. At the end of this week, if we still have this problem, I will have the honor of inviting you all to return." I stared at each of the men again before continuing. "One of you will draw one of these papers from my hat. Then I will shoot the man whose name is on that paper. Right here. Did you all hear what I said?" Seven heads bobbed. "You can go home now," I said.

I was an enemy of corruption and against everything those merchants stood for. In a way, that was something that I had in common with my enemies, the North Vietnamese communists. The difference is that I believe in human nature, and the communists do not. They believe in a system without the profit incentive, a system where poverty is shared equally. I believe that most people will try to better themselves and ought to be encouraged to make better lives for their families, to benefit from their efforts. In this way, while some will have more than others, the wealth of our society will increase. Everyone will share the prosperity.

But I am a son of Buddha, so I also believe that government must protect the weak from the strong. Money is a kind of power, and in a developing country like Vietnam, the rich, or at least most of them, acquired their wealth through corruption, by oppressing the weak. I grew up in a middle-class family, and my closest friends came from similar backgrounds. In Vietnam, I never let a rich man get too close. This was well known, and when I became premier and had power, the wealthy and corrupt became frightened. They tried every way to get rid of me.

They had good reason to be scared. I was trying to change my country, to curb the corruption that had stifled Vietnam's progress, that kept all of its citizens from uniting against the North Vietnamese invasion. Corruption is as old as civilization, and we Vietnamese have long experience with both. One might say that in Vietnam, as in many poor Asian countries, corruption was almost an art form. The war brought inflation averaging 30

percent a year but no increase in the salaries paid soldiers or
civil servants. It also brought hundreds of thousands of free-
spending American soldiers and hundreds of millions of dollars
in U.S. aid. And so corruption attracted more people than ever.
Most government officials, very nearly every one, including the
most lowly functionaries, squeezed small sums out of everyone
who came under their authority. They could be truly heartless.
Soon after I became prime minister, a woman came to my office,
the widow of a sergeant with whom I had served in 1950, when
we fought the Vietminh guerrillas in North Vietnam. Her husband was killed in action in 1963, but the official responsible for
dispensing widows' benefits, a modest, lump-sum payment, refused to allow her the money—unless she gave him half of it. I
fired that parasite, but there were thousands more, equally venal.

It wasn't merely extortion. Senior policemen owned phar-
macies that sold illegal drugs. They were partners with gangsters
in bars, brothels, and gambling dens. And they protected these
establishments not only from official interference but also from
competition. In my time, the richest cop in Vietnam was sup-
posedly responsible for enforcing vice laws in Saigon's Chinese
quarter, Cholon. He paid $130,000 for his police appointment,
but was making a profit inside two years.

Not only police profited from graft. Soon after I took office
I learned that Pham Van Dong, military governor of Saigon,
perhaps through his wife, was protecting an illegal casino in Cholon. It operated quite openly, protected by well-armed soldiers.
Dong, whose name in Vietnamese is spelled and pronounced
different from that of the former leader of North Vietnam, deployed his toughest troops around the casino and dared anyone
to challenge them.

When I had satisfied myself that the reports about Dong
were true, I sent word to him that I didn't care how many troops
he had, if he continued to protect the casino, I would send tanks
to crush them and flatten the building. Dong knew that I was

not bluffing and immediately withdrew his protection. I arranged for him to retire, and in his place put Le Nguyen Khang, the Marine Corps commander.

Protecting criminal activity was not the only form of corruption practiced in the ARVN. Colonels commanding regiments accepted bribes from the wealthy fathers of conscripts and in return allowed their sons to remain safe at home instead of sharing the hazards of war. Other soldiers simply deserted—but their commanders never reported their absence, and tens of thousands of these "ghost soldiers" were carried on the official rolls. Their commanding officers pocketed their salaries and funds provided for their uniforms and meals. Officers stole troop rations and looted clothing, equipment, and supplies from warehouses and storerooms. Some even sold weapons and ammunition to the enemy!

The lowest lined their pockets and kept some, perhaps half, of what they squeezed. They passed the rest to bosses in exchange for the privilege of keeping their jobs, the privilege of squeezing money from the poor. It was like being in the Mafia, except that they operated under legal authority.

In the private sector, wealthy businessmen grew still richer by bribing officials for government contracts. Inspectors pocketed gratuities to ignore shoddy work. Bosses stole workers' pay, often by forcing them to work unpaid overtime, but also by keeping wages artificially low. Businessmen bribed officials for exclusive licenses to import milk, medicines, motor scooters—anything not made in Vietnam. With no domestic competition, they charged consumers whatever the market would bear.

Not that we Vietnamese had a monopoly on wartime corruption. In 1972 Sergeant Major of the Army William Wooldridge, the senior noncommissioned officer of the U.S. Army, was convicted of conspiring to defraud enlisted men's clubs in Vietnam through bribery and kickbacks. Several senior noncoms who were involved with Wooldridge went to prison. A ring of air force enlisted men smuggled heroin out of Vietnam and into the United States by concealing it in hermetically sealed containers used to transport dead soldiers for burial. Thousands of U.S. troops sold cheap consumer goods from their PXes on the black market, or smuggled small quantities of drugs into their homeland. Many South Korean and Thai volunteers, men who battled the communists side by side with Vietnamese soldiers, bought cheap appliances in American PXes and either shipped them home to be sold on the black market or sold them to a Vietnamese for triple their cost.

But these men were guests in my country, and whenever the police arrested foreign troops for black marketeering or smuggling, I gave instructions to treat them leniently. They were wrong, they were breaking the law, but they were not big criminals. They were poor and underpaid, and I understood from personal experience why they did wrong.

...

Since our nation began in 1954, South Vietnam's currency, the dong, was not welcomed by other nations. Only so-called hard currencies—U.S. dollars, West German deutschmarks, Swiss francs, the British pound sterling—were accepted. Vietnam secured such currencies by exporting commodities. As those currencies were always in short supply, Vietnam imported almost no foreign luxury goods. To conserve hard currencies to purchase such important items as heavy machinery, few Vietnamese were allowed to travel abroad. If you were close to one of Mr. Diem's relatives, however, or if you had Can Lao party connections, you might get permission to leave the country, but there was always a price for this.

Earlier in my career, when I commanded the First Air Transport Wing, only my unit was allowed to make frequent overseas trips. We flew all over Southeast Asia, to Bangkok, Malaysia, the Philippines, Singapore, and Hong Kong, which in the late 1950s offered the best shopping in Asia—low prices and the best brand names. My duties included training new pilots, so I flew many of these missions. When we flew to Hong Kong or Singapore, my pilots crews got thirty or forty dollars a day in U.S. currency for per-diem expenses. Instead of eating fancy meals or staying in good hotels, they used some of these dollars to buy cameras, tape recorders, transistor radios, perfume, ladies' clothing—small luxuries not available at home. My men were therefore able to bring in goods without paying import duties. Technically, this was illegal. But a pilots' salary was almost nothing—a few dollars a month. A man could make twenty dollars by selling a wristwatch or a radio, fifty for a camera—more than his monthly salary. But the pilots were not getting rich. They and their families were barely getting by.

Rumors of this practice spread widely; soon almost everyone knew what was going on, even the high command. So one day I called my pilots together and said, "I understand your situation. I will allow you to do this, but only if the extra money goes to support your families. I am willing to protect you, but I will not allow anyone to get rich by smuggling."

Even so, I personally never brought back anything from these trips—not a bolt of Thai silk, not even a single foreign cigarette. Until one day, just before I left for Singapore, my mother asked me for a small Japanese transistor radio, a particular model. Of course, I could not say no.

Singapore was still quite small in 1957, and even poorer than Vietnam. The city got few foreign visitors; tourists mostly went to Hong Kong and Bangkok. Even then, however, it was a free port: There was no duty on goods purchased for export. Because we visited often, local businessmen recognized us as Vietnamese pilots and treated us with great courtesy.

After the flight to Singapore, I changed into civilian clothes and went to a shop, where I was greeted by two or three salesmen, Chinese fellows. I looked around until I found the radio that my mother wanted. "This one," I said.

"How many?" one of the salesmen asked.

"Just one."

"Only one?" asked the manager, astonished. "You know Captain Tinh? He buys three hundred radios!"

Evidently they did not know that I was Tinh's wing commander—or that I did not allow such greed. "Yes, of course I know him" was all I said.

The next morning I had breakfast with my crew, including Captain Tinh. Everyone behaved as usual, except Tinh, who did not eat. Finally I asked, "Captain, are you not hungry?"

He just shook his head.

I could only imagine the scene at the shop the previous afternoon when he stopped in to pick up his radios. Probably the manager or owner came out to greet him, and very likely he said something like "I met your friend. How come he buys only one radio?"

And Tinh would have said, "Who is that? Which friend?"

"I don't know his name. The guy with a big mustache."

Not many Vietnamese wore a big mustache.

After we had eaten, I said, "Listen, gentlemen, for the flight back to Saigon we are carrying extra fuel. We will be very heavy for takeoff. So remember, don't buy too much in the shops. If we are too heavy, we cannot take off, and we will crash and everyone will die." Later the crew told me that Tinh had hurried to the shop and canceled his order.

In time, most of my people realized that although I allowed them the privilege of bringing in a few items, except for buying my mother that little radio, I did not participate in these activities. On one flight, however, one of my pilots asked me, "Why don't you ever buy things for yourself? Do you have fifty American dollars? Let me buy some White Horse [scotch] for you. Back home we can sell it in Cholon and you can make a few dollars."

I gave him the money, and he bought two cases of White

Horse. Two days later he came to my home and said, "I found a buyer in Cholon! What are you going to do with your profits?"

I said, "Use my share to buy me some Marcel Cognac."

"But you must be careful," he replied. "A lot of fake liquor is sold in Cholon."

"You are right," I replied. "Don't sell the whiskey. Keep it. Let's have a drink."

After word of that little maneuver got around, my pilots never again bothered me with offers to buy foreign goods.

But while I could permit such small matters as a junior air force officer, when I became prime minister, I made up my mind to oppose corruption of every sort. To do otherwise was to admit defeat in our national struggle.

I had read Machiavelli as a young officer and I was also familiar with Lord Acton's maxim that power corrupts and that absolute power corrupts absolutely. I felt that I understood this—but not until I was actually prime minister did I truly comprehend just what Acton had meant or appreciate the true extent of power's corrupting effects or the many insidious ways that corruption presents itself. Temptation was present every day and in every segment of my life, official and personal. A parade of people literally came begging to give me money, and it would have been very easy to enrich myself. I would not have had to work at it. I would not have had to force anything upon anyone. All I had to do was take the money and say yes or no. And everything I touched was potentially worth money! A duty assignment closer to home for a major, or far away for someone's romantic rival. A license to import some goods, to build a factory or close one, to start a business. A construction contract. An easy job for a relative. An exemption from the draft or from service in a combat unit. A lenient sentence for a convicted criminal. A pardon. For nothing at all right now, but later, someone might ask me to remain silent. Anything one could imagine—someone was eager to pay me for it. A million dollars a day, if

I wanted it. A hundred million? A matter of months, and no effort at all.

I did not want it. People whom I had respected told me that I was silly or naive because I would not take their money. Even after months in office, even after those who worked with me daily knew that I would not be bought, still people came bearing bribes. For centuries in Vietnam, the emperor or president or prime minister or colonial governor general—who ever stood at the pinnacle of power—had taken whatever was set before him, and most people simply could not believe that anyone in my position would refuse.

And in Vietnam, enriching oneself from the power of their office did not even require touching cash. When Mr. Diem was president, he appointed his brother, Ngo Dinh Nhu, to head national security. It was a license to steal.

Thus did Nhu's wife acquire millions through her family connection. Madame Nhu had a palatial villa at Bac Lieu, a market city deep in the Mekong Delta. Some of the family's millions went to buy a large yacht; its masts were too tall to pass under the bridges along the canal leading to her villa. So one of her in-laws ordered several bridges torn down. One new bridge was built, with room beneath it to allow the boat to pass. It was bad enough that public funds were used to build the bridge, but Madame Nhu made the lives of thousands of poor people even harder. With only one place to cross the canal for several miles, they were forced to walk far out of their way, and the high, steep arch of the new bridge made it difficult to carry or cart heavy loads across it. She held no office, but Madame Nhu was probably the most powerful woman in Vietnam—more powerful than a prime minister, because she had no responsibilities. No one could criticize her official conduct. She whispered in her husband's ear, and people fell over themselves to pay her.

Because nepotism is the corruption that multiplies itself, I went out of my way not to allow this virus to infect my own family. On my first day as prime minister, my predecessor's young secretary presented himself. I recognized him immediately: my sister's son. I ordered him transferred. Soon after that, at a cabinet meeting, the minister of communications and transportation gave a report on the sorry state of our country's national railroad system. There were many problems, he said, and enumerated several.

"Fire the man in charge, and find a good man to replace him," I ordered.

Later in the day, the same minister came to my office. "The chairman of the national railroad organization is Nguyen Ngoc Lam," he said.

"So what?" I replied.

"I have learned that he might be some kind of cousin to you," he replied.

With a small shock, I recognized the name. He was the eldest son of my father's oldest brother, and in our culture that made him head of our clan. He had moved south soon after the end of the Japanese occupation and had gone into the railroad business. We called each other "brother."

"So what?" I said. "He is unfit for his position, and I told you to fire him." Cousin Lam, who died in Canada about 1988, never spoke to me again. Too bad for him.

A few months later, reviewing his annual personnel roster for promotions and rotations, the foreign minister submitted a recommendation for the appointment of Phan Quan, then first secretary in the Ministry of Foreign Affairs, as ambassador to Japan. "If this Quan is the husband of my sister Phung," I replied, "then perhaps I know him better than you. He is not qualified for such an important diplomatic post." My brother-in-law, who also died in 1988, never spoke to me again, although his wife, my favorite sister, and their children remain very close.

Many years later I learned that some of my wife's relatives had asked her to help them with a problem: Their son had sought to avoid the draft by enrolling in a Parisian university. His family had bribed the mistress of the minister of the interior and obtained a false passport, but when they failed to get him a French visa, he entered Cambodia, hoping to get a visa there. Instead, the Cambodians arrested him. Now my wife's relatives asked her to get my help in freeing him. My wife did not dare to ask me such a thing and turned them away. Eventually they found the money to bribe Cambodian officials, and the boy was freed. He went to Paris and completed his studies there.

...

I was determined to be the first top political leader in Vietnam's long history who did not corrupt himself, either by enriching his friends and family or by accepting bribes. For a long time, nobody could believe it. In Saigon's exclusive neighborhoods, behind the thick walls of villas protected by private bodyguards, the rich whispered to each other that when I said "no" I actually meant that they had offered me too little. Nothing I said or could say would persuade these rumormongers that I was different from my predecessors. With no evidence, American journalists wrote that I made millions by using my air force to smuggle drugs. A lie, but many still believe it.

I had no need to smuggle. On the day that I assumed office, I discovered a slush fund, a so-called black account, that appeared on no official budget. The money came from a tax on horse racing; there was the equivalent of about $46 million in this fund. By law I, and only I, could draw upon it. There was no accountability. It was completely legal. I could have taken it all, sent it to Switzerland. Why bother smuggling drugs?

One more word about temptation: Until you decide that you will not be tempted, that you just won't take money, no matter how much is offered, each new offer brings an inner struggle. You may say no the first time, but what about the second time? What about the fifth and sixth and seventh and tenth and the hundredth, the thousandth time? When I came to know how hard that would be, I decided that I would never again think about it. Thereafter, when money was offered, I didn't think. Because if you consider each offer, if you take the time to think, even for a minute, you are lost, finished. One day you will find a reason to say yes, and from that moment you are corrupted. So I decided never to negotiate with myself. I had only one answer for those offering cash: No.

Several months after I became prime minister, Tam Giac, an old friend and a leading Buddhist monk, invited me and my wife to dine at his home. After our meal, he said that a Japanese motorcycle manufacturer was eager to build a factory in Vietnam and that if I granted them a license, they would donate dozens of small cars that could be used as taxis. I could give them away to poor people who wanted to start a business, as part of a program I had initiated.

If you want to know what people in any country are thinking, what they are talking about, what is bothering them, you must join them on their way to and from work. In Paris I rode the Metro and the city buses, and in Saigon, even after I became premier, I sometimes left my car and hailed a cyclo, one of the thousands of pedicabs that most Saigonese used to get around the city. One day I asked my driver, an older man with ragged clothes and weathered skin how much he made, and he said that on a good day he might take in about ten dollars. "But after I pay rent to the man who owns this cyclo, I have only three dollars left," he added. "And even if I take in only six dollars, I must still pay seven dollars rent."

"But why not buy your own cyclo?" I asked.

"They cost hundreds of dollars. How could I save that much when everything I earn goes to buy food for my family?" he replied.

I was very disturbed by this. This grandfather sweated from dawn until the midnight curfew, seven days a week, but his family barely survived on his wages. I asked my staff to check and soon learned that it was true everywhere in Vietnam. There were only a few cyclo companies, all owned by rich men, and drivers made almost nothing. I decided that this had to change. I proposed to my cabinet that the government buy hundreds of cyclos and sell them to poor people at our cost. We might have simply given them away, but I wanted people to have the dignity and satisfaction of earning their own way. But to ensure that even the poorest could afford to buy, my government financed these purchases, with no money down and at a very low interest rate. It was not my original intention, but in selling cyclos on the installment plan, I created Vietnam's first consumer credit system.

That became a successful program, as far as it went. But cyclos were powered by human muscle. We needed more motorized vehicles, pedicabs augmented with small motorcycle engines. These would be much cheaper if they could be built in Vietnam by Vietnamese workers. So I was glad to hear from my monk friend that a Japanese company wanted to build a factory.

Then the monk dropped his other sandal: If I granted this company an exclusive license, they would give me, personally, several million dollars.

"No," I said. "Let the company submit a bid, like all the other Japanese companies that are interested. My cabinet will consider all the bids and grant the license to the best-qualified company." I stopped talking to that monk.

When I became premier, I was the tenth to hold the position in less than three years. Nobody expected that I, a small-town boy, a pilot with no political experience, would last a month. Some said that I would be gone in one week. But politics is the art of the possible, and I have always been a very practical man. When I see a problem, I have to find its solution. When I took office I was without a cabinet, without trusted advisors. I could do almost anything merely by issuing a decree: If I signed a directive, it became the law. The biggest problem I knew was corruption, so my first decree established a special court to deal with corruption, black marketeering, and profiteering. I asked Nguyen Cao Quyen, the chief justice of the military court, and my closest friend since elementary school, to serve as its presiding judge. According to this new law, those found guilty by that court were to be publicly executed. To show that I meant business, I ordered sandbagged execution stands built in Saigon's central market and in the central markets of every provincial capital.

I hoped that by establishing these courts, appointing an incorruptible chief judge, and building execution stands, the message would sink in: I am different from any Vietnamese ruler you have known, I will not permit corruption. Stop your stealing! But if there were people who still didn't believe me, I intended to show everyone that I meant what I said. I instructed the special court to ignore the small fry and concentrate on the most notorious, the most blatant, the most corrupt. And when they had examined the evidence and convicted them, I intended to sign death warrants for at least three men in each province: a corrupt civilian, a corrupt senior military officer, and a big black marketeer or smuggler.

It was a very harsh decree, but it was necessary.

We were at war. Every week hundreds of American soldiers—but *thousands* of Vietnamese soldiers and civilians—lost their lives. Many thousands more lost their homes and livelihoods and were forced to live the fearful, miserable lives of refugees. The corrupt enriched themselves at the expense of their countrymen. They provided aid and comfort to our enemies. I place great value on all life, especially human life. But if you have a diseased finger, and medicines will not cure the infection, you must cut off the finger before you lose the hand, before you lose the arm, before you lose your life. So I would execute the most flagrantly corrupt, in the hope that I could save many more from making the same mistake.

The first man to be convicted by the special court was Ta

Vinh, a Chinese Vietnamese and one of Vietnam's richest men. Vinh had contracted to build a U.S. Army officers' quarters but stole much of the structural steel shipped in for this project. He reaped millions by selling it on the black market.

After Vinh's death sentence was announced, ambassadors from several nations came to beg me to spare his life. I also received various members of his family and many of his friends. I don't know how much money I turned away, but every Vietnamese who came to plead for Ta Vinh seemed to act as if I were holding him for ransom and that with enough money in my pocket I would let him go. They were wrong.

He was to be executed early in the morning. The night before the execution, for the first time in my life, I was unable to sleep. Vinh was in his forties, and I thought about his wife and about their children, who would now grow up without a father. I recalled how my mother had struggled for years after my father died, and I felt very sorry for those young people and for their mother.

Also, it is one thing to shoot at the enemy on the battlefield, where it is kill or be killed. One fires in self-defense, and there is never time to think about whether it is right or wrong. Often the enemy is an abstraction, faceless, and impersonal. Ta Vinh, however, was a civilian. I knew much about him. I had the power to save his life, and of course I had to think about that. Although he was very corrupt and had stolen from his fellow citizens, I did not hate him as a human being—no one is perfect. The women who came to beg for his life asked me to forgive him. Put him in prison and confiscate his fortune. And I thought about this—I was tempted, not by money but by mercy. But Vinh was the very first person condemned under the new anticorruption law. If I spared him, then everyone would be sure that it was because he was rich, that he had bought me. As a political leader, I had few assets beyond my reputation for integrity, a reputation that no top Vietnamese leader in memory could match. Spare Vinh, and that reputation would be tarnished forever. And because he was the first to be sentenced, if I failed to keep my word, failed to enforce my own law, then who would take me seriously? Who would believe that I was determined to end this terrible disease that was destroying my country, this leprosy called corruption?

And so others would ignore the law, and if I continued to press this point, then I would have to shoot the next man convicted of corruption. As soon as his sentence was handed down, I would be back to the same situation: people lining up to beg me to take their money, to beg for another man's life.

Make no mistake: I did not allow this execution without a great deal of soul searching. In the end I decided as I had when I wrote the law. Corruption must end. Corruption was sapping the national strength, undermining our efforts to fight the Vietcong and the North Vietnamese, to drive them out of our country. If I let Vinh live, it would weaken not just my position but my whole government. It would probably cost many lives. Why spare Vinh and condemn some innocent young father to death in battle? Or by starvation? As the Buddha wrote, "Kill one cat, save the lives of a thousand rats."

Vinh's sentence was carried out before sunrise and reported in every Vietnamese newspaper and around the world. To this day, however, many people continue to believe that perhaps the firing squad used blanks or another man was shot, that the whole affair was a sham, a trick, and that Vinh was spirited out of the country with a new identity. How could I execute a rich man?

Corruption would not suddenly come to an end, of course, because one thieving profiteer was shot. If my message was to be understood, I would also have to crack down on the military. For this purpose I selected one of the few completely honest and incorruptible men in Vietnam, Nguyen Ngoc Loan, and made him head of military security and head of the national police.

Loan was from Hue, and among the most highly educated men in the military. Like me and so many others, he had been drafted at age twenty. After infantry service, he was selected for France's elite air force academy, Ecole Delair Salon, in Provence, where he graduated first in his class. After pilot training, he returned to Vietnam, where he rose rapidly through the ranks. When I became head of the VNAF, I chose him to serve as my chief of staff. Balding and short, he was fearless and carried out my orders with a great sense of responsibility. He always said what was on his mind and never worried about what anyone, including the U.S. media, wrote about him. And he was honest. Dirty money is thrown at every policeman, and as the military's chief law enforcement officer, the opportunities for graft and bribery were limitless. Loan never took a cent. The proof of this is that, after the war, when he went into exile near Washington, D.C., Loan spent his last years ekeing out a living in a tiny pizza restaurant where his wife cooked and he waited tables. I am sorry that his last years were so difficult, but when I began looking for an honest cop, Loan was exactly the kind of man I needed to help me cleanse Vietnamese society.

On his own initiative, Loan even investigated one of my own sisters, Thi Ly, regarded by some as the black sheep of our family. Ly is ten years older than I. She was a rebellious and undisciplined teen who left home at seventeen to marry someone that we, her family, had never met, then moved to Haiphong. During the last days of World War II, when bombing forced many to flee to border areas, Ly moved to Laos. I neither saw nor spoke to her for more than twenty years. During that period it became common knowledge that many Vietnamese living in Laos were involved in smuggling gold or opium. Because of this, at the time in my life when I had many powerful and important enemies, rumors were spread that Ly and I smuggled drugs into Vietnam. It is possible that she was involved in this illicit trade, but if so, I knew nothing about it then, and I know nothing of it now. What I do know is that after I became prime minister, she paid a visit to Saigon. On his own initiative, Loan brought several men and searched her rooms! They found nothing incriminating. He nevertheless warned her: Not even my sister was immune from the law. Ly and I laugh about this now, but when I first heard of Loan's raid, I was very proud of him.

During the war, South Vietnam was divided into four military regions, known as corps, with I Corps in the far north, II Corps and III Corps below, and IV Corps in the Mekong Delta. General Dang Van Quang was IV Corps commander, and the foreign press, especially the Americans, wrote extensively about his alleged activities. He was widely reputed to be Vietnam's most corrupt general, with his fingers in every sort of illicit vice, including opium smuggling. Rumors are not evidence, however, and certainly not enough to have someone shot. I asked Loan to investigate General Quang, to find evidence of corruption.

Such investigations take time. If Quang was guilty of only a tenth of his rumored crimes, then he was at the center of a vast network of corruption, a web of hundreds, perhaps thousands of people involved in criminal acts. Because the very people who could provide the best evidence against Quang were themselves criminals, each had good reason to conceal his crimes. There was also the matter of retribution: Quang ruled the delta region virtually as a warlord. He had the power to crush anyone who threatened his safety or to take action against their families. It was not easy to find witnesses to his corruption. Still, if I had remained in office even a few months longer, I have no doubt that enough evidence would have been found to convict him. When I stepped down in 1967, however, President Nguyen Van Thieu quietly ended all investigations of ranking officers. I am sure this saved Quang's life.

Later in this book I will have much more to say about Thieu; here I need only point out that his salary as a senior general and then as president never came to more than a few thousand dollars a year. He went into exile a few days before the end of the war with so many tens of millions of dollars that President Gerald Ford sent word that he was not welcome to live in the United States.

Although I was unable to try Quang, the execution of Ta Vinh made many senior military officers uneasy. They said nothing, however, because they all knew that my course of action was right. Many generals suspended their illicit activity, waiting to see what I would do next.

So, I was surprised to read news reports in the Vietnamese press that instead of mounting combat operations, the commander of the Second Division, Major General Nguyen Van Toan, was using his troops to harvest wild cinnamon growing in the jungles near Quang Nam and then selling it. I got a helicopter and, with his corps commander, General Hoang Xuan Lam, made an unannounced visit to Toan's headquarters. This division commander was well over six feet tall, a muscular and imposing figure—and he began to tremble when I showed him the newspaper.

"Here is a story about you using military people to go to the jungle, cut cinnamon, and sell it," I said, looking him in the eye. "Is it true?"

People have told me that I have a very intimidating way of asking hard questions, and so when I confronted General Toan, he could not deny the truth.

"But why? Why do you do that?" I asked, as curious as I was angry.

"My troops need the money to take care of their families," he replied. "And for some social activities, a feast to celebrate the new year, that sort of thing."

"How much do you need for these kinds of activities?" I asked. "To help the soldiers' families and this and that? How much each month? Give me a number."

Toan named a figure—a few thousand dollars.

"From now on, every month I will give you that money," I said. "As prime minister I have a special fund available, and I will use some of this to improve troop welfare and morale. Every month I will send it.

"Now, concerning your own family," I continued. "I know that your army salary is not enough for a general officer. So tell me how much you need for your children, for your family. Give me a number."

Toan gave me a second figure, not much more than a hundred dollars. "From now on," I said, "every month you will get this extra pay. I myself will send it to you. But also from now on, if I hear that you are making your troops cut cinnamon in the jungle, or anything else like that, you will be executed." And I gave him that hard look, the same look that I had used before, so that he understood that I meant exactly what I had said. "Do you understand?" I asked.

When I got back to Saigon I ordered my aide to make arrangements to give similar funds to every division commander, both a personal allowance and monies for troop welfare, including better food, and more of it. I knew that I had to support the troops in this way. I would deal with corrupt officers harshly, but if most ordinary soldiers were not in a position to be corrupted, they had to eat. If the army didn't give them enough food for their families, they would take livestock or rice from the farmers—from anywhere they could. I wanted their bellies filled so that they would not steal from the peasants. I wanted their families to have enough to eat as well, because I had learned that so wretchedly poor were the lower ranks that some of their wives had been forced into prostitution. And so, from the time of the cinnamon incident, whenever I visited a military unit and someone asked for money, I gave it to him.

About the same time, a man turned up at the main gate to the Presidential Palace and asked to see me. The guards tried to send him away, but he refused to go. I had made a public statement that as prime minister my door was open to everyone, and eventually my aide heard about the man at the gate and brought him to my office. When he told me where he had come from—Camau, the southernmost tip of the country, hundreds of miles away—I knew that he was truly desperate, because he had only one arm, one leg, one eye. I cannot conceive of how he had managed to travel all that distance without a dong to his name. He was an army veteran, and he said that although he had tried everywhere, he could not find a job. "I need some money to start a business for my family," he said.

"How much would you like?"

He was dumbfounded. He had not even thought about how much to ask for. I gave him 300,000 dong, about $250 at the official exchange rate, and surely far more than he had imagined possible. I didn't like the idea of him traveling with so much cash, so I sent him home in my helicopter.

Word got around. Wherever I went, people asked for money. The special fund was not *my* money, it was the people's money, so I never questioned anyone, never demanded to know why they wanted it. Instead I said, "Tell me how much you need." Most were afraid to ask for too much, so they usually responded that the amount was up to me. I often gave them a blank check. "I trust you," I said. "Take what you need." I dispensed several million dollars that way, yet I know of no one who ever abused the privilege of a blank check.

Usually, when a commander visited a subordinate's unit, he was showered with valuable gifts. That was the ancient custom, to offer tribute. But accepting such presents is a form of corruption: The gift-giver hopes to receive something more valuable in return. So I stood that custom on its head. On my trips abroad as prime minister or vice president, I bought Rolex watches and expensive fountain pens. When I visited a unit to celebrate a hard-fought victory or to give a brave soldier a medal or a promotion, my aide gave them a watch or a pen as a souvenir. By rewarding the brave and the meritorious, I hoped to make the point that courage and honesty would pay off. I hoped that by setting an example, junior commanders would emulate it. And many did.

The day that I visited General Toan to ask him about cutting cinnamon, I came across one of the oldest soldiers I had ever seen. He was walking guard duty in the rain, and when I saw a man with that many years who was still a private, I was very surprised. I stopped and asked him how long he had served. I've forgotten exactly what he said, but it was about ten years. I turned to his commander and said, "How come this guy is still a private? Is he a poor soldier? If he gives you trouble, makes problems, then kick him out. We don't need that kind of soldier."

"No," said his commander. "He is a good guy—a good soldier. I requested his promotion many times, but it was never approved, and I don't know why."

I knew why. I called one of my bodyguards over, a sergeant, and borrowed one of his epaulettes. "Come here," I said to the old man, beckoning with my hand. I buttoned the epaulette on and shook his hand. "Now you are an NCO," I said. "You are a big boss." When we got back to Saigon the next day, my aide had the paperwork sent to this man's unit. After that, whenever I was in the field, I looked for others who had been privates too long, those who could never scrape enough together to bribe the right boss for a promotion, and righted things on the spot.

I never had a second meeting with the rice merchants. A day or so after they left my office, Minister Truong stopped by. "There is plenty of rice in the markets, and it is selling at the official price," he said. Did I trick the rice merchants? Not at all. Had they supposed that I was bluffing, had rice not returned to the markets at a fair price, I would have shot one. And if that had not brought supplies and prices back to normal, I would have shot another.

As it happened, only the luckless Ta Vinh was executed for his crimes. The Americans, as well as many of my colleagues, put a lot of pressure on me not to shoot any others. When I left office, things went back to normal. Everything and everyone was for sale—and so, in the end, everything was lost.

Now I believe that I was too soft. There was no lack of candidates, no shortage of corrupt officials, businessmen, or military officers. If I had stayed with my plan and allowed a few more profiteers to be executed, there surely would have been less corruption. And then, perhaps, things might have turned out differently.

10
CRISIS

As efforts to eliminate corruption attracted notice, my government acquired more popular support. Just as important, by autumn of 1965 the U.S. First Cavalry (Air Mobile) and the Republic of Korea Tiger divisions had arrived to drive back the enemy in II Corps. After several bloody battles, a desperate situation reversed itself. Now it was the communists who hid beneath the monsoon clouds, hunted by well-trained and highly motivated troops. There was a bitter price to pay: While the communists suffered their highest casualties of the war, hundreds of Americans, Koreans, and other allied soldiers were killed or wounded each week. Even today I am moved by their valor, by the depth of their commitment, by their personal sacrifices.

Due in large measure to these heroic efforts, as 1965 drew to a close I could see almost day by day how South Vietnam grew militarily stronger and more politically stable. Those who had said in June that within weeks I would fall to yet another coup—among them many senior Americans—fell silent. Just before Christmas, Jack Valenti, now chairman and chief executive of the Motion Picture Association of America but then a senior advisor to President Johnson, suggested

> that we [the Americans] focus our political energies in Saigon—and seek Korean assistance—in building a widely based South Vietnamese political party . . . The critical missing ele-

ment in the stabilization of politics in South Viet Nam is an effective political party engaging the major groups which constitute now—and will constitute in the future—an effective majority . . .

We all understand the deep splits in the political and social life of South Viet Nam: Northerners v. Southerners; French trained Catholics v. more indigenous Buddhists; etc. We are doing what we can in Saigon to urge them to come closer together; Ky is considering a representative advisory group; and the most wholesome political fact about South Viet Nam is that the Vietnamese are beginning to talk and worry about what the Communists will do to them if they remain split and peace (or negotiations) breaks out.

. . . our experience in Korea over the last five years indicates that [creation of a party] . . . may prove the device for crystallizing minimum national unity. I am now convinced, for example, that it was the creation of the government party in Korea that converted Park from a well-meaning soldier into an effective politician and, even, a statesman—laying the base for the true Korean "miracle" now under way.

To my certain knowledge, our people were almost as hopeless about Korea in 1961, after the young officers' coup, as they now are about politics in South Viet Nam. The Koreans were about as fragmented, inexperienced, and helpless in making a political life as the Vietnamese have been . . .

I do know there are glimmerings of a desire among the Vietnamese to pull together . . .

Moreover, we should enlist the Koreans in the effort. Their experience is the closest parallel to that in South Viet Nam. They, too, began with a mandarin autocrat; then had squabbling civil politicians; then a young officers' coup . . . We should approach General Park and suggest that he write directly to General Ky explaining fraternally the lessons of his

June 27, 1963. South Vietnam's ruling family. From second from left: Madame Ngo Nhu, Archbishop Ngo Dinh Thuc, Ngo Dinh Nhu, and President Ngo Dinh Diem. At right, Nguyen Van Thuan, Diem's nephew and now a cardinal of the Roman Catholic Church in Rome. (AP/Wide World)

August 26, 1963. U.S. Ambassador Henry Cabot Lodge presents his credentials to President Ngo Dinh Diem. (AP/Wide World)

January 31, 1950. Former emperor Bao Dai. (AP/Wide World)

February 16, 1965. From left to right: Chief of State Phan Khac Suu and Prime Minister Dr. Phan Huy Quat, at Saigon's Gia Long Palace. (AP/Wide World)

June 21, 1965. Outgoing prime minister Dr. Phan Huy Quat gestures toward Air Vice Marshal Nguyen Cao Ky, the Republic of Vietnam's new prime minister. At left, Major General Nguyen Van Thieu, the new chief of state. (AP/Wide World)

General Nguyen Cao Ky with Chiang Kai-Shek in Taipei, 1965. (author's collection)

Divine Wind Squadron Leadership, Tan Son Nhut, 1965.
(author's collection)

General Nguyen Cao Ky.
(Courtesy of the Vietnam
Archive, Texas Tech
University)

February 20, 1965. Brigadier General Le Nguyen Khan, Vietnamese Marine Corps commander. (AP/Wide World)

June 6, 1970. Major General Nguyen Ngoc Loan, former Chief of National Police, welcomes Vice President Ky back from an official visit to Cambodia. (AP/Wide World)

November 29, 1963. Chief of State General Duong Van Minh. (AP/Wide World)

October 17, 1966. Brigadier General Vinh Loc, II Corps area commander, in traditional Montagnard garb. (AP/Wide World)

September 11, 1964. Prime Minister Major General Nguyen Khanh during a press conference in Saigon. He has shaved his goatee "to be a completely new and different man," according to a bodyguard. (AP/Wide World)

April 5, 1967. Major General Nguyen Duc Thang, South Vietnam's minister for revolutionary development and head of the pacification program, during a trip to the countryside. (AP/Wide World)

October 5, 1966. Buddhist leader Thich Thien Minh (right) at Saigon's Buddhist National Institute. He was the only leader to comment publicly on Prime Minister Ky's decision to remain in power another year with his military government, cautioning Ky to keep promises. (AP/Wide World)

Venerable Tri Quang, leader of a militant Buddhist antigovernment faction.
(AP/Wide World)

July 9, 1966. Lieutenant General Nguyen Chanh Thi, one of five generals who cooperated with Buddhist dissidents in an uprising, He was sentenced to sixty days in prison and forced into retirement. (AP/Wide World)

January 15, 1962. General Maxwell D. Taylor. (AP/Wide World)

February 1976. Ambassador W. Averell Harriman. (AP/Wide World)

June 19, 1975. CIA Director William E. Colby. (AP/Wide World)

April 22, 1966. Prime Minister Ky and Prime Minister Harold E. Holt of Australia review an honor guard of Vietnamese marines at Tan Son Nhut Airport. (AP/Wide World)

May 16, 1996. Thailand's King Bhumibol Adulyadej. (AP/Wide World)

March 14, 1966. Businessman Tah Vinh was executed by firing squad for black marketeering and bribery. (AP/Wide World)

General Nguyen Cao Ky awards medals to Major General Robert M. Shoemaker (left) and Brigadier General James F. Hollingsworth. (Courtesy of the Vietnam Archive)

General Nguyen Cao Ky (at top, middle) with National Security Adviser Henry Kissinger and (below, left to right) President Richard Nixon with President Nguyen Van Thieu. (author's collection)

June 1970. As Prime Minister Tran Thien Khiem looks on, Vice President Nguyen Cao Ky talks with newsmen at Saigon's Tan Son Nhut Airport. (AP/Wide World)

experience in building a stable civil government in South Korea over recent years; the role of the government party in that process; and offering to send to General Ky men who will explain in detail how his national political party was organized and how they made the transition in Seoul from military to civil politics.

The glimmering of desire to work together in Saigon was real, and since I would have been responsible for its absence, I will take credit for its presence. The political situations in South Korea in 1961 and South Vietnam in 1965, however, were quite different. Korea, for millennia a hermit kingdom that shunned foreign contact, was a former vassal of China subjugated by Japan but never colonized by Europeans. With all Indochina, Vietnam experienced the benefits of regional commerce and cultural intercourse for hundreds of years but suffered a century of colonial rule. Korea was historically a homogeneous kingdom without ethnic minorities and relatively insignificant regional rivalries mitigated by a shared Confucian sensibility. Moreover, Korea's Buddhists never involved themselves in politics, while in addition to Vietnam's many ethnic minorities, our religious pantheon included competing Buddhist sects.

Most important, in 1961 Korea was at peace, a peninsula protected by the world's best navy and a large, well-equipped and battle-tested army. We, however, shared a porous border with nations controlled or neutered by the communists. Enemy forces roamed every province of my country. The comparison was strained, if revealing.

I feel sure that Jack Valenti, a World War II bomber pilot whom I would come to know and like, had the best intentions. His thinking on that subject, however, did not reflect the realities of our situation as much as it did the American tendency to oversimplify complex issues that they don't understand.

In any event, I did not hear from General Park in this regard, and when we met several months after this idea was floated, he never mentioned it.

...

As it became apparent that my government could adapt to the changing military and political situation and was not in imminent peril, President Johnson invited me and leading members of my government to confer with him in Honolulu on February 7, 1966. He made it plain that our principal purpose was to become personally acquainted, which, we both hoped, would make it easier to work together toward our mutual goal, a free and independent South Vietnam.

Although I was still a relatively new prime minister, and this was my first meeting with the most important man in the world, I didn't worry for even a moment. As with everyone whom I meet, I assumed that Mr. Johnson would either accept me or not, as he wished; there was no reason for any elaborate preparation on my part. I told my people that I would take the occasion to share my thinking with Johnson.

As chief of state, Thieu would share the spotlight—but I would deliver the speech. I knew that America would help us fight the communists, so I decided not to dwell on military issues. Instead I concentrated on four points: defeating the Vietcong, eradicating social injustice, establishing a viable economy, and building true democracy. I put my thoughts into Vietnamese, then worked with several bright linguists to translate them into appropriate English.

I spoke in a large conference room at CINCPAC headquarters to about a hundred people, Americans on one side of the room and Vietnamese on the other. When I finished, Mr. Johnson rose from his chair across the huge table. "You talk just like an American boy," he said.

"Fortunately, I am *not* an American boy," I replied, and laughter rippled around the table.

After lunch, working groups of Americans and Vietnamese discussed rural construction, economic stabilization, health and education, and diplomatic issues. That evening the Americans hosted a lavish reception. As I moved through the room, greeting friends, Mr. Johnson suddenly appeared.

"General, come with me," he said. We went to a private office, and when drinks had been poured, Mr. Johnson leaned toward me and lowered his voice.

"General, I think everything that we do in public, whatever we say in public, is just for the public," he drawled. "Let me propose that from now on, every time we want to do something, or we have to discuss something between America and Vietnam, we'll do it at the individual level. Just you and me. Together we'll make the important decisions, things that we don't want the public to know."

"That is fine with me," I replied. I was left with the idea that I had made a good first impression on Mr. Johnson. Later on, after getting to know him better, I decided that I liked him very much. The next day at lunch, he took me aside again.

"What would you like me to do for you right now?" he asked.

Once more I was taken by surprise. Without thinking I said, "We have radio but not television. Personally, I enjoy watching cowboy movies. When I was a young boy in Hanoi, I only went to the theater when there was a western. Can you give us a TV broadcasting station?"

He guffawed—and then I explained why we really needed television. I often used radio to talk to my countrymen, especially when there was some important issue that everyone ought to know about. But television would be more effective, I explained, in helping to build a national consensus and maintain political stability.

Within an hour Mr. Johnson had spoken with Jack Valenti, who said that it would take several months, perhaps a year, to build a television station in Saigon.

"Is it not possible to do it sooner?" I responded.

"Jack, don't we have a flying TV studio that we could send?" asked Mr. Johnson.

Within a week that station, along with thousands of black-and-white television receivers, was delivered to Vietnam. This was a broadcast facility in an airliner that was soon orbiting high above Saigon a few hours daily, broadcasting to television sets that I had distributed to public locations nationwide. After several months, a permanent station went into operation. Alas, I was far too busy to watch cowboy movies.

Mr. Johnson and I had another private meeting, which included Thieu and a few American cabinet members. Mr. Johnson said that he liked my ideas for improving social justice, and then we discussed many things, including exchange rates between U.S. dollars and Vietnamese dong. We felt that the rate was too low and encouraged black-market speculation. Both sides agreed to have economists study the issue and make recommendations.

Mr. Johnson pressed Thieu and me about implementing several economic measures, and I agreed to announce them soon. I also told Mr. Johnson that I intended to split the Ministry of Economics into a Ministry of Trade and a Ministry of Industrialization because I thought the present ministry had too much power and offered too many opportunities for corruption.

Then Mr. Johnson lectured on the importance of the Chieu Hoi program. I agreed that it deserved emphasis and explained how I had already taken several steps to strengthen the "Open Arms" program that helped Vietcong defectors adjust to their new lives. Mr. Johnson then did something I thought strange: He made an issue out of us getting prominent Vietcong to defect so that we could put them on radio for propaganda and psychological purposes. He pressed us to develop better contacts with the communists to gain increased understanding of the movement.

I never doubted that putting defectors on the air would have a great impact on those listening. Unfortunately, relatively few Vietnamese, and fewer Vietcong, owned radios. Another difficulty was that most of the "prominent" Vietcong were either infiltrated northerners or figurehead southerners; as a group they were undistinguished men who, before they became Vietcong, had commanded little respect. Moreover, any defector who allowed himself to be used in this way would also sign the death warrants of his family and closest friends. As this was not a good idea, we ignored it.

On the second point: There were many in government and the military who had regular contact with Vietcong, often close relatives. Some of these talks yielded valuable intelligence, but most merely served a communist agenda. As for gaining a better understanding of the movement, I am as certain now as I was then that I understood the Vietcong well. They made brilliant use of propaganda and understood truth as whatever served their purpose of the moment. Their goal was to control Vietnam and transform it into a "dictatorship of the proletariat." I write this more than twenty-five years after communists subjugated my country. My people remain among Asia's poorest, a society afflicted by corruption where individuals have few rights and fewer hopes. I understood this perfectly in 1966.

Because I saw no point in confronting Mr. Johnson in front of his advisors, I merely listened. The president also suggested that we create a program to encourage defectors from among "very young members of the VC." Again, I could only nod.

As our meeting broke up, Mr. Johnson urged me to carry out more reforms in the ARVN. And he suggested that I spend more time in the countryside "acting like a politician instead of just a general."

After lunch, Mr. Johnson asked if I could take Vice President Hubert Humphrey back to Vietnam on my aircraft "to start right away, to give a little push to those new programs." Mr. Humphrey stayed just long enough for a look around the country and a briefing—a few days. Upon his return to Washington, however, he briefed President Johnson and members of the cabinet. Mr. Humphrey reported that my government's goal was to stop communist aggression and "bring a better life" to all people. He said that while none of us saw an easy solution or predicted a speedy end to fighting, we all felt that we could win by defeating the enemy, ending subversion, and starting a social revolution. At the same time, he said, "It is difficult to talk of victory in this country. Some people resent victory . . . If we don't weaken, and help South Vietnam build a better society, our objective can be accomplished." On the subject of stability, he pointed out that during the first two years of the Marshall Plan after World War II, France had six governments. The vice president praised my leadership, along with Thieu's, but added that he didn't know how long we would survive. "These men are trying to do what is right," he concluded.

I was not impressed with Mr. Humphrey. On the long flight from Honolulu to Saigon, and at each of our subsequent meetings, he stopped spewing grandiloquent phrases only long enough to pause for breath. I tried to engage him as a man, but he responded as a politician. I always had the impression that whatever came out of his mouth was a prepared speech, that he spoke with calculation, with some hidden intention or agenda. He was never spontaneous. Even when there were only the two of us, Mr. Humphrey was on a stage, trying to convert me to his politics. I got very little sense of the man behind the politician. Maybe that is the reason that some years later, when he needed my help, I withheld it. With Johnson, Henry Cabot Lodge, and later Henry Kissinger and even Richard Nixon, when we were in private we spoke as men, without pretense, from our hearts. But Mr. Humphrey never let down his guard with me. If there was a human being behind that façade, I never saw it. Wrong or right, I never felt that there was a man inside that suit.

Our meetings in Honolulu, however, left Mr. Johnson impressed with me in much the way that I was impressed with him: We respected each other, although our views of the world were quite different. On the evening of February 10 he spoke with B. K. Nehru, India's ambassador to the United States, by phone. Mr. Johnson said:

I knew nothing about Ky and Thieu, the Chief of State [*sic*], and what I learned was quite favorable. The impressions, the titles, the military backgrounds, the generals, the air marshals, the field marshals, so on and so forth. They never have been very impressive to civilians in Johnson City, Texas, cause we didn't have many storm troopers out there. And we haven't had many of them in our government. And I was amazed, as Alex Johnson [a state official] said, whatever else may be, he [Ky] certainly knows how to talk. Whether he knows how to do as well as he knows how to talk is different. The declaration that we wrote was really his speech and it said in effect that we are going to act to prevent aggression, to defeat aggression. He didn't take in any more territory. He was defeating aggression. And we're going to defeat social misery, with considerable details along the line of his January 15th speech. And Ky was a young man who was going to lead the revolution in his country and build a new society and a stable society, and he was going to seek and obtain an honorable peace. And there's not anything in those four points that any country, I think, wouldn't apply to themselves: to prevent an aggressor, and try to defeat social misery, and establish a stable society, and seek an honorable peace. And it was so eloquent and so simple and so young [*sic*], [but] we have no illusions and we've seen a good many governments come and go and we don't know what'll happen that night. It was quite different from the General [Chiang Kai-shek of Taiwan] marching around with a sword at his side. And when we had the technicians, sixteen of 'em, with Orville Freeman [Secretary of Agriculture], sit down and meet with him [Ky], they all, every Ph.D. there, came away rather stimulated at this man's exciting interest in the quality of the rice seed and how you're going to increase its production. And his demand that we get eight million more school books in there next year. And his telling us how to handle the economic aid that Dave Bell has given him. And he just traded back and forth with Dave Bell for an hour on how to build classrooms. And he said that the American contractors come in and put 'em up overnight, and the Viet Cong come in and burn 'em down a week later. And they say, "We burned down American schools." But he said, "You give me some materials. We take the materials and put our own people to building the schools, and when the Viet Cong come in to get the school they will say 'you cannot touch our school.' "

. . . we have tried for two years to get these people to thinking in terms of building a better society there and not just strictly a military operation but a political one, too. And you can't do it unless you can get Lodge and Westmoreland and the Prime Minister to adopt the baby as their own. And we did that.

When I returned from Honolulu I reorganized my cabinet somewhat to focus on what I felt were new priorities. The Honolulu summit assured me of Mr. Johnson's personal support, and this was of vital importance in dealing with a domestic crisis: a covert alliance among Buddhist troublemakers, communist infiltrators, and one of my key corps commanders that held the potential for crippling my government and handing a huge chunk of territory to the communists.

Before I had served even a hundred days as premier, the Buddhists had begun to stir the pot. Despite my willingness to hear their complaints and the steps I had taken to support the pagodas, Tri Quang was not satisfied. He seemed to act as if he were invincible, that he actually was, as an American newsmagazine had put it, "the man who shook the world."

In August Tri Quang granted an interview to the *Far Eastern Economic Review,* a Hong Kong newspaper, in which he denounced my government in general and Thieu in particular, claiming that "the people" were against the government. While this is the sort of thing I had come to expect from that monk, I was not pleased that he also said that he hoped the war could be stopped as soon as possible by a cease-fire or "by any negotiations which would have the people's support." He was further quoted as saying that a small country like Vietnam could rely only on itself and "certainly on no outsider."

Yet only a few weeks earlier, Tri Quang had told foreign visitors that we should pursue the war more vigorously, bomb the North harder, even if it meant taking on the Chinese communists!

So when Tri Quang subsequently told U.S. Embassy officials that he had "discouraged" antigovernment demonstrations in Hue, none believed him. Probably because of the public support that my government enjoyed in the capital, the Buddhists focused their efforts on Hue and Da Nang. Hue, the former imperial capital, was a few miles from the demilitarized zone (DMZ) separating North and South Vietnam. Da Nang was headquarters for the I Corps region.

I Corps was commanded by Nguyen Chanh Thi, the paratroop commander whom I had saved from Diem's wrath after the failed coup of November 11, 1960. The CIA described Thi as an extremely complex individual. I never considered him complex. He grew up in a family of impoverished peasants, had almost no schooling except in the military, and often acted as if he felt out of place among educated people. After escaping from Diem, he bickered with the other Phnom Penh exiles, complaining that they had dragged him into a lost cause. His exile was a bitter brew; he survived on handouts and menial jobs from those whom he considered inferiors.

After Diem was deposed, Thi returned to Saigon feeling that he was owed a promotion and other rewards for his role in the failed coup and the tribulations of exile. Instead he got his old rank and was assigned to I Corps, commanded by another who had come late to that first move against Diem, General Nguyen Khanh. Khanh used Thi's connections to the airborne brigade to organize the coup that overturned Big Minh. Once Khanh was in power, however, he kept Thi in Da Nang instead of bringing him to Saigon, as promised, to serve as his right-hand man.

Thi was given command of the First Division, headquartered in Da Nang. Later Khanh promoted him to corps commander. Still in that post when I became premier, he became a member of the Directorate. Before and after, however, he rarely displayed much loyalty to Saigon. He had allowed antigovernment rallies in Hue that led to the downfall of the Huong government and had done nothing to prevent an embarrassing demonstration during Thieu's first visit to Hue as chief of state.

My take on Thi is that he is a classic example of a man with low self-esteem. He is susceptible to flattery and thus could easily come to believe he is the potential savior of his country. Competing with these ambitions, however, was the self-doubt of the peasant who finds himself far above his father's station in life. Not so complex as the Americans imagined.

Recall that when the civilian leadership returned power to the Armed Forces Council in June 1965, and Thieu had declined my nomination to serve as prime minister, I had immediately nominated Thi. He too had declined. Soon after I became prime minister, however, Thi began to conspire with such retired officers as the St. Cyr–trained General Tran Van Don (who once famously said, "I feel that we shall achieve victory in 1964."), a crony of the perpetually ambitious Big Minh. Don was said to have once abetted a secret French effort to force U.S. troops out of Vietnam and would have liked to return to the army, where he could further enrich himself.

Thi was not subtle. In his September 28, 1965, telegram to the State Department, Ambassador Lodge noted:

> In his conversations with Mission officer [probably Lansdale] regarding his destiny, Thi has . . . said on one occasion that he would hope that Ky, on becoming aware of his incapacity to lead, would turn to him and say, "I tried, now it's your turn," and quietly return to his air force. Such remarks by Thi must be weighed carefully, because they were meant for American consumption with full knowledge of our anxiety that governmental stability be maintained. Given Thi's mercurial nature, one must conclude that the circumstances of the moment would determine whether he made his play within or outside the framework of the existing government. In any event, were he to assume either Thieu's position or Ky's one would have to expect many changes in personnel (Thi has always wanted his own men around him), programs and probably even in fundamental GVN [Government of Vietnam] policy.

Thi's ambitions did not sit well with Lodge:

> It is our judgment that Thi would be seriously deficient in either military backing or popular support were he to try and assume power. One can imagine a situation developing within the Directorate itself through which he might be named either Chairman or Prime Minister, but he would face virtually insurmountable difficulties from outset in attempting to allay any broad base support . . . there would be sharp reaction within the northern Catholic refugee bloc. In addition, the southern mass would probably find this impossible to stomach. His only assets would probably be in the center and even

these are uncertain if he were unwilling to accept guidance from Tri Quang. (Thi and Quang are possessed of personalities which are not dissimilar and potentially antipathetic.)

In view of foregoing, we will . . . hope that we can convince him that he can best serve the nation in present role as I Corps Commander and by lending his support to the principle of continued unity within the Directorate. Defense Minister Co has told us that he was sent to Da Nang while Hue protests were going on for the purpose of reaffirming Thi's support for the government about which certain members of the Directorate were worried. Co claims to have gained Thi's understanding and that Thi continues to support status quo.

As I Corps commander, Thi often displayed lapses in judgment, and had done nothing to advance such vital programs as pacification or revolutionary development. As his delusions of grandeur grew, he seemed to go out of his way to provoke top government officials; he often returned their written orders with scribbled notes like "this crazy government." By the time I returned from Honolulu, it was obvious that the national government no longer controlled a quarter of our nation, an intolerable situation.

I was kept apprised of Thi's extracurricular activities by some of his underlings, who told me that he met secretly with Buddhist leaders. The monks encouraged his grandiosity by suggesting that someone of his talent and virtue ought to be a king, running his command as he pleased. In response, Thi lent tacit support to their antigovernment demonstrations.

I had shared a Hue speaking platform with Thi in September 1965. He took that occasion to castigate those who caused trouble on the home front while troops were dying in the field. As he spoke, however, I wondered if his words were for my benefit, to buy himself time before I confronted him. In the interest of unity, I gave him more rope.

I suspected that Thi had forged alliances with other generals, and so on this occasion I sought Ambassador Lodge's counsel. He was gracious enough to see me on very short notice, and when I explained the situation, he remarked that Thi reminded him of the warlords whom he had encountered in China in 1929. Lodge said that as a representative of the U.S. government he could not interfere in an internal Vietnamese matter. As a personal friend, however, he advised me to have lawyers build an airtight case against Thi, documenting his insubordination and malfeasance.

This was undoubtedly good advice for an American general, but the situation in Da Nang was such that there was little time to waste on such formalities. I decided that it came down to one issue: I had granted each of the corps commanders enormous powers, including authority to hire or fire everyone from provincial governors on down. In return I demanded loyalty to my government. Either I was prime minister and responsible for the conduct of my government, including all four corps commanders, or I was not really prime minister.

When I returned from Honolulu, I learned that Thi had openly complained to the Americans about my leadership, suggesting that I ought to return to the air force. On March 10, 1966, I went to Hue with General Huu Co, the minister of defense, for a routine and previously scheduled visit. It began with a meeting at the Hue city hall with top I Corps military and civil officials. Throughout the country, on every such previous occasion, the corps commander personally conducted the briefing. This time, however, Thi gave this task to the deputy governor. Most of what this civilian said was critical of the Saigon government—*my* government. It caught me by surprise. As I sat listening, I began to wonder, How is it that this third-rank civilian dares to challenge me? Why does the rat come to play with the tiger? Something is wrong.

Later that day, after a tour of I Corps facilities, Thi and this same underling accompanied me and my entourage to the Hue-Phu Bai Airport, where I boarded a plane for the return trip to Saigon.

The ground crew sealed the hatch. As we started to taxi away, I glanced through the window and saw Thi and his hench-man exchanging the Vietnamese equivalent of high fives—they were shaking hands in a congratulatory way, as if they had just won the World Series or the World Cup.

I turned back to Co and said, "As soon as we are airborne, use the aircraft radio and send a cable to Thi, relieving him of his command."

Co, stunned, asked: "What did you say?" I repeated myself, and a few minutes later he sent the cable.

I did not need anyone's permission to fire Thi. Nor did I need to send the cable myself. As minister of defense, Co was authorized to make such military personnel changes on his own authority. Whether he was a member of the politburo or not, Thi was a military officer, a corps commander subordinate to the minister of defense. I exercised my prerogatives under the law, and there was nothing Thi could do but obey.

The next day, to use a phrase favored by many Americans of that era, the shit hit the fan. In Da Nang, small groups of Buddhist and student protestors were joined by uniformed I Corps soldiers. Demonstrations accompanied by strikes and school shutdowns grew in size and spread to Hue and elsewhere, including the first public protests in Saigon since I took office.

At first the I Corps demonstrations focused on Thi's removal, but as they spread to Hue the demonstrators began to make additional demands. One by Thich Tam Chau, leader of a mil-itant Buddhist faction, included the return of Vietnam to civilian government and the holding of national elections. Tam Chau demanded creation of a national assembly and representative political institutions, reinstatement of retired military officers, and implementation "without delay" of the "social revolution related to the life of the masses," as U.S. news media dutifully reported.

Buddhist leaders knew very well that my government was already working hard to accomplish all these things, but nationwide elections, for example, do not just happen. They require planning, preparation, and time. With the Directorate's concurrence, I had scheduled a second round of provincial and municipal council elections in the spring of 1966. In the autumn there was to be a national referendum to elect representatives to draft a constitution, followed by national elections in 1967.

But the Buddhists, motivated by personal and political ambitions and by fundamental antipathy to almost any conceivable government, had only the vaguest understanding of what it took to achieve stability and national unity in a time of war.

To be fair, some who joined the protests had legitimate concerns. The military could not rid itself of corruption overnight, yet there was still no viable democratic civilian alternative. The underpaid civil bureaucracy remained riddled with corruption, especially at its lowest levels. Meanwhile, the effects of the war, including hundreds of thousands of comparatively well-paid foreign troops, had sent inflation spiraling to new heights, making difficult lives even harder.

Still another reason for the unrest was that the Buddhist leaders, who regarded themselves as Vietnam's major political force, took offense because I did not consult them before reorganizing my cabinet after the Honolulu conference. They also perceived that meeting with Mr. Johnson strengthened my convictions about the correctness of my policies. In short, the more successful my government was, the more determined they were to get rid of me.

In Thi's place as I Corps commander the Directorate put General Nguyen Van Chuan. Although no longer in command,

Thi continued to exercise influence over the violence in the northern provinces. As the situation deteriorated, Lodge described his view of events in a telegram to Mr. Johnson:

> From the standpoint of the ability of the Government of Viet-Nam to influence events and promote stability, last week was bad and so is this week.
>
> On the one hand are certain Buddhists who are making impossible and preposterous demands. They actually say they want to change the government and yet are utterly unable to give the names of anyone who would be able to step in and run the government. Tri Quang even says: "Overthrow the government and then elect Ky Prime Minister." These Buddhists actually say that they want to hold elections now when there is no election law, no suitable election machinery, and when the country is evidently totally unready.
>
> This Buddhist attitude undoubtedly reflects Communist advice, subtly planted among Buddhist priests [*sic*], who think themselves very clever but who actually are lacking in knowledge of the world. They have all been told time and again by me personally and by other Embassy officers that to follow the course which they suggest would look crazy to Americans. But they are so parochial and so limited in their outlook that it apparently leaves them indifferent.
>
> Now we have the beginning of an anti-American flavor in Hue, with widely untrue and improbable charges being made, which I am certain reflects Communist activity among the students . . .
>
> If I were required to prove what I said about Communist influence, I could not do it. But the logic of the situation drives me to that conclusion . . .
>
> The Buddhists have in effect infiltrated the government in many posts. The government radio is publicizing Buddhist meetings, and government broadcasts are actually stimulating

opposition to the government. I worry lest the Directorate may be coming apart . . .

One reason Hanoi thinks it can win, I believe is because it knows the fragility of the government structure here. They are counting on this to weaken American enthusiasm. They realize that the average American at home cannot possibly understand the social structure in Viet-Nam and the lack of a tradition of national government in this country, even though there is a strong sense of peoplehood and a strong and courageous desire not to be a victim of aggression. This governmental fragility is what Hanoi is depending on, and if I were advising them, I would advise them to do just what they are doing to encourage the natural divisiveness in South Viet-Nam.

We are at the stage here when everything you try to grab is like quicksilver. Moreover, as the Buddhists go further, the chances of Catholics and Southerners (Cochinchinese) getting going increases and instead of the delicate balance we have had for 8 months, the scales will start wildly clashing up and down.

So now I find myself thinking the same thoughts that I was thinking in October 1903, that is, "What can be done without a civil government?" I think it is clear that military operations could go on for quite a while but everything which requires forward planning, such as "revolutionary development," would start grinding down. But also everything else today is so much better than it was in 1963 that there is scarcely any comparison . . .

As far as the general public is concerned, it appeared interested in but not worried about the dismissal of Thi. In the southern delta there appears to be little interest in the maneuverings by the Buddhists and by various center [*sic*] Viet-Nam personalities. Even in the Hue–Da Nang area there appears as yet to have been no genuine popular interest in the strikes, meetings and speeches of the past week which have been the work of individual Thi partisans, students and certain politicians interested in stirring things up for their own purposes.

Among influential middle and upper class Vietnamese . . . the optimists believe that the agitation in the wake of Thi's dismissal will blow over after a certain amount of jockeying for position among the Buddhists and the Generals. The pessimists, most of whom are journalists or intellectuals, fear that the agitation may drag on for several months with unfavorable effects on government stability.

All parties seem agreed that if the government maintains the initiative in moving towards a more representative base and avoids making a martyr of anyone, the Vietnamese public attitude will not change appreciably.

Lodge's intuition about communist influence was correct. After the fall of Vietnam in 1975, documents surfaced that showed that 300 shaven-headed Vietcong agitators wearing monks' robes had infiltrated the so-called Buddhist Struggle Movement. After Thi was placed under arrest, Colonel Wilson, the tommy gun–toting CIA operative who a year earlier had unknowingly backed the Vietcong double agent Colonel Pham Ngoc Thao, asked me to let Thi go to Washington, where the U.S. government would "take care of him." I agreed, even though I suspected that Thi was being groomed for some CIA contingency plan.

As March lengthened toward April, the I Corps antigovernment movement began to behave and sound more and more like an anti-U.S. movement. My government teetered on a delicate balance. Clearly I had to take some decisive action, but to restore order too soon or too forcefully would create still more opportunities for Vietcong agents provocateurs, for incidents, for bloodshed, and for the creation of martyrs. Three years earlier

Diem had responded to a similar situation. His choices cost him his life and threw our country into a chaos from which we had only begun to recover.

But if I waited too long, the "struggle" forces, which even without proof I believed to be under Vietcong influence, if not control, would become more and more boisterous. There would be more and more opportunity to provoke further incidents, leading inevitably to bloodshed and martyrs. This was obvious to Lodge, who also worried over the safety of the thousands of U.S. Marines based in Da Nang if my government failed to restore order.

I wanted to negotiate a peaceful solution, but the Buddhist leaders avoided making commitments, and even when they did, they felt no obligation to keep them. When I learned of Lodge's concerns, I met with him to assure him that I was committed to protecting all Americans from mob violence. Here is some of what Lodge wrote to Johnson about that meeting:

> If one omits the very fallacious estimates which Ky and Thieu both made regarding the reaction to the relief of General Thi, it must be said that, since then, Ky has said many right things and said them quite well, as regards· moving toward constitutional democracy, restoring law and order, dividing the Buddhists, and uniting the Directorate. He is thinking hard and seems to be thinking straight. He also maintains his poise and appears to be in good health.
>
> But to me, as a typically impatient American who naturally wants action, most of the things he says come about a week too late. He seldom gives dates or specifications. Also, one always wonders whenever a Vietnamese says something intelligent and true, whether he is in any way able to do anything about it. One must, to be sure, concede the dangers of moving too fast and he is, as he says, following the advice of Confucius "first to try protocol (negotiations) and then to use force."

(Incidentally, this is his second reference to Confucius.) Maybe his timing is right, although I believe strength tends to beget strength and that he has lost precious time. But I'm glad to have gotten this promise out of him as regards our Marines—and I impressed him with the vital necessity of moving quickly and sure-footedly when the time comes to move.

I, therefore, think the situation is precarious and, although there are a few hopeful signs, I fear serious developments unless the government moves in to restore order . . .

While there is a non-Communist element in all this, brought by the envy which the "outs" feel for the "ins" and by their reckless selfishness, there is no doubt that the Communists have subtly taken advantage of the "struggle." There is also a believable report of French trouble-making and Communist collaboration. Having been hurt on the field of battle, seeing the Chieu Hoi rate [Vietcong Deserters] going so much against them, and observing the promising beginnings as regards revolutionary development, they are trying out their political arm.

Buddhist (and presumable [*sic*] VC) agitators have tried—unsuccessfully so far—to start trouble in Saigon. They will surely keep trying despite some signs that Buddhist moderates such as Tam Chau are exerting a dampening influence. It is vital to keep Saigon and the South calm. If the pot boils up there, the gravity of the government's position will increase immeasurably . . .

I remain certain that Lodge's desire for a resolution to the I Corps situation was underlain by a genuine desire for my government to succeed. I could do a few things to try to prevent the spread of unrest without appearing to cave in to Buddhist demands: I put the establishment of a constitutional preparatory council on a fast track, and on March 25 the Directorate agreed that this body would be composed of one representative from each of the forty-three provincial and municipal councils, plus forty-three members selected from religious and social organizations. A few lawyers would act as the council's secretariat to ensure that things were tidy.

In this way I hoped to eliminate some uncertainties about the transition to civilian rule and to neutralize those who demanded immediate return to civil government by removing the rallying cry of their mob agitators.

I also tried to force a wedge between the Tam Chau and Tri Quang factions to discourage further Buddhist agitation. And I tried to enlist the support of other political elements, to limit the authority that the Buddhists could hope to seize by challenging my government.

But these were stopgaps; sooner or later I would have to deal more directly with the mess in I Corps. Because I judged it unlikely that I Corps forces would follow government orders, I made plans to dispatch Vietnamese marine battalions to Da Nang. To discuss this move, I invited Lodge to my office after lunch on April 2. "We have waited too long," I told him. "Now we must be very firm. All these different groups and minorities and sects make an infernal combination . . .

"I informed the Directorate today that either I would resign or that we would all stay. We have decided to remain together." I then told Lodge that I would go on radio and television that night and announce a nationwide state of siege, accompanied by twenty-four-hour curfews where appropriate. As another temporary measure, all schools and universities would close.

Teasing me, Lodge said that "some thought that Tri Quang was a communist, but I remembered that Prime Minister Ky had said he was an 'illuminé,' a visionary."

I replied that perhaps I had matured considerably in the last few weeks; I now thought that if Tri Quang was not a communist, he was certainly a Vietcong tool. "We face a great conspiracy to take over the government, ask all Americans to leave, and turn the country over to Hanoi," I said, adding that I now realized that even after making many concessions, even after talking with Thien Minh day and night, no prime minister could ever satisfy the Buddhist leaders. Minh had demanded a job for Thi, to which I was not opposed. But then he demanded that Thieu issue a formal reply agreeing with all Buddhist demands. Instead I had sent word to Thien Minh that as proof of their good intentions, by eight that evening orders must be issued to all monks to sit down and discuss ways to achieve our common goal. I was sure they would not meet that deadline, nor any deadline.

The Directorate meeting earlier that day had been thoroughly military and professional. We had staffed out plans for psychological warfare, including leaflets, sound trucks, and mobile radio stations, all designed to wrest the propaganda initiative from the Buddhists and communists. But we also needed American support.

"I want to move some marine battalions to Da Nang and bring up a division from IV Corps for additional security in Saigon," I told Lodge. "I will fly to Da Nang tonight with General Vien. He will remain at the command post when I return to Saigon, probably tomorrow." We needed American airlifts to reinforce Da Nang, however. "I know that Military Assistance Command, Vietnam [MACV, the U.S. supreme military HQ] is ready and that they need an order from you. Will you give it?" I asked.

Lodge agreed and notified Westmoreland. The next day, April 4, Westmoreland told the marine commander, Lieutenant General Lewis Walt, that two Vietnamese marine battalions, field police and military security elements, psywar teams, and a command group would move to Da Nang that evening on U.S. aircraft.

My plan was to retake Da Nang first and use this example

of government power and resolve to strengthen the national backbone to resist the troublemakers bent on causing dissension. Finally, I told Lodge, there was no longer any doubt in my mind that in view of the rapid reversal of their military success, Hanoi's plan was to use the events in I Corps as a springboard for a *soulevement*, a general uprising along the lines of the Russian revolt of February 1917 that deposed Czar Nicholas II.

"If I am weak they will succeed," I said. "But if I am strong they will not. History will judge if I do well or not, but I am ready to make the supreme sacrifice." As we parted, tears glistened in Lodge's eyes—and perhaps in mine as well.

11

HIGH NOON

IN Saigon I had Lodge's support and goodwill. Things looked different from Washington, however, where presidential advisors and State Department officials traded position papers suggesting such bizarre alternatives as asking the Dalai Lama to intervene with the dissident Buddhists. A telegram sent at the direction of U.S. secretary of state Dean Rusk to Lodge and Westmoreland on the evening of April 4 declared that "US forces should not be used in any way within Da Nang or Hue or against dissident GVN forces. Nor should any endorsement be given to the GVN claim that the Struggle Movement was 'Communist-dominated,' a claim 'contrary to any evidence we have.' "

Alarmed by what they perceived to be my government's imminent demise, Mr. Johnson's closest advisors met in secret to put forward alternatives, including, I would learn many years later, returning Thi to power in Da Nang. Vice President Humphrey offered his opinion that "Thi is pleasant, Buddhist and clever," he said, adding that "Ky is jealous of Thi. Some of our Mission people think Thi is able. [CIA agent Colonel] Sam Wilson thinks he is competent."

Defense Secretary Robert McNamara chimed in. "The way I see it, Ky is gone, the last gasp. Doubt he can pull it off. When he goes, there'll be hell in this country. Let's get a government we can appoint and support. We need a tough advisor."

Things looked so dark that Valenti penned a personal note to Mr. Johnson:

I truly believe we need to find some way out of Vietnam. All that you strive for and believe in and are accomplishing is in danger, as long as this war goes on. If there were a way out, some hint of the end with honor, I would believe it best to stay there till the bitter conclusion. But there is no reasonable hope. All your military advisors insist you must double your force, and still they give you no prophecy of victory, however shapeless, however mild.

Another telegram to Lodge discussed possible alternatives to my government: ". . . our first choice would be keeping the Directory [*sic*] united and bringing in someone else to replace Ky," it said, with "Chieu at top of tentative list for this purpose."

I was not quite so ready to leave. I had learned that many of Tri Quang's supposed monks had acquired rifles, often by enlisting in ARVN units, then deserting with their weapons. Often local bureaucrats helped them. I thought that officials who committed acts of disloyalty to the government and thereby aided and abetted the enemy were traitors who ought to face a firing squad. As I told a Saigon press conference before I went north, that included Dr. Nguyen Van Man, mayor of Da Nang, who had publicly encouraged rebellion.

By April 5 Saigon remained comparatively quiet, although army troops broke up an unruly demonstration near the Buddhist Institute by firing over demonstrators' heads. Da Nang, however, still seethed. I intended that the marine battalions that had flown in to the air base would confront the Buddhist troublemakers; before such action could be taken, however, the I Corps commander, who had been told that marines were en route, sent troops to join militiamen from regional and local self-defense units and the so-called Struggle Forces. Together they manned roadblocks between the air base and the city. Moving the marines along that road would have touched off a civil war; the only winner of such a conflict would be Hanoi.

Since I was not an expert on army personnel, I had gone along with the Directorate's recommendation that General Nguyen Van Chuan replace Thi as I Corps commander. The appointment was short-lived because he was unable to cope with the political situation. Next General Huynh Van Cao was given a chance, but he fared no better. The fourth I Corps commander in two months was Ton That Dinh, who, alas, shared many of Thi's sympathies and also succumbed to the Buddhist leaders' flattery.

Dinh came to the air base to confer with me, but as I had lost the element of surprise, I postponed any attempt to confront the troublemakers. Reassured only that I Corps was not yet under Vietcong control, I flew back to Saigon.

About the same time, however, some six hundred "students" demonstrated in front of the MACV billets demanding removal of barricades along the main road that impeded Hue traffic; when barriers were removed, the demonstration quietly dispersed.

Then Lieutenant General Lewis Walt, commander of the Third Marine Amphibious Force in Da Nang and also the senior Military Assistance Command Vietnam advisor, recalled MACV advisors to the ARVN First Division and ended U.S. air support for the division. The U.S. consul general in Hue, Thomsen, fearing that MACV's recall might provoke the Struggle Forces to attack Americans in Hue and Quang Tri, ordered all U.S. civilians except consulate and essential staff evacuated to Saigon.

The violence spread southward. In Nha Trang, demonstrators burned the U.S. Information Services library and the adjacent Vietnamese Information Services offices. In Da Lat, where a mob had seized the government radio station, ARVN troops regained control of the facility.

After I returned from Da Nang, the Americans continued to discuss alternatives, to look for some way to accommodate the Buddhists. As before, I took the time to meet with Buddhist leaders, many, many times. I told them that out of respect for Buddha and Buddhism, and in the interests of the country, I was willing to give them whatever they wanted, anything within reason, if they would stop making trouble. I even invited Tri Quang to have dinner with me, to talk out our differences.

I realized that it was too late for talk, too late for either side to find a middle ground. Despite my efforts to mollify him, Tri Quang kept pushing. It was clear that to accede to his demands was not only the end of my government, it was also the end of my country. Tri Quang had called me out: It was to be me or him. It was time to stop thinking like a politician and start acting like a fighter. I must strap on my six-shooter and face this unmannered bully in the street at high noon. Like Gary Cooper's reluctant-but-determined Marshal Will Kane, Marshal Cao Ky had now to act in the interests of his community. Gunplay was always dangerous, a last resort, but I knew that I served a righteous cause. I had much hope that when the echoes of our gunshots faded on the wind, I would be the one left standing.

I continued to talk with Buddhist leaders, but only to buy a little time. As Confucius put it, "First diplomacy. Only after [it fails] fight." My previous movement of marines to Da Nang, intended to place a decisive force there at my disposal, had been countered when the rebellious commanders learned of my plans. I knew that whatever I shared with Lodge or Westmoreland would be passed along to those like Colonel Wilson, men so ill informed that they considered Thi useful. There were also loose tongues in my own government; some belonged to powerful men with personal agendas. I could trust no one, including Thieu. I had to act fast, and until I had done so, my plans and intentions would remain between my own ears.

When I was nearly ready to move, I decided to give the bully one last chance to get out of Hadleyville. I invited thirteen leading monks, representing all major Buddhist factions, to my home. We sat around a long table, and when tea had been served, I said, "I am sure that I know what you want and what you intend. You all think that since you could destroy a man like Diem, you could also destroy me. After all, I am much younger than Mr. Diem, so I don't have his experience or credibility. So, yes, I will be easier to overthrow.

"But perhaps you have forgotten one thing, one difference between me and Mr. Diem. He allowed himself to be killed by his enemies. But before I let you kill me, it will be my pleasure to shoot each of you personally."

The monks recoiled in wide-eyed horror. "Oh, no, don't speak that way, don't use such words!" cried one. "We are friends!"

"No, no, nobody has to be shot," wailed another.

"Now that you understand what I mean, you can go home," I said, and that ended my conversations with Buddhist leaders.

A week later, nothing had changed; the situation in Da Nang had deteriorated even further. "Buddhist dissidents" controlled the city's radio station, most of its municipal buildings, and many army headquarters. Even more ominously, "dissidents" had begun to distribute weapons to the populace and organize block and neighborhood committees, replete with spies who reported on each household's activities and political leanings. In short, the situation reeked of Hanoi-style communism.

At nine in the evening of May 14 I called General Cao Van Vien, chief of the joint general staff, and Colonel Loan, who served both as chief of military security and head of the national police, to VNAF Headquarters at Tansonnhut and an office that I knew held no CIA listening devices. They arrived separately, and when the door was closed I described the situation. "In the interests of the country, we must now move. Are you with me?" Both replied that they had been expecting this, that if I waited a few more days it would be too late: I Corps would be under communist control and the war lost.

Even before I brought Vien and Loan together, I had set in

motion the first elements of my plan, again moving two marine battalions to Da Nang. I had done this by telling the marine commander, General Khang, to carry out a routine rotation of his troops by swapping a battalion at Quang Nam with another based near Saigon.

The marines I had dispatched to Da Nang in April had flown on U.S. Air Force C-130s. *This* rotation, however, would be accomplished by the VNAF. The First Transport Wing was commanded by Lieutenant Colonel Luu Kim Cuong, the finest pilot, and loyal to me. I told him that his aircraft were to pick up the marines at Quang Nam and Saigon for a routine rotation of forces—but when they were all back in the air, he was to divert them to Da Nang. Hauling both battalions with combat equipment, however, exceeded the wing's capacity, so I mobilized some DC-3s and DC-6s from Air Vietnam and placed them under Cuong. As usual, the pilots were VNAF.

After describing these arrangements to Vien and Loan, I told Vien to go to Da Nang and at precisely seven o'clock the next morning, occupy I Corps headquarters. Loan, who had other tasks to complete, would accompany him. Both would arrive at 6:00 A.M.; the marines were to land an hour earlier, ready to follow Vien's orders.

Probably the best ARVN unit in Da Nang was a Ranger battalion. Intelligence sources told me that its commander, Major Nguyen Thua Dzu, sympathized with the Buddhist cause. He had told the monks that he and his men were willing to die fighting against Saigon. In the Tansonnhut office that night, I told Loan about Dzu. "You know this guy, right?" I said.

"We all know him," he replied. When we were junior officers, before the war began to consume our lives, we had often made the rounds of Saigon's first-rate nightclubs together, dancing and drinking the night away. Oh, yes, we knew Dzu.

A day earlier, I had his best friend, Major Ly, flown to Da Nang. I gave him a message for Dzu: "General Ky remembers you from the old days, and he likes you. But what you are doing now is wrong. General Ky said that he is willing to overlook the activities of the last few weeks, but from now you must be and act completely loyal to the government. You must take your orders from Saigon and not the rebels. If you do not—one battalion is nothing, and we will destroy you and all your men."

Dzu knew me, so he was aware that I said what I meant and meant what I said. The Buddhist leaders, who believed that I Corps' most elite unit was in their pocket, were in for a nasty shock. Once I was assured that Dzu was under control, I had put the rest of my plan into operation.

Vien and Loan took off for Da Nang and I returned to my office around midnight. Never have I felt so lonely as that night. Thousands of men were winging through the darkness, and I knew that the morning would bring great danger and many surprises. I had set forces in motion, and I was very much aware that if I had miscalculated or forgotten something, I would forfeit not only my life but also those of many of my bravest countrymen. If I failed and the northern region fell to the communists, my nation would quickly disappear from world maps. My name would be cursed for generations.

I remained in my Tansonnhut office. About one in the morning I summoned Truong Van Thuan, the minister of communications. When he arrived, still rubbing sleep from his eyes, I said, "In one hour you are to cut off all civilian communications inside and outside Vietnam. No one is to be able to communicate with anyone."

He stared at me. "What has happened?"

"Do it, or I will shoot you," I replied, waving him away.

An hour later it was impossible for someone in Saigon to telephone Bien Hoa, much less Da Nang or abroad. None of the foreign news reporters could file stories, even through their bureaus in Tokyo, Hong Kong, or Bangkok. I knew what reporters under deadline pressure do when they cannot confirm rumors and wild guesses: They report gossip and speculate over its meaning. I didn't know how long it would take to restore I Corps to government control, and the last thing I needed was rumors and muddle-headedness elevated to gospel because they were anointed by foreign news reports.

Once the long-distance circuits were down, I telephoned my minister of youth, a young, French-educated activist named Vo Long Trieu, who had excellent ties to the Catholic community. This was the fellow who had done such a good job getting houses built for the poor. For the first time in my life, I had to act like a politician. I told Trieu that tomorrow I would move against the Buddhists. If things went against me, I wanted to see thousands of Catholics marching in the Saigon streets, men and women and students with placards and posters demonstrating support for my government.

"Are you okay with this?" I asked

"Oh, yes," he said. "It is time to end this rebellion."

Two civilians now knew of the impending clash, but I did not tell Thieu or the military leadership. I could not risk pulling the plug on army communications; if Thieu or another general decided to second-guess me, there was still time to alert Da Nang.

So I spent the next several hours alone in my office, sipping endless cups of coffee and smoking way too many cigarettes. At 7:01 my desk telephone rang. Vien's voice in my ear told me that I Corps HQ was in his hands. Dinh, the commander, had taken refuge at the nearby headquarters of the U.S. Marines.

I had to smile at the thought of General Dinh in his underwear, startled awake by the thunder of engines. Once he saw that line of planes stretching miles out of the rising sun, whooshing down to disgorge hundreds of troops, he must have thought the sky was falling on him.

"Continue with the plan," I said to Vien. "Occupy the area,

including all of Da Nang. If you encounter any resistance, destroy them, whomever it might be." Then I called Thieu and told him what I had done. As usual, he was noncommittal.

A quarter of an hour later Vien called again: One of the I Corps field artillery units, alerted by the noise of the landing, had begun to move its big guns and aim them at the airfield. I called a VNAF squadron commander at Da Nang, and a few minutes later one of his planes dropped a message pouch on artillery HQ: One shot from any of those cannon, it said, and my aircraft would pulverize the battery and everyone in it. The cannoneer understood, and there was no fire. I gave instructions for more planes to loiter over Da Nang, just in case any of the rebels missed the point.

But at 9:00 A.M. Vien called to say that there was another problem: Walt, the U.S. Marine commander who also served as chief U.S. advisor to I Corps, had demanded that Vien halt operations. He also insisted that all VNAF aircraft supporting Vien's troops be grounded immediately. If not, said Vien, the Americans would use their F-4 Phantom jets to shoot down our A-1 Skyraiders.

Even as we spoke, a confrontation was taking place high above Da Nang. A little earlier two so-called Struggle Movement machine guns had fired at ARVN troops, and a VNAF Skyraider fired rockets at them. Three of the rockets fell short and hit a U.S. Marine compound, wounding eight Americans. General Walt had then ordered a pair of Phantoms aloft and sent word to the local VNAF commander to ground his aircraft.

Instead, Colonel Duong Thien Hung, the VNAF base commander and one of our best pilots, sent four more Skyraiders to orbit the skies above the two USAF Phantoms, which were circling above the two VNAF Skyraiders. Walt launched another pair of Phantoms, which promptly began to circle above the latest Skyraiders, four layers of aircraft carrying tons of bombs and rockets.

Only the American planes, however, were armed with air-to-air missiles.

"What are my instructions?" asked Vien.

"Get six of the biggest howitzers you have and put them in front of General Walt's headquarters. Have those guns trained on the building and loaded, and then have the crews stand ready.

"If the Americans shoot at our planes, you have my order to destroy the U.S. Marine headquarters."

"Oh, yes," said Vien. I knew he would follow orders.

I hung up and immediately called Lodge. "Please come to my office, it is very urgent," I said. When he arrived I explained the situation, including Vien's latest report. "Is this action by General Walt the policy of the United States of America?" I asked. "Is his order confirmed by the White House, or is it only General Walt's order?"

"No, no," replied Lodge. "This is not from my government."

"In that case, can you send a message to your marine commander in Da Nang to the effect that this is a purely Vietnamese affair, and we don't want U.S. interference?"

While Lodge used another phone to send this message, I called Vien again and told him that I was on my way up there. The Americans had been good enough to provide the VNAF with several A-37 Dragonfly trainers, two-seat, twin-jet aircraft that we used as light attack planes.

Lodge seemed very nervous, perhaps because I did not share any details of my plan for dealing with I Corps. But we shook hands warmly.

"General, you would have disappointed me if you had not made a move," he said.

I climbed into an A-37 and headed north at 450 mph, landing at Da Nang Air Base a little after 11:00 A.M., where I borrowed the base commander's office. Within minutes one of my aides said that General Walt had telephoned to invite me to his headquarters.

"Tell him that I have no time," I replied. Very soon Walt called again. This time he told my aide that he wanted to come to the air base to meet with me. "Send the same reply," I said. "I am busy and have no time."

When he called the third time, Walt said that he was acting at the request of Dean Rusk. "Okay, tell him to come," I said.

About thirty minutes later Walt arrived. He was big and burly, dressed in Marine Corps camouflage fatigues and trailed by a much smaller man who spoke fluent Vietnamese. I had watched films of this man, a U.S. consular official in Hue, participating with Buddhists demonstrating against my government.

When they walked into my temporary office I remained in my seat while they saluted. "Sit down," I said. "General, what do you want?"

"I want to know about operations. There are troop movements and I want to know what has happened," he said.

I stared at him for a long moment. "General, how many years have you served in the military?" I could see that my question had taken him off guard.

"Twenty-three years," he said.

I looked at him a while longer. "You have over twenty years in the military and yet you have no notion about the chain of command!" I said. "Why do you think that *you* have the right to ask *me* questions about operations? As commander in chief, there are times when, if I choose to do so, I can tell my subordinate what I will do even thirty days in advance. Or maybe I will let him know when I have begun the operation. Or maybe I will tell him later. But it is all up to me. My subordinate has no right to ask me—that is the military chain of command. Do you know who you are talking to?"

"Yes, the prime minister."

"So why do you think you have the right to ask me such things?"

My question hung for several seconds in the cool air of the base commander's air-conditioned office. Tiny drops of sweat appeared on Walt's face.

"Oh, because I am also the advisor to the I Corps commander," he said at last. "Everything is peaceful here, there are no problems. Why, suddenly, did the government move?"

"General, you are an advisor to the military for military matters. *This is a political and internal affair of Vietnam!* You have no right to interfere. Do you understand that?" Now perspiration poured from Walt's face to stain his collar.

"Now, General," I continued, "I understand that you have threatened to use American forces to fight us. You know that I can use this telephone to call Mr. Johnson, your commander in chief. If I make that call, I can guarantee that in five minutes you will be packing to go home. Now that you understand me, you can leave."

Walt stood, saluted, left the office. His entourage followed.

Walt's actions had made me wonder if my government's difficulties lay entirely with Buddhist agitators and Vietcong infiltrators, if perhaps the I Corps situation here was more than a revolt within the ARVN. Obviously my problems also included American officials, civil and military. The question was, had they acted on their own—or were they following orders from the White House or the State Department or CIA? Maybe some ranking Americans had mistaken my desire to avoid bloodshed for weakness. Or perhaps they had decided that, like Diem, I had outlived my usefulness. Possibly they believed that the Buddhists held the highest cards, so I would be discarded in order that they could play their Buddhist hand.

As I would learn many years later, the perceived shortcomings of my government were subjected to U.S. State Department scrutiny, and those who would not be sorry to see me fail were already considering options. For example, consider excerpts

from a memo by Ambassador-at-Large W. Averill Harriman re-
garding his conversation with Robert McNamara on May 14,
1966:

> Bob McNamara believes the Government in Saigon will be-
> come weaker and weaker as time goes on. On the other hand,
> the Viet Cong are showing signs of poor morale and also the
> bombing seems to have caused more difficulties in the North.
>
> Under these circumstances, he feels we should get in
> touch direct with the NLF, also the North Vietnamese, but
> particularly the NLF, and begin to try to work up a deal for
> a coalition government . . .
>
> He agreed with me that we must have some way of forc-
> ing the South Vietnamese government to avoid taking these
> disastrous actions, such as firing Thi or Ky's recent press con-
> ference . . .
>
> I asked him why we shouldn't get the military committee
> to put someone else in as Prime Minister, rather than Ky, and
> he at first seemed to agree, and then said perhaps we better
> wait until after September 15 when the elections are held . . .
>
> I told him that I had not been satisfied with the political
> actions in Vietnam, that I couldn't understand why Lodge
> hadn't prevented the firing of Thi, and it certainly was a mis-
> take to carry Ky's troops to the North.
>
> He agreed. He said he would be quite willing to tell Ky
> we would take our troops out if we really meant it. I suggested
> we devise sanctions, tough, but less complete than that . . .

While I was quite unaware of such thoughts in 1966, Walt's
actions made me feel the need to test the American commitment
to my government. I telephoned Lodge and said that I wanted
more big tanks to reinforce my troops in Da Nang. Could he
arrange the use of some big aircraft to fly them in from Saigon
tonight?

"Oh, yes," said Lodge. After two gigantic USAF C-124 Globemasters flew in from Japan that night to bring my tanks to Da Nang, I again believed that my government enjoyed Mr. Johnson's confidence as well as Lodge's support. As I would learn from diplomatic documents declassified many years later, however, my move in Da Nang really shook up Washington. Lodge left Vietnam for a few days, and Rusk flashed a cable to Deputy Ambassador William J. Porter:

It is intolerable that Ky should take such far reaching move as that against Da Nang without consultation with us.

However, immediate problem is how to pick up pieces and prevent a major debacle. Most urgent need is to insist that principal figures in Da Nang area (such as Ky, Vien, Dinh, Lam, Nhuan and Thi) agree at once to prevent further fighting among SVN elements pending further discussion of more lasting solution. This may require rough talk with several of them but United States can not accept this insane bickering. I recognize this is tall order but you, MACV, General Walt, Thomsen and others must do your best in next few hours.

I cannot emphasize strongly enough that the disarray among South Vietnamese leaders has been rapidly undermining support of American people for war effort. The question "what are we being asked to support?" is becoming insistent and is becoming more and more difficult to answer.

We must rely heavily upon you at this moment and assure you of our full confidence.

I did not learn of this telegram for many years, but Thieu and I met with Porter in Saigon after I confronted Walt. Porter said that his government was "extremely annoyed that [we] would carry out operation of this importance without in any way consulting or informing us."

I understood Rusk's anger, but I did not regret, then or now, my decision to act in Da Nang. Rusk, Harriman, and other American diplomats spent much time and energy thinking about negotiating with this group or that group, of how to bring Vietnamese factions together. For me it was much less complicated: stability and order. I was like a priest who believes so strongly in his God that he will do anything to protect Him. My deity was stability; whosoever attacked this God, I would kill. I believed in my country and in my people, and both required strong and stable authority more than anything else. I would fight anything that threatened this.

Moreover, I was prime minister of a sovereign nation and not obliged to discuss internal matters with U.S. officials. While I served as prime minister, I gave no American cause to suppose that I was their puppet. When U.S. officials became extremely annoyed, they liked to leak word of their unhappiness to the press. Perhaps they thought this might bend me to their wishes or cause me political problems. *Au contraire*: I wore each American insult as a badge of honor. The more insulting, condescending, or offensive the Americans were, the more popular I was with the brown and yellow peoples of the Third World.

In sum, as prime minister, I had the right and obligation to remove anyone who threatened the authority of Vietnam's lawful government. I did not need the permission of the I Corps commander to fire the I Corps commander. I would learn, later, that Lodge, a loyal and wise American, agreed with me.

...

After my return to Saigon, events continued to unfold in I Corps. Vien's marine battalions were supported by the tanks Lodge had flown in. Skyraiders from Da Nang and elsewhere provided air cover, and by nightfall two battalions of paratroops under General Dong arrived to reinforce the marines. This force moved quickly into the city. When Loan, in his role of chief of police, asked the rebels who had held the radio station for months to surrender, they refused. Instead of making a direct assault, which would have produced many casualties, Loan had an M-48 Patton tank brought up. One shot carefully placed into the roof and everyone came out, hands reaching for the sky.

When they saw our trucks moving into the city, about two thousand young Buddhists sought refuge in the central pagoda. These were youngsters, some as young as fourteen, who had been trained to use grenades to commit public suicide. I am certain that they hoped we would assault the pagoda, which would have yielded a fine crop of propaganda pictures to prove that we were anti-Buddhist, antireligion.

Instead of attacking, Vien asked them to surrender. When the kids refused, Vien called for my guidance. I said, "If they shoot first, shoot back and then go in and get them out." But I was sure that the Buddhists would not initiate violence. At my order, Vien brought up several tanks and used them to establish a *cordon sanitaire*, a sanitized zone. He telephoned the pagoda and said that no one would be allowed in or out until they all surrendered. This temple was not large; a few hundred people inside would have felt cramped. It was already very hot, a typical summer day in central Vietnam. After two days without food or water or sanitary facilities, they all came out. We gave them food and water and sent them home after individual face-to-face lectures. "Do not make more trouble," we told each. "Next time, you will die."

When Vien had occupied all of Da Nang, the rebel ARVN commanders surrendered. Suddenly General Westmoreland turned up. "What are you going to do about Hue?" he asked. Westmoreland made a big point of telling me that Da Nang was not important, that the center of the rebellion and the Buddhist stronghold was Hue. And he asked me what I intended to do about Hue.

I still smile about this. Of course, Da Nang, with its port and military facilities, was the serpent's body. The head was Hue, where the bonzes—Buddhist monks—controlled everything.

But not one of my troops had to set foot in Hue. The Buddhist troublemakers would come to me. Throughout the Hue area lived thousands of members of the Kuomintang, the Vietnamese Nationalist party. They were happy to see us and more than fed up with all the unrest, disorder, and interruptions of commerce caused by the extremist Buddhist leaders. I sent people to visit their villages in the areas around Hue and asked for their help in stopping anyone who tried to leave the city. I distributed arms to the Kuomintang for their members, who were very happy to help us. We isolated Hue completely. No trucks brought gasoline, food, or anything else into the city from Highway One, which my troops controlled. No sampans could move on the Perfume River without being intercepted by my aircraft or boats. After three days, Tri Quang and General Phan Xuan Nhuan, commander of the First Division and the last rebel leader, surrendered.

I sent Loan in with troops and police to keep order in Hue. Most Asian homes maintain a small altar, honoring Buddha, some national hero, or departed ancestors. As Loan's police entered Hue, they found the streets filled with such altars. Since traffic could not move without crushing or destroying these artifacts, it was obvious that the Buddhists sought to force a confrontation to produce martyrs and fuel new propaganda.

Loan called to ask how to avoid this symbolic desecration of Buddha. "Today we are all Buddhists," I replied. "Have your troops offer a short prayer at each shrine, and then move it and the Buddha to police headquarters. If they want to keep or sell the altars, let them."

These altars and Buddha statues were antiques, some hundreds of years old, many worth a fortune. Police carted the first few away, remarking loudly about their good fortune in finding such treasures abandoned in the street. By the time they had loaded two or three, people came running out of their homes to reclaim family heirlooms. In ten minutes the streets were clear, and traffic began moving again. The rebellion was over.

...

I ordered Tri Quang flown to Saigon. The monk did not want to get on the C-47 that I sent, so he was carried aboard. Much of the flight was over the sea; at some point about halfway to Saigon, one of the flight crew brought Tri Quang an orange to eat. "Are you going to drop me into the sea?" he quailed.

"No," said the crewman. "Our orders are to bring you to Saigon."

Tri Quang was not the only one anxious about his life. Before the flight, Westmoreland came to see me and asked, "How are you going to treat Tri Quang?" He feared that I would shoot him.

I said, "Don't worry." I gave no further answer, didn't explain, felt no need to do so. If Westmoreland wanted to lose sleep over a troublemaker, that was his problem.

I had plans for Tri Quang. I knew of a Saigon physician, a fanatical supporter of the Buddhists and an accomplished amateur troublemaker in his own right. But although Dr. Nguyen Duy Tai supported the Buddhist movement and was an outspoken advocate of the reverence-for-all-life bonzes, this wealthy doctor operated the Duy Tan Clinic, notorious for the number of abortions it performed. Maybe supporting Buddhist political ambitions was Duy Tai's way of buying respectability.

When I got word that Tri Quang was aloft and heading toward Saigon, I invited Dr. Tai to my office. I told him, "I understand you are a very staunch Buddhist," and he nodded warily. "I am going to bring your leader, Thich Tri Quang, to Saigon. After so many years of struggle, he is very weak. I need someone to take charge of his health, and I think the best place is your clinic. From now on, you are in charge of his health care.

"But Thich Tri Quang must remain in the clinic at all times.

There will be no guard, no police surveillance, nothing of the sort. I trust you to keep Tri Quang healthy and under house arrest. Because, if anything happens to him, if he leaves the clinic or becomes seriously ill, I will shoot you and your wife and your whole family!

"Do you understand?" I asked, and the doctor, now ashen, nodded weakly. "You can go," I said.

When Tri Quang landed at Tansonnhut, he was driven to the clinic. Twenty-four hours later Saigon newspapers reported that he had begun a hunger strike to protest my actions in squashing his revolt. Day by day the newspapers reported that he continued his fast. When Lodge expressed concern, I said, "Mr. Ambassador, don't worry. If Tri Quang was merely a monk, then maybe he would fast until death. But he is a politician. Have you ever seen a politician die of hunger?"

Lodge laughed.

"Between us," I continued, "I will tell you that he doesn't eat, and he refuses intravenous nutrition, but don't worry. His doctor will take very good care of Tri Quang."

My prediction was confirmed. A week later Dr. Tai came to see me, very nervous, to report that his prize patient looked better, his color was better. The man whose mission in life was to bring down governments had vowed never to eat until justice came to Vietnam—yet this medical miracle had lost not a single pound. He had all the fresh fruit juice and protein shakes that he could hold, and Dr. Tai assured me that Tri Quang could live thirty years that way. When the war ended in 1975 Tri Quang was imprisoned by the communists for many years. At this writing he is free and in good health. I am glad that I didn't have to shoot Tai.

With Tri Quang's arrest I ended the so-called Buddhist movement. From that day, Vietnam's Buddhists have displayed no further political passion.

I promoted General Hoang Xuan Lam, commander of the

Second Division, who had remained loyal to the national government, to I Corps commander. Then I dealt with the mutinous ARVN commanders, who had all come crying to me for mercy. I told several that if they remained in uniform they must face courts-martial. Instead, I suggested, they should retire and try civilian life. Others I cashiered without a pension. I had grounds to send several officers to the firing squad; I decided instead to put them in jail for a while, to serve as an example to others.

About a month after my confrontation with General Walt, I was asked to return to Da Nang to decorate him for outstanding service as I Corps advisor. His marines had accomplished miracles in both fighting the Vietcong and pacifying the countryside, so to show that I held no hard feelings, I agreed. As sometimes happens, in the months that followed we became friends. When I remarked at lunch one day that Tabasco Sauce was my favorite condiment, he volunteered that back home in Louisiana, he was a friend of the family that made it. For years thereafter I received a case of Tabasco Sauce every month or so.

When Walt left Vietnam he became assistant commandant of the Marine Corps. Later he got a fourth star. We met a few years later at a Washington dinner that I gave to honor American generals who had served in Vietnam. Afterward, with tears shining in his eyes, he thanked me for showing him how to act like a general, how to be a better leader.

When the dust had settled on the confrontation in I Corps, I began to see that the Americans, for the first time, showed respect for my powers of judgment. By acting decisively and keeping my intentions secret, I had demonstrated to the Directorate and to the world that despite my youth and inexperience, I was capable of leading the country.

Even Vietnamese politicians who opposed me when I was in power now express admiration for what I accomplished in Da Nang.

I have had many years to reflect on those desperate days in

May. While I have had my differences with Charles de Gaulle, it was he, writing in another context, who best summed up the lessons of my personal High Noon: "Every man of action has a strong dose of egoism, pride, hardness, and cunning. But all those things will be regarded as high qualities if he can make them the means to achieve great ends."

The infusion of disciplined and highly motivated American and allied troops in 1965 and 1966 had put the communists on the defensive. We still faced many problems, but overall, South Vietnam enjoyed a better position than it had held for several years. My next great challenge was to maintain this momentum through an orderly transition to a popularly elected government.

Viewing those desperate days in May 1966 through the lens of time, it is clear that my victory in Da Nang ended the period of instability following Mr. Diem's demise. For more than three years, Vietnam teetered on the edge of anarchy and internecine war. By crushing the revolt, I established the Second Republic and prolonged our national existence for many years. Many Vietnamese, and especially those who share the bittersweet life of the exile, now regard this as my supreme achievement.

12
ELECTIONS

IN June 1940, following France's defeat by Germany, an obscure fifty-year-old French colonel went to see British Prime Minister Winston Churchill. Unsure of who this Charles de Gaulle fellow was, Churchill had his secretary inquire about his caller's identity. De Gaulle replied: "Tell him, *'Je suis la France*—I am France.'" Gaul was the ancient name for France, so this was undoubtedly a play on his name, but also, perhaps unintentionally, a reference to Louis XIV's remark: *"L'état c'est moi*—I am the state."

Unlike de Gaulle or the Sun King, I never considered myself the embodiment of South Vietnam's nationhood, but I did accept the burden of leading my country. And while the armed forces had put me in office, I considered myself prime minister of *all* the people, not just of the military. I saw neither justification nor cause to pander to the self anointed leaders of various political groups and religious factions. At best they represented the selfish interests of their supporters, and many stood only for themselves. And so I had resisted Buddhist demands for immediate elections and turned a deaf ear to such calls from the various political parties.

By the middle of 1966, however, I had crushed the so-called Buddhist Struggle Movement and retired all the mutinous generals. I had restored order and unity to the army and to my country, and after the infusion of American and Korean combat troops countered the North Vietnamese invasion of the Central Highlands, I felt it was a good time to plan elections.

Lacking a constitution or legal code, I had ruled by decree, promulgating new edicts to fit each situation. I knew that over the long run this was not a suitable basis for the government of a modern state. In order to survive and prosper, we required a formal legal system.

I might have written a constitution myself, or convened a committee of sympathizers to do so, then submitted the resulting document to a national referendum. Many nations have done this. But such an approach did not suit my notion that Vietnamese should train themselves in democracy by participating in democratic events. Also, because we had no national democratic institutions, social justice demanded that we create them.

So I decided that the people should elect representatives to write their constitution. Vietnam had held several elections since the end of World War II, but few reflected a free expression of the people's will. In October 1955, for example, Diem held a referendum asking voters to decide between himself and Emperor Bao Dai. These were the only choices on the ballot, and Bao Dai tried to prevent the vote. Several months later Diem held an election for a constituent assembly, and in 1959 and 1963 voters elected a national assembly. Diem also held a presidential election in 1961, but he selected the other candidates. Each of these votes was carried out under Diem's control, and while the rigging of results was never so blatant as in the few elections held in the North, many Vietnamese had become skeptical about the fairness of any election.

I had another reason for holding an election: I wanted to know what people really thought about my government and its policies. Counting the votes is far more accurate than any opinion survey, especially in Vietnam, where those surveyed are likely to tell the poll-taker what they think he wants to hear. So I put General Nguyen Duc Thang in charge of the election for a Constitutional Assembly and explained that I wanted it completely free and honest. I also instructed General Loan that the most important mission of his police was to ensure that no one interfered with a fair election. Thang did such a good job that I put in him in charge of rural development and Chieu Hoi.

The Vietcong preferred a military government in Saigon because it allowed their propaganda to focus on the people's fear of a dictatorship; a popularly chosen government invalidated their claim that America had established a neocolonial regime in Saigon, that I was a U.S. puppet. So communist guerrillas attacked voters, polling places, and even candidates. One of those who won a seat was murdered by the Vietcong immediately after the election.

Even so, in September 1966, 85 percent of the eligible people in South Vietnam registered to vote, then elected 118 men and women to serve as the Constitutional Assembly. As I had suspected, the voting illuminated another dimension of South Vietnamese politics: Few of those elected were affiliated with a political party. Now everyone could see that the religious factions and petty politicians who had caused so much friction and animosity represented no more than tiny minorities.

Most elected to the assembly were between thirty and forty years of age. After the election, many of these young, earnest, patriotic representatives of the people invited me to lead them in forming a new national political party, but I declined.

The document they were to write was not Vietnam's first constitution, but it was the first written by representatives of the people. Under Diem's rule, a constitution was prepared by a chamber of 123 deputies. It seemed like a fair set of rules— until one reads the last article, which permitted Diem to suspend normal democratic freedoms during the first term of the new legislature. Even after that, Diem never allowed most of the democratic provisions of this document to be implemented.

After the assembly of 1966 convened, many of its younger

members, not yet fully grasping the idea of democracy, came to see me and asked what kind of a document I wanted them to write. "Write what you think will best serve the people who elected you," I said.

The United States Constitution was drafted by a committee representing, primarily, the property-owning elite. After its first version was put to paper, the hard bargaining began. The Southern states had economies based on slavery, while those in the North found slavery repugnant. The smallest states were wary of the biggest. To accommodate these and other competing interests required protracted negotiations. The final document, which has proven marvelously malleable and therefore continues to serve after more than two hundred years, incorporated many hard-fought compromises.

So it was with the constitution drafted in Saigon from late 1966 through early 1967. As a tangible step toward civilian government, and to share development of a national consciousness with leaders from outside the military, I persuaded the Directorate to add several civilians to its membership. Oddly, these civilians were less receptive to the constitution than most of the military members of the Directorate.

The draft presented to this body contained a few provisions that we felt needed to be modified or eliminated, and there was a period of strenuous negotiations between the assembly and the Directorate. The CIA, as was often the case, got *some* of this story right:

> Premier Ky was able to secure the approval of the constitution from both the Constituent Assembly and the Directorate . . . by personally taking on the task of compromising the extreme positions of the Directorate and the assembly. In the process, however, Ky may have posed strains on future Directorate unity . . .

The compromise is the direct result of Premier Ky's private parleys with selected assemblymen in a series of nightly meetings . . . which were apparently not attended by the rest of the Directorate. The acceptable formula was achieved on the evening of [March] 16, and Ky and the assembly delegation then proceeded to sell the compromise package to the Directorate and to the rest of the Assembly . . .

In the final meeting between Ky and the assembly delegation, the main point of disagreement was election of a president. Once the deputies [*sic*] bought Ky's formula to keep the Directorate in power until the election, Ky granted the assembly practically every other concession it had desired, including the election of province chiefs and the authority to vote "no confidence" in the cabinet . . .

In his personal bid to arrange quick, final agreement on the constitution, it appears that Ky risked future Directorate unity for the sake of presenting a finished document to the US at the Guam conference. The reaction in the Directorate, at least from Thieu and the civilians who had pursued a less lenient policy with the assembly, was one of irritation, according to the US Embassy. In approving the document, the Directorate has set aside private differences at least until after the Guam conference . . . the civilians on the Directorate are considering resigning after the constitution is promulgated, possibly in protest over their lack of influence on the final decision.

Rather than *expending* political capital to get the Directorate's approval, however, I *invested* it. My position with military members was strengthened by the negotiating process, which revealed the degree of respect accorded my leadership by the assembly and by the events that soon followed.

A few days after the constitution was approved I had my second meeting with President Johnson, in Guam. He seemed very glad to see that what I had said of my intentions in Honolulu was more than empty words, that my pledge of social justice reflected what was in my heart. But I did not hold the election or have a constitution written to please Mr. Johnson, or Lodge, or any American. I held them, as I have explained, because it was the right thing to do at that time.

On the second day of the conference, after a review of the many improvements in the political and military situations in my country, I proposed a way to bring a speedy and just conclusion to the war.

After briefing the Americans on the disposition of North Vietnamese forces, it was apparent that most of the PAVN, the so-called People's Army of Vietnam, was deployed in the South. Beyond their small air force and antiaircraft units, only one combat-ready division remained in the North. So I proposed that after the election, I would resign as prime minister and lead the invasion of North Vietnam by South Vietnamese forces. I believed then, and I do now, that this would have ended the war. Any incursion that threatened Hanoi would have forced the communists to recall forces from the South and sue for peace.

We could not do this without American support, but I did not ask for a single U.S. soldier to set foot in North Vietnam. My plan required U.S. air cover, naval artillery support, and a logistics package to equip the ARVN for sustained offensive combat. Our infantry was equipped with cast-off American weapons from World War II; I wanted them to have the same lightweight firepower that U.S. troops carried into combat. Finally, with most of the ARVN fighting in the North, the United States would have to secure our rear by defending our major population centers. I remain convinced that it would not have required a long-term effort.

I concluded my presentation by pointing out that South Vietnam had the legal right to defend itself, and because the United

States would not be part of the invasion force, international criticism would be muted, except, as usual, from the communist bloc and their amen chorus of "nonaligned" nations.

My presentation seemed to scare the hell out of the Americans, especially McNamara. As he had at our previous meeting in Honolulu, the secretary of defense failed to inspire me with his intellect. Americans praised him as a big brain, but I saw no signs of it. Perhaps I was wrong. Maybe he is so much smarter, a living computer who cannot relate to us humans. After a few minutes with him I dismissed him from my mind as unimportant, an impression reinforced whenever we met. Unlike Johnson, whom I was proud to call a friend, I felt that Robert McNamara was not worth the effort to cultivate. I neither loved nor hated him; he left me utterly uninvolved.

While lunching with him and Johnson, I suggested an alternative. "If you cannot support us for an invasion, what about mass bombing to destroy every airfield and military facility in North Vietnam? How about blockading Haiphong?" I asked.

"Mac, tell General Ky why we don't go in," replied Johnson.

"All those airfields are very well defended," said McNamara. "We'll suffer heavy casualties."

This was not the answer that I had expected. If he had said, "If we go in, the Chinese will join the war," or the Russians, I could have understood it. But he said, because they are well defended. If you go to war believing that you will not suffer casualties, why go in the first place?

Therefore, a little later, I said to Johnson, "Mr. President, with the big buildup in this region, including your navy, air force, and army, there are now almost six hundred thousand U.S. troops. The size and composition of your force is better suited for a conventional war than for a guerrilla war.

"In conventional war, the goal is to find the enemy, fight them, destroy them. But if your policy is only to fight a counterguerrilla war, why don't you bring your conventional forces home and help us to sustain a counterguerrilla war for maybe ten or fifteen years?

"President Johnson, if your only purposes are self-defense and counterguerrilla warfare, why do you need so many American troops? What is their purpose?"

Johnson abruptly changed the subject. I wonder now if he did so because, deep within himself, he saw my logic. Or if this had already occurred to him. Perhaps he thought that his administration had come too far down one road to risk paying the political price of acknowledging a strategic mistake.

On the subject of strategy, it was clear that many Americans worried that history would repeat itself, that the Chinese would intervene, just as they had in Korea in 1950. And so I told Mr. Johnson, as I had told McNamara, Rusk, Westmoreland, and Lodge many times, "Don't worry about the Chinese. Even if we invaded North Vietnam, the Hanoi communists cannot ask for a million Chinese to come fight. And even if they did ask, I don't think the Chinese want to risk a war with the U.S."

I don't think they believed me. But by then, anyone with a shortwave radio knew that China was in no position to fight the United States. To fend off his army's grab for power, Mao had unleashed the so-called Cultural Revolution. The country was in turmoil, rival factions at each other's throats. It was a struggle for China to support Hanoi with food, war munitions, and military technicians.

A few years later, when the United States had pulled out of Vietnam and Hanoi occupied the South, the historic enmity between Vietnam and China and deep doctrinal differences between North Vietnamese communism and the Chinese version erupted into a nasty border war—and the Chinese lost. If China couldn't beat economically depressed, war-weary North Vietnam in 1979, how could it have opposed a nuclear superpower in 1967?

As to the airfields that I asked Johnson to bomb, when Nixon became president he finally ordered attacks against them. By then, of course, the enemy had added Soviet missiles to their antiaircraft defenses, and U.S. casualties were far greater than if we had attacked in 1967. A lot of brave American pilots lost their lives or years of freedom on bombing missions that a few years earlier would have been far less risky.

Even so, Nixon never used the massive bombing of North Vietnam to help us invade, but only to force Hanoi to negotiate an "honorable" withdrawal of American troops. In McNamara's memoirs, he said that by 1967 he had decided that the United States would lose the war. That explains why from Johnson to Nixon never had any thought of *winning* the war. The United States fought only to keep from losing, a classic example of the self-fulfilling prophesy. How can anyone, even a superpower, expect to win a purely defensive war?

But all that was far in the future when I returned from Guam. The next meal on my plate was a national election to choose Vietnam's first freely elected president. I would run, of course. I wanted my position validated by the people as much as I wanted them to feel good about their government.

I also must confess here that as much as I felt the necessity for elections in 1967, I have had many years to think about this, and I believe now that they were a mistake. I was young and idealistic, and in this matter I honored my feelings more than my intellect. We were at war, and if I had simply continued governing and guiding the country as I had, many serious mistakes, including my own, might have been averted. The war might well have ended differently. More generally, no political system is better than the heart of its leader. Usually the people will be better off under a king with a good heart than under a corrupt but democratically elected president.

In 1967 some Americans understood that elections were a risk. A CIA intelligence summary put it this way:

The present government has always been viewed by all concerned as a transitional government. It is inherently unstable because it is government by committee, and because it depends on continued accord among the Generals [*sic*] for its existence, because it has until very recently had little meaningful civilian participation, and because it has no demonstrable popular mandate. Nevertheless, the Ky regime has proved the most stable and most durable Vietnamese government since Diem. Changing it, even by legal, democratic processes, is a risk. The mere prospect of change has already made the Ky regime a lame duck. For a nation at war, such a risk is not small.

While the objective of the exercise was to let the people choose their leaders, I knew, both as a military man and as the one holding the reins of authority, that the military must continue to have a primary role in government. I have stated that when I came to power in 1965, only the military was capable of governance. Here is what the CIA said in a mid-1967 intelligence summary prepared for Johnson:

Since 1963 the military have provided Viet-Nam with whatever stability and unity it has achieved. The military have acquired extensive experience in civilian administration. As a group they are the best-educated, best-disciplined and most talented among the elites of South Viet-Nam. They cannot be excluded from constitutional government without depriving the nation of much-needed talents and skills. They also cannot be excluded from constitutional government without incurring grave risks of military coups, of further political instability and weakness. But neither can they by themselves resist communist political strategy and achieve political support. They must have civilian political support.

I agree. And so, while I was committed to the democratic process, I felt it important that a military candidate win the presidential election. After Guam, the question looming largest in the Americans' minds was whether Thieu or I would seek the presidency, or if both of us would run. Dozens of declassified State Department documents report or speculate that Thieu and I were maneuvering against each other.

As was so often the case with American perceptions, this was a half-truth. I did not need to maneuver against Thieu. As prime minister, I controlled his official life down to the budget for his office: His staff could not buy even a box of pencils if I did not allow it. I could have fired or transferred any member of his staff—or all of them.

The leadership committee of the Directorate, which I privately referred to as the politburo, consisted of ten generals. Aside from Thieu and myself, its members were the army chief of staff, the four corps commanders, and the ministers for interior, communications, and Chieu Hoi.

The corps commanders' duties transcended those of most military leaders. Under Diem and during the months of unrest and national disunity that followed his death, they had conducted themselves as virtual warlords. Under my government, each functioned much like a regional civil governor, with many important administrative responsibilities. As prime minister I worked closely with Vinh Loc, Hoang Xuan Lam, Le Nguyen Khang, and General Nguyen Manh Thanh, the corps commanders, allocating and prioritizing national resources to support each of their efforts.

The others included General Cao Van Vien, the army chief of staff, and Generals Linh Quang Vien, Nguyen Duc Thang, and Nguyen Boa Tri, who were in my cabinet. Together we functioned as if we were a single body, with me as the head and them as my limbs. After working together more than a year, we understood and respected one another; except for Thieu, each member of the Directorate was entirely in sympathy with me and my goals. They knew who had brought national stability, who had delivered a measure of security for the countryside, who had the confidence of the armed forces. They believed in my leadership, and we never failed to reach consensus on any important matter.

Once I had achieved stability of government, once America began pumping billions into our country and promised more, Thieu, who had not been willing to assume the risks of serving as prime minister in 1965, saw something that he wanted: the power and wealth that would come with the presidency.

Without consulting the Directorate or even the politburo, Thieu announced his candidacy for president. I was appalled. I was certain that Thieu could not win an election against me. The respect paid him when together we made an official visit or entertained at a state dinner was directed entirely to his office, not to his person. I treated him as a figurehead. I made every major decision, including the transfer or retirement of corps commanders or firing the secretary of defense, and told Thieu what I had decided. If he sometimes offered an opinion, he understood his role and never attempted to interfere once I made a decision.

For example, in the middle of 1966, I learned that one of my most trusted colleagues, General Nguyen Huu Co, was plotting against me. In September 1965 I had promoted him from chief of the Joint General Staff to defense minister and deputy premier. After the Buddhist crisis ended, I began to hear rumors about the activities of members of Co's family and quietly initiated an investigation.

Soon after that, Co went to Taiwan for a brief official visit. Afterward he stopped in Hong Kong. On the same day that he was to return to Vietnam, I left on an official visit to Malaysia. At the airport I told General Cao Van Vien, who had come to see me off, to have Thieu send a cable to Hong Kong. "Tell Co he cannot return to Vietnam."

Days earlier I had learned that Co was conspiring with several other southerners to kill me. Fortunately, they carried out their scheming in the presence of their junior aides. These young, idealistic officers were appalled. They knew what I had done for Vietnam and feared the chaos that would follow if I was deposed. Co's captains and majors were pals with my own junior aides. They alerted my men, who immediately told me.

"Can't we wait until you come back from Malaysia?" asked Vien. As chief of staff, Co outranked him.

"No," I said. "Just tell Thieu that I want him fired." I got on the airplane.

Chief of State Thieu, a lieutenant general, carried out my order.

After Thieu announced his intention to run for president, several top generals from the politburo met with him privately to ask him not to run. They told him that I had held the top job long enough to prove that I knew how to get things done and that I had deep and broad support from the ARVN. "Let Ky run the government, handle the politics, and deal with the Americans, and you can become army chief of staff," they told him.

"No," he responded. "If you don't want me as the army's candidate, then I don't care about the military, I will run myself."

Finally General Nguyen Duc Thang, the minister for Chieu Hoi, went to see him. He repeated the Directorate's guidance: Let Ky run for president and handle politics and government, and return to take care of the army. Thieu began shouting "Don't try to deceive me! The reasons you offer are not true! You are trying to trap me!"

Thang, an honest and very open sort, exploded in anger. "You treat me as a liar? I am a general officer! You think I am trying to deceive you?" They nearly had a fistfight.

After all these meetings, every member of the politburo

knew Thieu's attitude. As the deadline for announcing the military's candidate approached, I called the politburo together. The time for trying to convince him not to run was over, I explained. "Whom do you want, Thieu or me?" I asked.

"We want you," said each general in turn. It was unanimous.

"Very well, I accept," I said.

"How are you going to do it?" they asked.

"Easy," I replied. "Thieu will need military support if he is to have any chance at all, so we should retire him. Let him run for president as a civilian, if he wishes."

Everyone nodded agreement.

"Then the chief of state's position will be vacant. The best choice is Cao Van Vien, don't you think? He is senior." Vien was army chief of staff, and all the corps commanders supported him. He was a fine man, one of my strongest supporters, but very much the soldier, not as worldly as some of the others.

Thieu, of course, soon learned of this meeting. He had already told anyone who would listen that if he ran without the support of the military, he would get only two votes, including his wife's. Nevertheless, he continued to insist that he did not need the military's support to run as a civilian candidate.

By this time six or seven civilians had announced as candidates. For all the reasons described above, I had no need to maneuver against Thieu or anyone else. I was confident that I would get the most votes; I even dared to hope that it would be more than 50 percent. Once Thieu decided to risk a run for president, however, he began to maneuver against me. According to declassified U.S intelligence documents that I obtained for this book, Thieu secretly approached the two leading civilian candidates, Tran Van Huong and Phan Khac Suu. Apparently no deal was finalized, but they discussed the strategy of Thieu representing himself as a military candidate in the hope of splitting the military vote, thus allowing a civilian to win. In return, the winner would name Thieu prime minister. Suu and Huong were both elderly and infirm, and a smart politician like Thieu would have wasted little time making himself the real power behind their throne.

Henry Cabot Lodge returned to Washington in May 1967. His replacement was Ellsworth Bunker, seventy-two years of age, tall and very erect. With his icy demeanor, Saigonese soon began to call him "Mr. Refrigerator." Bunker had served with distinction during the 1965 crisis in the Dominican Republic, when 25,000 U.S. troops landed on the Caribbean island republic to prevent a communist victory in a civil war that was about to start. It was easy to send in troops but hard to take them out; American diplomats failed to find a political solution to the internecine rivalries that had brought the country to the brink of chaos. Bunker negotiated a solution that suited President Johnson, the troops left, and Bunker got a medal. So when he turned up in Saigon, we knew that he had come with the same instructions that took him to Santo Domingo: Find a way to negotiate a settlement and bring our boys home.

Officially, Bunker's policy was no interference in domestic Vietnamese matters, most especially including the military's choice of a presidential candidate. Because we had many differences, I was very surprised to learn from reading Westmoreland's memoirs that Bunker and almost all other senior Americans preferred me to Thieu. The traits of my character that in 1965 had been described with words like "flamboyant" and "impetuous" were now repackaged as "charisma."

The sole exception to supporting me, wrote Westmoreland, was him. He said that he had observed Thieu's career and his rise from command of a division to chief of the Joint General Staff, corps commander, minister of defense, and chairman of the Military Council, and that it reminded him of his own career. "Among all possible candidates, I saw Nguyen Van Thieu as the real hope for the country," he wrote in 1976.

I must admire Westmoreland's honesty, if not his judgment.

Thieu's career was nothing like Westmoreland's. After he involved himself in the coup against Diem, and until he became chief of state, Thieu held no military position for more than a few months and accomplished nothing. Before World War II, Westmoreland served five years in the field artillery. He was among the first American officers to complete the grueling paratroop training, and he commanded an elite airborne battalion during the bloody invasion of France and later a regimental combat team that parachuted into South Korea and fought with distinction.

In contrast, after he was elected president, Thieu would arrange to be tutored in parachute landings for a few hours. He would make one jump. In honor of his own courage and dogged determination, Thieu would order a table, complete with a fine linen tablecloth, erected on the drop zone. Westmoreland, with many more than a hundred jumps, would pin on Thieu's Parachutist's Badge. Then the new paratrooper would toast himself with champagne and feel entitled to wear the red beret of the airborne division.

All that was far in the future when the politburo chose me as the military's candidate for president. I wanted the entire Directorate to officially ratify this decision, and then I wanted the Armed Forces Congress to approve it. I convened the congress, hundreds of colonels and generals, in an auditorium at the chief of staffs compound. General Loan's troops secured the compound; I wanted things to happen as in a movie: There would be no accidents, and any sign of rebellion would be quashed at once.

The congress waited while the Directorate met in Cao Van Vien's office at about 7:00 A.M. I told the Directorate, "You are going to decide our fate, so to allow you complete freedom to discuss this matter, General Thieu and I will wait outside."

We sat in silence in the reception area, waiting. I knew what was going on in that room, and he knew it too. But a clock was ticking in Thieu's head. He knew that his fate had already been decided informally. If he was going to make any kind of a move, he could delay no longer.

Behind closed doors the Directorate decided formally as the politburo had already agreed: I would be their candidate for president, Thieu would be retired, and Cao Van Vien would temporarily become chief of state. Vien's door opened and the generals trooped out.

Before anyone could say anything, however, Thieu leaped to his feet. "I am still in the military. I belong to the corps, so whatever your decision, I will accept it," he said very politely. This was a radical change of attitude. He had always said, "I don't need the military." Now he saw where that road led and humbled himself.

My eyes were riveted on Thieu's face; I felt that he was about to weep. "Stop," I called. I did not take time to think. In one ten-thousandth of a second, faster than the blink of an eye, in the space of a single heartbeat, words flew straight from my heart to my tongue. I heard myself speak as from a distance. "Don't say anything," I said to Vien and the others. "Don't announce your decision. *I* will make the decision. I am going back to the air force, and you can name Thieu as the military's candidate for president."

I cannot think of any logical reason why I spoke as I did. The world would be different if I had instead bitten my tongue.

In the years since that moment, I have heard many stories about what happened in Vien's office: There was pressure from the Americans. I was subjected to blackmail about this or that. I was bribed or promised something to withdraw. But what really happened in that fraction of a second remains a great mystery, even to me. Perhaps I was engulfed by pity and bowed to my Buddha heart in sorrow for this man who hungered so greatly for power, a proud man who could shed tears over the loss of that for which I cared nothing: power and money.

Because Thieu was present, no one could raise an objection

or attempt to discuss the problem. Hoang Xuan Lam, the I Corps commander, broke the stunned silence that followed my announcement. "We all appreciate your sacrifice for the unity of the army," he said. One could not doubt his sincerity. Before I became prime minister, and even under Diem, there were no such sacrifices for unity among military leaders. Each of the generals in Vien's waiting room had served in the army for years and saw how the older generation had contended with one another for power and position.

"But why do you give just fifty percent to the army?" Lam continued. "We need one hundred percent from you. Continue to be a team with General Thieu. If he runs by himself, I think one of the civilian candidates will defeat him."

With a little shock I saw that Lam was crying. He reached up and removed the stars of his rank from his epaulets, then held them out to me. "If you do not agree to team with Thieu and run for vice president, then I will retire, because then I will no longer want to be part of the army."

Things were happening so fast. I took a deep breath. "Okay," I said. "If that is what you all think, I will do it." Without discussion the others agreed that I should support Thieu, and we all went down to the auditorium.

I took the stage and announced that I was not running and that I wanted everyone to support Thieu. The room was stunned, silent. Those officers had come to cast a vote in the belief that they would be putting their stamp on my candidacy.

A colonel rose. "I never imagined that General Ky has such a sense of unity that he was willing to make such a big personal sacrifice!" he said. "I ask everyone to stand up and show appreciation." Everybody got to their feet and applauded. I think Thieu was embarrassed by this spontaneous outpouring of respect and affection for me.

Thus I snatched defeat from the jaws of victory, the biggest mistake of my life. I cannot recall a day since 1975 when I did not regret it, and I have said so on Vietnamese radio. Until now, however, I never revealed my reason for withdrawing.

Later that day I heard that some of the younger officers, outraged and suspecting that some backroom deal had been struck, said that if Thieu accepted the nomination, they would arrest him. I sent word to not do this, that there was no need.

About one that afternoon I returned to my home on Tansonnhut to find William Colby, a CIA agent whom I had known for years, waiting. "Is it true?" he asked. "Did you make that decision?" When I said yes, he became very agitated. "Why are you so silly? So stupid? We just got the green light from Washington to support you in the election! How can you do this?"

I could tell that he was disgusted, but I thought that he was out of line. "Hey! This is *my* business," I said. "Why should I discuss it with you?"

"Can you retract?"

"No. I made my decision public, and there is nothing I can do to change it. Nor do I want to."

Looking back, I see that even then, the Americans had been studying Thieu for many years and knew him better than me. They did not like him at all. I wish that they had advised me, but I can see why they did not.

Colby thought for perhaps a second. "If you cannot reverse your decision not to run for president, and you are going to run as a vice president, why join Thieu? What about if you run as number two with Big Minh? We will support you!"

That turned my stomach, of course. But on later reflection I realized that the Americans preferred even a man who would deal with the communists to Thieu.

Months later, after the votes were counted, Thieu and I won about 35 percent of ballots cast. According to our new constitution, these results had to be certified by the new congress before the vote was official. A large majority of the members did not want Thieu, and as a last resort they sent a secret delegation to me. They said, "We will refuse to certify these results and invalidate the election. Then we will hold a new election, and you can run for president!"

"No, no, don't do that," I said. Such underhanded maneuvering goes against my nature. Even worse, such a stunt would have cost all my credibility in the world community and discredited my entire country.

I sent the congressmen away with the message that I would not allow such shenanigans. To make sure they certified the vote properly, I send General Loan, whom everyone knew to be incorruptible, completely loyal to me, and quick to act against lawbreakers, to the congress. "Sit where you will be seen," I said, "so everyone will know you are there and no one will invalidate the vote."

How foolish I was! I had so many chances to stop Thieu, even at the last moment. Now I feel like a chef who created a grand recipe, personally went to the market to select the perfect ingredients, labored long at the stove to prepare the dish—and then casually presented it to an oaf who stumbled into the kitchen crying for a meal.

But even then I thought that Thieu was more or less like myself, that even if he was of an older generation, at his core he was a patriot who would act in the best interests of his country. After years of fighting alongside so many true comrades in arms, sharing hardships and dangers along with life and death, relying on one another, trusting each other with our lives, I came to feel that every good soldier had these qualities. I felt a responsibility for and a duty to my people and my country, and I never considered that a comrade in arms could use his position of power to betray his countrymen by pocketing their money. But really, I should have known better.

At least in this regard, there were wiser heads among the

Directorate, men whose respect for me was infinitely greater than for Thieu. Before the election, Thieu was forced to sign a secret protocol designed to keep him under military control.

This was not my idea, but I embraced it. Only the generals who signed it knew of this paper and the council that it created. Composed of the most trusted military members of the Directorate, this council was responsible only to itself, and not bound by the constitution. The protocol specified that in any election, the council would select the military candidate for president. Even after that candidate was elected, however, he remained a member of the council and would act under its guidance always. In this way we sought to ensure that even after he became president, Thieu would continue as the army's representative and that during time of war the military retained ultimate responsibility for running the nation.

At the first meeting of this council, which included Thieu, we all signed the pact. Then we voted, and I was elected chairman. Thus when Thieu was elected president, he shared power and authority with the council. As council chairman, I held more power than Thieu himself.

The Americans never knew about this. They observed, however, that even as vice president I retained much power. The declassified documents that I would read decades later show that U.S. officials ascribed my authority to a clique of officers loyal to me personally. In a way, they were right, but as I have shown, there was much more to the story. Thieu, his prime minister and cabinet, as well as the military remained under the secret control of the chairman of the committee.

...

I have recounted many examples of how the Americans did not truly understand either Vietnam or the Vietnamese people. This was the source of much friction between fraternal nations who shared a common goal and between individuals. But if Americans, who came to my country by the millions, never came to understand Vietnam and Vietnamese, then my people, few of whom had then even visited the United States, also failed to understand America.

I accept responsibility for this failure. At Honolulu, Mr. Johnson suggested that Thieu and I study the criticisms and policies of "anti-Vietnam" Americans, including "journals like the *New York Times* and members of the Foreign Relations Committee."

"You need to know what our pressures are, just as we need to know what yours are," he said. Traveling by air throughout Asia as a young man I had been exposed to the foreign press, but my personal paradigm for mass media was strongly influenced by the Vietnamese organs. Few Vietnamese put much trust in newspapers, and I certainly had none.

I had spent months in Alabama at the Air War College, but this did not equate to much exposure to American society. I had not learned to appreciate the power of American media in shaping public opinion.

As prime minister and later as vice president, I dealt with the top American leaders. After reading years of their official correspondence and reports, I am convinced that most knew what we were fighting for and that I, along with many members of my government, devoted my full energies to the struggle.

I was preaching to the choir. America is a democracy. Its governments come or go at the will of the voters. And in America, the voters did not get it at all. They knew that their sons, husbands, brothers, and fathers were serving and too often dying in a far-off country, but they never really knew why. Americans trust their media. They are persuaded to buy soap and feminine hygiene products and cars and all sorts of unneeded products through mass-media messages. But the Vietnam war was never marketed to the American public, and thus it never attracted enough popular support.

The most glaring example: A primary justification for the war, according to Mr. Johnson's administration, was that the United States had intervened in order to bring democracy to Vietnam. True enough—but not nearly the whole story. The American media, however, delighted in pointing out all the instances in which Vietnamese governments, including mine, failed to act in a democratic way. When I suspended some elements of the new constitution because of the military situation, the suspension was reported fully, but my reasons were all but ignored.

Having lived in the United States since 1975, however, I realize that I made a fundamental mistake. Instead of relying on American politicians to tell their constituents about Vietnam, I should have taken my message to the American people directly through the mass media. It would have been hard, but there was no other way to convince U.S. voters that the war could be won, that things could get better, that with patience and fortitude the communists could be defeated. I have confidence in my powers of persuasion, and I believe that I could have communicated, along with much useful information, my sincerity and strong beliefs to the American people.

During my tenure as prime minister, the Americans shifted from a mainly advisory role to a partnership and then to serving as the principal strategic and political architects for the conduct of the war. But we abandoned the political dimension to the Americans. Our side didn't do enough. For example, I did not ask my Ministry of Information to research public opinion outside Vietnam. Much was written and broadcast about me, my government, and the war in American media, but while I saw a few newspaper and television reports, I never had a good picture of what Americans thought about me or about the Vietnamese government or the war. I had almost no picture at all.

As South Vietnam's premier I had the respect, understanding, and goodwill of most Asian leaders and governments. I was admired by many people. Why? Because I made several trips around Southeast Asia and Oceania. I spoke with newspaper reporters and was seen by local television audiences. But I never had a state visit to Europe. I never met informally with European leaders or media. I should have visited London and Paris, at least.

I might well have emulated Chiang Kai-shek and his heirs, who maintained public support for Taiwan over decades by cultivating America's powerful and politically connected.

After proving myself, I won the support of the U.S. leadership, who respected my integrity and saw that I was getting results. The antiwar elements that denounced me and my government got most of the coverage in American media. But instead of visiting America to explain to the public what was going on in Vietnam, we left this to the White House, the Pentagon, and the State Department. That was a mistake: I should have hired a top American public relations agency to deal with this issue. I should have created a program to send our most effective speakers, including myself, to meet with the mass media and speak to groups of Americans, including those who opposed us. I should have cultivated relationships with the Hollywood film industry, with the top people in the legitimate theater and in the music industry. I should have visited America often, not to go to the White House or the Congress or the Pentagon, but to speak with the people of America as I did with the people of Vietnam.

Along with nearly all my countrymen, however, I thought that America was President Johnson and his ambassadors, that when we spoke to congressmen, cabinet secretaries, and top generals, we were talking to America.

We were 100 percent wrong.

But if I, the prime minister, a widely traveled general who

had been to America, didn't realize this, how could the average Vietnamese understand it?

So it is wrong to blame the American side for not understanding Vietnam. *We never understood America.* We didn't understand its system or how its society thinks or processes information and ideas.

If I had it to do over, I would spend more of my time in the United States. It is only eighteen hours of flying, and like American politicians, I would campaign across the country. I would go to the Midwest and meet with farmers, to the South to talk to textile workers. I would visit the families of American soldiers who had been killed and personally convey my country's condolences and gratitude. I would do anything that could bring Vietnam and Vietnamese closer to the American people. We didn't need to be close to Johnson, to be pleasant or comfortable with McNamara or Bunker. We needed the man in the street, the taxi driver who had spent a year in Vietnam; the schoolteacher whose students faced the draft after they graduated; the small businessman who had fought in World War II. If I had done that, as I could have, America would have supported Vietnam for a long, long time. We ought to have won.

There was one more thing I failed to do. I should have paid far more attention to the selection of my ambassador to the United States. I should have sent abroad only our best-educated people, true intellectuals, patriotic men and women who would represent not just what Vietnam was but all that we aspired to become. Looking back, nearly all our ambassadors were mere bureaucrats, functionaries thinking only about bettering themselves, about the privileges of an easy life in Washington or Paris paid for by the government.

What we needed instead were cadres, fighters, men and women motivated to tell Vietnam's story to the world, people who would work night and day to gain the sympathy and understanding of our allies—people who would make powerful friends for Vietnam, who through daily efforts would invite admiration for their nation.

...

Late in 1967, Thieu moved into the Presidential Palace. I did not know it, but it was the beginning of the end of everything that I held dear. I blame only myself.

13

TET

IN the presidential election of November 1967, seven civilians ran against Thieu. Had they put aside their greed and displayed even a little intelligence, they would have held a caucus, selected one of their members to lead a coalition government, and beaten him. Even with me on the ticket as vice president, he won only 35 percent of the votes cast. But they were politicians, and thought only of themselves and their immediate goals.

The election drew enormous attention around the world. Hundreds of observers representing U.S. churches, citizens' groups, and other nongovernmental organizations fanned out through the countryside to observe the process. While they reported few irregularities, and of these far more occurred from ineptitude than from malice, the Western press faulted our commitment to democracy because the election commission refused to let a candidate with well-known ties to the communists run. The American media raised a stink about how this undermined the election's integrity.

I was not aware, in 1967, of how much attention this got in the West, but now I will address the matter: The only communist party of South Vietnam was the so-called NLF, or National Front for Liberation—the Vietcong. Their goal, clearly stated, was to overthrow the government and unite the country with the communist regime in the North. Not that we thought that a communist candidate might win, but to allow them to participate would be to endorse their legitimacy. Would the communists in Hanoi have allowed a pro-American South Vietnamese to participate in an election in North Vietnam? If we had invited the North to participate in our election, would they have fielded a candidate? *For how many years was membership in the Communist party of the United States illegal?*

Although the balloting of 1967 was important, I would have preferred an election that united North and South. As I once told Nixon, if there was a fair contest between candidates representing North and South to award the victor leadership of a reunified country, I felt certain that any staunch anticommunist would beat any communist candidate.

"How can you be sure?" Nixon asked.

"Neither I nor any other anticommunist is as well known in the North as Ho Chi Minh," I replied. "But in a democracy, people know that if they are unhappy with their government, they can insult it in the press, curse it in the street, replace it, and nothing bad will happen to them. Anyone who is overheard saying bad things about a communist candidate will go to prison, or worse. I think that if we have a truly free election, the Vietnamese people will reject the communist way and choose the noncommunist candidate."

"That is so simple," Nixon said. "Why is it that until now, nobody has told me?" He borrowed my pen and made notes.

...

Soon after I became prime minister in 1965, I was encouraged to move into the magnificent new Presidential Palace, probably the finest such structure in Asia. It was built on the site of a French edifice destroyed when Diem was overthrown, and included spectacular grounds and a spacious apartment.

I preferred to live more modestly. My wife had expended great efforts in making our house at Tansonnhut, converted from a barracks, into a cozy home, and she did not look forward to moving, even into a palace. My home also included an office for air force business.

As prime minister I needed a larger office that was more convenient for visitors, so I used one in the palace and commuted from home in one of two Bell UH-1B helicopters that General Westmoreland gave me. Before the 1967 election, I landed early each morning on a pad on the palace roof. A few weeks after the Thieus moved in, however, Madame Thieu found occasion to tell me that she had changed her mind about a roof garden: The rotor wash from my helicopter would destroy her plants.

This was her oblique way of pointing out that their fourth-floor bedroom was immediately below this garden. I am an early riser, and I knew Thieu was not; I realized immediately that each time I landed, I woke him up. I immediately switched to a landing pad elsewhere on the grounds. I mention this incident to illustrate two points: Thieu's character was such that he was unwilling to confront me even over such a trivial matter and that he did not feel, even after the election, that he held power enough to tell me to do anything.

Immediately after Thieu's election, the U.S. government initiated a public relations campaign to rally America behind the Johnson administration and the war. They called this campaign the "Success Offensive," and it took the form of a series of optimistic statements about the direction of the war from credible Americans. These pronouncements were meant to convey the idea that the war was being won and would soon be over. As Johnson said in a November 17 press conference: "We are making progress. We are pleased with the results we are getting. We are inflicting greater losses than we are taking . . . The fact that the population under free control has constantly risen . . . is a very encouraging sign . . . overall we are making progress."

This was true, as far as it went. But even the most optimistic in South Vietnam's government felt that it would be several years before we could defeat the Vietcong and expel the last North Vietnamese invader. Ambassador Bunker told the press that 67 percent of South Vietnam was under government control and only 17 percent was controlled by the Vietcong. In this way he strongly implied that two-thirds of the nation was under complete government control. The reality was somewhat different. The United States designated an area "under control" if the Vietcong did not contest the local government presence. Bunker's statement, however, was not meant to make me or my countrymen feel more confident. Johnson, who planned to run for another term, meant these words for U.S. opinion leaders, and Bunker did not clear his speeches with my government. Even if he had told us his intentions, however, how could we have told Johnson's representative what to say to his own people?

General Westmoreland, commander of U.S. forces in Vietnam, made an influential speech on November 21 at the National Press Club in Washington. He said that 1968 marked the start of a new phase where "the end begins to come into view," and added that the United States would soon turn over a major share of Vietnam's defense to ARVN troops.

After the speech, Westmoreland told newsmen: "It is conceivable to me that, within two years or less, it will be possible for us to phase down our level of commitment and turn more of the burden of the war over to Vietnamese armed forces, who . . . will be prepared to assume this greater burden."

Some in the Johnson administration were more realistic. General Earle Wheeler, chairman of the Joint Chiefs of Staff, addressed the Detroit Economic Club on December 18. He said, in part: "the North Vietnamese are not yet at the end of their military rope. Although North Vietnam—as well as the Vietcong—is feeling a manpower pinch, they still have the ability to send additional troops to the south. Thus there is still some heavy fighting ahead—it is entirely possible that there may be a communist thrust similar to the desperate effort of the Germans in the Battle of the Bulge in World War II."

Although this speech was in marked contrast to the official optimism of the Success Offensive, it drew little attention because it was delivered far from Washington. Only two days later, however, in a cable to the Pentagon, Westmoreland echoed Wheeler's prediction: "the enemy has already made a crucial decision to make a maximum effort. The results of this effort will determine the next move."

On January 22, Westmoreland told Johnson that he believed that "the enemy will attempt a countrywide show of strength just prior to Tet." Such warnings were not made public in the United States, Nor were they shared with the South Vietnamese government.

As January 1968 drew to a close, the whole country prepared for the lunar new year observed throughout Asia. Vietnamese celebrate Tet, the lunar New Year, as a sort of secular Christmas and New Year's rolled into one. We visit our families, exchange gifts, feast on the best food we can get, have a few drinks, shoot off fireworks, and generally try to have a good time. Since the war against the Vietcong had begun almost a decade earlier, both sides usually called a truce during Tet.

Westmoreland canceled the 1968 truce twenty-four hours before the start of Tet and placed U.S. troops on full alert. The ARVN was told only that this was because of increased enemy activity around Khe Sanh, a U.S. Marine firebase in the northwest corner of I Corps, near the border with Laos.

There was indeed a buildup around Khe Sanh, but as the CIA would disclose over three decades later, weeks before Tet, U.S. intelligence had concluded that a major enemy offensive was imminent. CIA historian Harold Ford's report "CIA and the Vietnam Policy Makers: Three Episodes 1962–1968" is based on researching the files of the National Security Agency (NSA), the supersecret organization that intercepts and analyses enemy communications. The Ford report, published on the CIA's Web site, describes how the first indications of "impending major enemy activity" came from signal intercepts in the second week of January 1968.

The NSA issued several more alerts over the next few days, "culminating in a major warning disseminated widely in communications intelligence channels" on January 25. The title of this warning: "Coordinated Vietnamese Communist Offensive Evidenced in South Vietnam."

In 1998 Westmoreland told an interviewer that he was "well aware of the NSA reports" as well as other intelligence predicting an offensive. "I knew the attack was coming, but I did not want to let the enemy know I knew."

That may explain why the United States failed to share such alarming intelligence with its South Vietnamese counterparts: The Americans probably feared that this information would be leaked to the enemy. But the enemy was quite aware of their impending attack! Even in hindsight, it seems peculiar.

Tet came at a time of transition. I was vice president, not prime minister. On New Year's eve, as was my custom of many years, I hosted a reception at my home for VNAF and army friends and their wives. As midnight approached, officers stopped by to have a drink and wish each other a good year. At one minute after midnight we heard a distant crackle like gunfire. We thought nothing of it, supposing that it was merely firecrackers or happy soldiers shooting into the air to celebrate the new year.

The firing went on and on, however, and then my phone rang. It was General Khang, the marine who commanded the Capitol Military District. Then came calls from other bases around Saigon. Everyone had the same message: They were under heavy attack—and they could not reach Thieu. Within a few hours I had similar reports from corps commanders up and down the country, from I Corps in the north to IV Corps in the south, and every place between: The enemy was attacking in great strength.

Catastrophe loomed. In expectation of the usual Tet truce, half the ARVN had gone on leave. Even worse, most of the army's combat forces were not deployed in or near big cities. The Vietcong, who until now had avoided attacking major population centers, used some 80,000 troops in a coordinated assault against thirty-nine of South Vietnam's forty-four provincial capitals, against almost every allied airfield, and against Saigon. Before we could organize the capital's defenses, a Vietcong hit squad penetrated the sprawling grounds of the U.S. Embassy and almost shot their way into one of the buildings. Other communist teams attacked the headquarters of the general staff, the Presidential Palace, navy headquarters, and the radio station.

Thieu could not be found, so I took charge. Fortunately, the Vietnamese armed forces had excellent communications. When I knew that it was a general attack of great intensity, my first decision was to declare an immediate curfew. Vietnamese people normally take the first day of the year to visit pagodas, temples, churches, and relatives. I didn't want millions of people in the streets while communist guerrillas were roaming the city.

I ordered all commanders to hold their positions and sent my guests back to their units. At about 3:00 A.M. the base commander, Colonel Luu Kim Cuong, telephoned to suggest that I evacuate the base with my family: A strong enemy force had penetrated the barbed-wire perimeter and was inside the base.

"So, what are *you* going to do?" I asked.

"I'm going to stay and fight," he replied. "But I don't think we can stop them—my airmen are not trained as infantry." His small base security force had only sidearms and a few automatic weapons. "You'd better leave."

"If you stay, then I and my family will stay," I replied. I armed my wife and our three oldest children with rifles, pistols, and a submachine gun. Only my three-year-old was unarmed. I called General Khang. "Do you have any reserves that you can send to the airbase?" I asked.

"I have only one company left," he replied. "But I don't think the air base has priority number one. There are so many other places that need help more."

"What does it take to become the number-one priority? *The enemy is inside the base!* They are less than five hundred meters from my house!"

"Oh," he replied. "In that case, I will send you the last reserve company."

Those 150 paratroopers arrived ten minutes later and mounted a counterattack. While they fought, I dealt with more immediate problems: The Vietcong had broadcast messages that they had come to overthrow the Thieu-Ky "puppet regime." The transmission was oddly worded, and many who heard it thought that I had staged a coup to oust Thieu!

Our most immediate problem was the need to alert the populace to the attack, dispel rumors of a coup, and announce the curfew. I used a tactical radio to call General Loan, chief of police. He said that the enemy occupied the radio station in downtown Saigon.

"I don't care who has the station right now," I said. "I want it back, and in operating condition, by seven A.M. so I can broadcast to the public."

About 6:00 A.M. Loan called to say that he was about to launch his counterattack. He had dragooned whatever army troops and police that he could lay hands on and would personally lead the assault. Forty-five minutes later he called again: The station was in his hands. I sent the station a tape with a recorded message announcing a nationwide curfew. Everyone was to stay home and allow the army and police to deal with the invaders.

The paratroopers were driving the Vietcong back, but I still couldn't find Thieu. Even though by this time he undoubtedly understood what was going down, he didn't contact me. Hours later I would learn from his office that he was deep into the Mekong Delta at My Tho, his wife's hometown, for Tet. Only his closest aides knew that he was gone, and I had to send my own helicopter to bring him back to Saigon.

Something very strange occurred during the first hours of the 1968 Tet Offensive: U.S. forces refused all our requests for fire support. Before this time, and again after the first hours of the Tet Offensive, whenever an ARVN or VNAF unit needed additional artillery support or an air strike, we asked the Americans. With few exceptions, they provided whatever we required. Over the years a tight, easy working relationship had grown between Vietnamese and their American advisors and between adjacent American and Vietnamese units.

Nowhere was this relationship closer than in the air force. VNAF liaison officers sat side by side with USAF counterparts in the operations center, working as one unit to coordinate operations between the two national command structures. When the VNAF needed support, we asked a USAF officer. If aircraft were available, a mission was immediately scheduled.

During the first hours of the enemy offensive, everything changed. According to a report from Colonel Cuong, the base commander, when a ranking VNAF operations officer asked his USAF counterpart for aircraft support, the American replied, "I have to check with higher authority." After a time the answer came back: "No aircraft are available." From my home I could *see* USAF planes parked in revetments across from the Joint Operations Center. They were nothing but available.

I thought that was strange, but later that day General Lam, commander of I Corps, called to report a similar situation: He had asked for B-52 support, and for the first time in his memory—or mine—the Americans said that none was available. And so it went throughout the country until ten in the morning: The entire American force, including offshore naval units, did nothing. During the perilous first minutes and hours of the Vietcong attack, we fought alone.

Then I got a report about 10:00 A.M. that the U.S. twenty-fifth Division, based at Cu Chi, had begun to deploy. In the next few hours the Americans slowly began to accept ARVN requests for fire support. The VNAF and USAF again functioned as a team. U.S. infantry ringed Saigon to prevent the Vietcong from reinforcing the unit they had infiltrated. The enemy fired heavy mortars and big 122 mm rockets into residential neighborhoods, killing and wounding civilians.

Although General Khang was in charge of the Capital Military District, he had his hands full. Many Vietcong infiltrators donned civilian clothes and mixed with the populace. Much of the street fighting fell to a mixed bag of police and soldiers commanded by General Loan.

A few days before Tet, Loan's men had found a cache of AK-47 rifles. On his own authority, Loan had ordered a state of alert: Eighty-five percent of Saigon police were in uniform and on duty when the attack began. The police, who were familiar with their own communities, were invaluable in identifying infiltrators. In these confused times, Loan did an outstanding job of coordination with Khang's troops.

On the second night of the offensive, Loan came to my house to say that a big battle had taken place in Cholon and that our troops, mostly rangers, had suffered heavy casualties. "I'm going down to see them," he said. "Want to come with me?"

I got in his Jeep and we drove to Cholon. As on the night before, the sky was lit with tracers, fires burned, and shooting was heard everywhere. This time, however, U.S. and VNAF aircraft patrolled the skies. We found the troops still mopping up, and spent time with the wounded, shaking hands, talking with them, letting them know how grateful we felt for their heroism.

The next day Loan again battled the Vietcong in the streets.

In house-to-house fighting, his men captured a man carrying papers identifying him as a Vietcong captain in the act of murdering a police sergeant, his wife, and three small children. This guerrilla wore civilian clothes. The Geneva Conventions do not extend the protections of prisoner-of-war status to spies, mercenaries, and guerrillas who fail to distinguish themselves from civilians. Loan, who was acquainted with the murder victims and whose first priority was directing combat operations, told a subordinate to execute the guerrilla. When his man hesitated, Loan drew his pistol and did it himself.

Unfortunately, both an American television film crew and Associated Press photographer Eddie Adams were on hand to capture this dramatic moment. Adams's heart-stopping image, reprinted all over the world without explanation of the circumstances, came to symbolize all that was perceived as wrong by those opposing U.S. involvement in Vietnam. In the click of a shutter, our struggle for independence and self-determination was transformed into an image of a seemingly senseless and brutal execution.

While most South Vietnamese heartily approved of Loan's actions, the picture ruined his reputation abroad, and especially in America. Nguyen Ngoc Loan was the rarest of Vietnamese birds, the honest cop. He was a brilliant intellectual and a brave pilot who continued to fly combat missions long after he became national police chief. A few days after executing the Vietcong murderer, Loan was severely wounded in house-to-house fighting, and ultimately lost a leg. He was a courageous fighter willing to risk his own safety to protect his homeland, and he was my friend. It is long past time that the stigma of that awful photo be removed. Loan deserves recognition for his career as a skilled, courageous, devoted, and principled patriot.

The image captured by Adams won the Pulitzer Prize for news photography. In 1980, however, Adams told my coauthor, who had served as a U.S. Army combat photographer in Vietnam, that he wished that he had never taken the photo. "It ruined General Loan's life," he said. "And he didn't deserve it. Joe Rosenthal [an AP photographer who captured a reenactment of the 1945 flag-raising on Iwo Jima] has a monument in Arlington [National Cemetery]. Mine will be in Hanoi."

...

Even as the shock of the surprise attack began to wear off, Thieu remained in the background. I took time to assess the situation. I was confident that we could kick the Vietcong out of our cities. On the third or fourth day of the attack, I went back on the radio and broadcast an appeal to the young men of Saigon. For years before the Tet Offensive, the army had many problems recruiting college-age men in the cities. Too many preferred riding around on imported motor scooters purchased with money from pimping, dealing drugs, or black-market trafficking to fighting the communists. Saigon was filled with draft dodgers, mostly sons of affluent families who bought exemptions or phony documents from corrupt officials.

Nevertheless, I appealed to their patriotism. "Here is the situation," I said in my broadcast. "The enemy has forced themselves into our home. I need your help to kick them out. Anyone who wants to volunteer, come to the public park, where I will come to talk with you."

I was astonished the next day when thousands of students from high schools, vocational colleges, the university, and thousands more college-age men not currently enrolled, packed the park. It made me proud. A hundred years earlier a French army had attacked Saigon—and the emperor had great difficulty raising an army because the young men did not want to die to defend his effete and corrupt dynasty. Now the park was full of young men who had ignored the communist propaganda to rise up against the government but had responded to my call.

After giving these youngsters an update on how the army

and police were handling the situation, I said, "Enemy troops are all over the city. I will give you weapons to defend your parents and your sisters, to defend your homes. Now, go back to your own street, to your own house, and watch for strange men and women. If you see armed strangers, if you think they are the enemy, even if you cannot shoot them, notify the police!" In the next few days Loan's police passed out thousands of rifles and ammunition and taught each young man the rudiments of marksmanship: how to load and safely handle a weapon. We had a similar program to this in the countryside, the Civilian Irregular Defense Corps, but not until the Tet Offensive did we see the need to apply this concept in cities.

On the military side, I issued an order to officers at all levels to stand and fight, to clear areas under their control of Vietcong. I called General Thang, an outstanding officer whom I had put in charge of the Chieu Hoi program, and said, "I need someone good to clear the whole Mekong River Delta. I'll give you three months. Can you do that?" He said yes, so I made him IV Corps commander.

Ninety days later, Thang called to say that he had cleared the last communist stronghold. He invited me to come down to Soc Trang for an inspection. If the whole area was clear, I reasoned, I would have no difficulty in *driving* down to Soc Trang. So I did, and with Thang I drove around visiting the people. Crowds flocked around our Jeep to greet us wherever we stopped. In one small town, where there had been a firefight the day before, the market was still burning. A few hundred people, mostly the elderly, women, and children, turned out to see us. "Were you scared?" I asked an old man.

"Oh, yes. But now it's good—the enemy are all killed."

I was struck by a sudden thought. These delta people usually celebrate the new year and other festivals with a cockfight. This year, however, the Vietcong had ruined their festivities. So I told

General Thang, "What if we stop here for lunch and ask the people to go to their homes and bring their birds? We could set up a little arena and have a cockfight." Thang agreed, and before long the people were having a wonderful time, chattering, drinking beer, wagering wildly, enjoying themselves as they had not for months. I know that cockfighting horrifies many animal-loving Americans—few of whom have ever seen a match—but for these simple peasants of the Mekong Delta, the freedom to spend a convivial day attending a local sporting event represented triumph over fear and oppression.

Another big victory came on February 26, when the U.S. Marines retook Hue. Even after that, however, stubborn pockets of Vietcong resistance remained throughout the country and in Saigon. The Vietcong had committed all its best-trained and battle-hardened guerrillas to what had proven a debacle. Even as casualties mounted and entire Vietcong companies and battalions were reduced to a handful of fighters, the survivors fought on. They had gambled and lost, but many believed their own propaganda and refused to give up.

If Mr. Thieu took no active role in clearing the enemy from Saigon, Mrs. Thieu did. A Vietcong squad had occupied a big clothing factory just off the end of Tansonnhut runway. From its roof and windows they fired at aircraft landing or taking off. The air base commander decided to mount an attack on the building, but before he could begin he got a phone call from Mrs. Thieu. She said that the factory and its inventory were worth $3 million and asked him not to destroy it.

Cuong called to ask me what to do.

"Don't worry about money," I said. "First, call upon the enemy to surrender. If not, just destroy them and the factory."

There was a little shooting, but when the Vietcong saw that we meant to bring the building down on their heads, they gave up. I later heard that Mrs. Thieu and some of her friends owned shares in that factory. A similar situation happened with a Cholon brewery. The enemy took hostages, apparently in the belief that we would not attack. I sent word to tell them that they had five minutes to release their hostages and leave the building. If not, we would level it. The brewery owners protested, but I ignored them. How could we think about money while the enemy was killing people? I was prepared to destroy the brewery, but just before I gave the order the hostages ran out, followed by thirty or forty Vietcong, hands in the air.

As the weeks went by and pockets of resistance were mopped up, we captured more and more enemy equipment. About three months after the start of the offensive an officer from the headquarters of the Capital Military District invited me and several senior officers to visit a Chinese school in Cholon to view a display of captured armament and ammunition. I told him to pick us all up around 8:00 A.M. the next day at the palace. Attending this sort of event was a common way of encouraging troop morale and espirit de corps. After a big battle, soldiers would display captured weapons as trophies, visible reminders of how hard they had fought. Senior officers often came to praise their efforts.

That night I had a strange dream. I was flying and suddenly my plane dived into a huge well. Overwhelmed with dread, I felt that I could not climb out of the well, that I would crash and die. At that moment Colonel Cuong, the Tansonnhut Air Base commander, spoke from the back seat of my aircraft.

Even in my dream, I was surprised, because months earlier, maybe a week after the start of the Tet Offensive, Cuong had been killed by the blast from a giant Vietcong B-40 rocket.

At the moment in my dream when I told myself that I was going to die, Cuong said, "Well, General, I'm going to bring you up," and then my plane soared toward the top of the well. Soon we were high in the air. Cuong pointed to some fighting on the ground. He said, "Look, you see that yellow smoke? Be careful, that is where they will strike."

"Yellow smoke means friendly troops," I replied. "Why send a strike against friendly soldiers?"

"You are right," he replied. "But heed my words."

Then he showed me a picture of seven dead men lying crumpled on the ground.

I awoke before dawn, covered with sweat and exhausted, feeling as if I had seen something that was impermissible, a forbidden scene, or that I had forgotten something important.

About 7:30 an officer came to take me to Cholon with the group. I said, "I feel ill today. Go without me," and went back to bed for a couple of hours. At 10:00 news came from Cholon: My closest supporters, who had gone to the Chinese school, were hit by rocket fire from an American helicopter. Six were killed, two seriously wounded. When I saw a news photo of the schoolyard, taken minutes after the incident, it was exactly the image that I had seen in my dream—except that in the dream there were seven dead bodies, and in the schoolyard there were only six. I don't know how or why, but I am certain that Cuong saved me.

I never learned who was at the controls of the American gunship that morning, or why a U.S. helicopter would attack friendly troops in a schoolyard in the heart of a pacified city. I have heard persistent rumors that Thieu was behind the attack, that he conspired with Americans in the hope of killing me. Years later I heard that a certain Colonel Tran Van Hai was aboard that aircraft. I know him slightly. Thieu made him chief of the National Police, replacing General Loan, who took months to recover from his wounds.

...

Our forces beat back every Vietcong attack and killed or captured their most experienced and capable soldiers. The Vietcong were defeated in the field, and it set the communist military agenda back two years. In dozens of communities temporarily held by the Vietcong, assassination squads worked their way through lists of names, murdering anyone they considered a possible enemy, mostly innocent people. Nowhere was this worse than in Hue, where several thousand people were murdered. Eerily foreshadowing the Pol Pot regime in Cambodia, they eliminated the petit bourgeois—merchants of every kind, school teachers and other "intellectuals," as well as anyone with any link to the government or military. This systematic savagery showed the people of South Vietnam exactly what to expect if the communists won.

The defeat that we inflicted on the Vietcong inspired all South Vietnam, and especially its military, to unprecedented unity of purpose. From their propaganda broadcasts and by interrogating prisoners, we learned that the enemy had expected the populace would rally to their cause and join them. Instead, the Tet Offensive was my country's biggest victory, both militarily and politically.

The offensive and its aftermath had the opposite effect in the United States. Because they had been told that victory was just around the corner, Tet shook America's confidence in the war and in its government. Just two months after Tet, President Johnson announced that he would not run for reelection. I did not know it then, but it was the turning point in the war, the moment when American public opinion began to tip against further involvement in Southeast Asia. In the months and years following Tet, the American media would document case after case of official misrepresentation. Top U.S. military and civilian leaders would be exposed for their lies about Vietcong troop strength and enemy casualties. As government credibility faded, America began looking for a way out of Vietnam. Peace with honor, they said.

The Prussian strategist Carl von Clausewitz (1780–1831) described war as "the continuation of politics by other means."

America's reaction to the Tet Offensive allowed the communists to stand that on its head: Politics became the means to win a war that they could not win in the field. Hanoi realized that all they had to do was absorb punishment, stay on their feet, and wait for the United States to tire and go home.

Ranking Americans had been looking for a way to withdraw from Vietnam from the time that I became premier. So I wonder now if the White House knew more about the Vietcong's Tet Offensive than it admitted to. Why did the Americans not tell us of an expected attack? Why, during the first few hours of fighting, did the United States refuse to support us? Why did they seem to avoid getting involved in the fight? But some now say that in the confusion of a surprise attack, Americans mistrusted radio communications. Units claiming to be ARVN might actually have been VC (Vietcong). It is so odd, and so out of character with what I know of American fighting men, that I am left to wonder if U.S. officials secretly decided to wait and see if the communists succeeded in seizing Saigon or several of the provincial capitals. The Americans might have thought that this would force us to cede territory and then negotiate a political settlement with the Vietcong.

That would have saved the face of the Hanoi regime: They could act like the big brother and sit down to resolve a dispute between the younger brothers—my government and the Vietcong. Then the Americans could say, "Okay, work it out among yourselves, and we hope you all get along. Good luck, and in the meantime, we're going home."

It was something like that, I am almost sure. Maybe I'll live to see this mystery solved.

...

As the fighting of the Tet Offensive tapered off, I went around the country to visit areas that had been cleared. It was immediately apparent that the attacks had created hundreds of thousands of refugees. People displaced by the fighting needed food, shelter, and medical attention. They needed to have their hamlets rebuilt or to be relocated to another part of the country. Peasants forced to live in cities had to be trained to earn a livelihood. I created an emergency committee to deal with all these problems.

From the first minutes of the offensive, I had been dealing with these matters, largely because Thieu did not and no one else stepped forward. Accordingly, the members of the emergency committee asked me to chair it, and for several months I went on doing what I had been doing: trying to ease the suffering of these people. I gave orders instead of requests, and because of my dual role as vice president and general, I could handily coordinate functions between the civilian and military bureaucracies. Things happened very fast and very effectively. After a few months, with a functioning infrastructure, I realized that the Ministry of the Interior, or some other government agency, could and should take over—once the crisis was past, there was no longer any reason for me to continue in this role.

When I told Thieu that I would resign from the committee, he told Bunker, who asked for a meeting. He said, "You must stay on for a year or so, you are doing such a very good job."

"This is not the vice president's responsibility," I replied. Soon after that I resigned, hoping to focus my attentions again on winning the war. While I had been out of Saigon, however, working night and day on refugee problems, Thieu had begun to consolidate his position. He put cronies into positions where they could make a lot of money, and he created a political party, the Dan Chu Dang. Little by little, the balance of power between us swung in his favor.

I had little confidence in Thieu's ability to inspire and lead, but he had been elected president, and I still trusted him in the sense that I felt that as long as he held such a sacred office, he would serve his country before he served himself. As vice president I wanted nothing more than that we all remain united against our common enemy and work together to solve our many national problems. In my heart I felt that it didn't matter if I was number one or number two or even number three. That was my mistake.

14
DIPLOMACY

ANGRY protestors lined the highway from the Canberra airport. Singing and chanting, they waved signs and placards labeling me a fascist and baby killer and urged Prime Minister Harold Holt to end Australian participation in Vietnam.

As South Vietnamese premier I made state visits to New Zealand, South Korea, Taiwan, Thailand, and Malaysia, but this was by far my most interesting trip. Holt met me at the airport and joined me in a motorcade to a press conference.

The opposition party had turned out 100,000 demonstrators along the route from the airport and surrounding the building where I spoke. They opposed the Holt government and its support of my government. Fielding a reinforced infantry regiment to fight in Vietnam had led to conscription, the first time since World War II that the Australian army had needed draftees to fill its ranks. So the demonstrations were not so much against me personally as against Holt's policies.

The leader of the opposition was Arthur Calwell, then in his late sixties, and a very well known figure to Australians. As his country's first minister of immigration, he worked to bring foreign settlers to Australia. But not just any settlers: He opposed anyone that would upset the country's predominantly European racial balance. "Japan, India, Burma, Ceylon and every new African nation are fiercely anti-white and anti–one another," he said. "Do we want or need any of these people here? I am one red-blooded Australian who says no and who speaks for 90 percent of Australians."

Calwell ran against Holt in the 1966 election with such campaign slogans as "Two Wongs don't make a White," and "Do you want a coffee colored Australia?"

On the way from the airport, Holt told me that every one of his close advisors, including his wife, opposed my visit. They felt that inviting a controversial figure like me would only compound strong opposition to his policies.

Holt held fast. Even before my Air Vietnam plane touched down in Canberra, Calwell had called me a butcher, a baby killer, and a dictator, among other less affectionate sobriquets. About five hundred reporters attended that first press conference. Almost the first question was "Calwell has called you insulting names. What is your reaction?"

I smiled and said, "Well, you know I am Asian, and there is an old Asian saying: 'If you respect old people, you will live a long time.' As for Mr. Calwell, I treat him as my grandfather. Whatever he says about me, no problem, I still respect him because he is an old man."

Everyone laughed, and the next day a leading Australian newspaper ran a front-page cartoon of a smiling, boyish General Ky pushing a snarling, dissipated, wheelchair-bound Calwell.

I held a press conference or gave media interviews every day—and everywhere I went, there were demonstrators. I stayed at the Governor General's Residence, where fifteen or twenty ladies picketed on the sidewalk. They carried placards with slogans such as "No War," "Ky Is a Dictator," and so on. On the second day I returned to the residence at about 6:00 P.M. to change for dinner. When I saw the picketers, I asked the driver to stop near the gates. My wife and I got out and walked over to the ladies, and I saluted. I said, "Hello, I am General Ky. Anything you want, you can tell me, I will answer your questions, we will discuss things." Then I introduced my wife, and we chatted quite amiably with the ladies. I explained to them what had happened in my country, what the war was about.

After about thirty minutes, one of the ladies said, "Oh, he is such a nice man."

"They are a lovely couple," said another.

"He speaks well, he is handsome," said a third.

"We were wrong to do this. We shall go home now," said their leader.

I was proud and happy—but there were more demonstrators the next day. After my speech at the National Press Club, one guy got up and said, "You represent nothing! From what I understand, three-fourths of South Vietnam is occupied by the National Liberation Front! You represent no one."

"I don't know where you get your information," I replied. "I am sorry that I don't have a map right here so you can show me the three-quarters that the communists occupy. But I can tell you that my government controls the majority of the territory. If you don't believe me, it will be my pleasure to invite you to come with me in my plane when I go home. Anywhere you want to go, you may go. I will even go with you, so you can show me the three-fourths of South Vietnam that communists occupy."

All the friendly press applauded—and this man said, "I accept your invitation." He flew back with me and spent almost two months traveling the country. When he returned to Australia, he wrote a report for his newspaper, the official organ of Australia's Communist party! He reported that the party was misinformed, that my government was in control of South Vietnam.

My trip to Australia was the most successful state visit of my tenure. On the day I left for home, the same newspaper mentioned earlier ran another page-one cartoon. This time I stood in the center of a boxing ring. Calwell is supine at my feet, arms akimbo, knocked out. The referee, Public Opinion, holds my arm aloft in victory.

And it really was a knockout. Calwell's party kicked him out of the leadership role, and that ended his political career. Holt told me that he was very proud to see that he had been right to invite me. Alas, he drowned in a swimming mishap the following year.

Apart from those who served in my country, most Americans only vaguely understand that fighting the communist invasion involved an outpouring of international support. Even many of the brave U.S. soldiers who fought for our freedom didn't know all the nations that supported our efforts. After America, by far the most help came from South Korea, which repaid its debt of honor for the help it received in repelling the communist invasion of 1950. The Republic of Korea sent two infantry divisions, with support units.

Tiny New Zealand, already committed to fighting communist guerrillas in Malaysia, sent an artillery battery plus engineer and medical units to Vietnam. Thailand dispatched a mechanized infantry brigade. About two thousand Filipino soldiers built roads and schools, drilled wells, and helped mend our war-torn countryside.

Of more importance, neighboring and nearby countries provided bases to support the war effort. None was more important than American naval and air bases in the Philippines and the USAF bases in Thailand.

As much as military support, South Vietnam needed humanitarian aid, especially medical. In 1967 we had only 859 doctors. Of these, 701 served in the armed forces, in administrative posts, as teachers, or had retired. That left 158 physicians to care for the needs of almost 16 million people! As civilian casualties mounted, our frail hospital network was overwhelmed. Medical assistance came from around the world. None was more welcome than the Australian nurses, compassionate volunteer caregivers who treated injured civilians and soldiers in provincial hospitals and in clinics they opened.

Much of this international support came as the result of U.S. diplomacy. Indeed, the seven-nation Manila Conference of 1966 was intended to show the world that the war against communist aggression was not exclusively an American effort, that it enjoyed broad regional support. As I was preparing to depart for this summit, however, I got a nasty shock: Seven ministers resigned from my cabinet. They were all young intellectual civilians whom I had appointed because I considered them both bright and compassionate. I granted them almost unrestricted power and latitude within their respective areas, and even when they moved more slowly than I had hoped, or did something in a way that I would not have chosen, I refrained from jumping in and telling them what to do. I also allowed them to appoint members of their own political party to positions in their ministries.

I believed that I had a very good working relationship with these men, so I asked each to come to my office in turn and explain his abrupt resignation. I told them that while I was sorry to see them go, I could easily replace them. Because of conscription, the ARVN's noncom corps included thousands of highly educated and experienced managers drafted from civilian careers. "I can go to the army and replace you all with NCOs," I said. "They will do a good job. But I don't want people making remarks about my 'NCO Cabinet.' " Each man seemed a little embarrassed.

"We have nothing against you—this is not personal," they said—and nothing more. They couldn't say so, but I was certain that I knew what was happening: It was the old problem of South and North. Most southerners think of themselves as open and good-natured and are wary of being cheated by northerners. In the North, southerners are seen as lazy and poor fighters.

But that doesn't really begin to describe the regional antipathy of Vietnam in that era. Think of how a Georgian might have regarded a native New Yorker in 1868, and you have some idea of how Tonkinese felt about Cochinchinese, and vice versa.

The most influential southern politicians considered me a carpetbagger, a Yankee gatecrasher. They did not want me to succeed. When I first took office, they did not expect me to be around for long—but as the summit approached, and they saw that I might well succeed, they sought ways to weaken me, to gain political leverage for their own narrow interests. My former ministers were all southerners, and by resigning en masse at the behest of party bosses, they tried to show other nations that my government did not have the support of the governed.

So once again, instead of serving their country, the best and brightest of my countrymen bowed to the forces of divisiveness. Fortunately, the ministers were easy to replace. Since I belonged to no party and needed no one's consent, I appointed a new cohort of technocrats. Most came from the ARVN, and collectively they did an excellent job. I went to Manila with a new government.

There I made or renewed acquaintances with Mr. Johnson and with Prime Minister Thanom Kittakachorn of Thailand, Australia's Harold Holt, New Zealand premier Keith Holyoake, and South Korea's Park Chung Hee. I was pleased and surprised that these statesmen, all much my senior in years, treated me both as a peer and with consideration and affection.

My wife and I were greeted warmly by our host, President Ferdinand Marcos. On an earlier state visit to Manila, Marcos had taken me aside to make sure that despite my youth, I understood the risks of power. "Always keep a suitcase under your bed," he advised. "I keep two, so I will always have enough to live on." I know that he meant well for me, but I did not stash any suitcases for a hasty departure. What would I have packed them with—socks and underwear? My children's toys?

I was on very good terms with my neighbor, Field Marshal Kittakachorn of Thailand. I also developed a warm relationship with His Majesty, King Bhumibol Adulyadej, King of Thailand. He is three years my senior, but while I grew up among the people, he was reared and educated in the traditions of the court. Because of his importance as a symbol of Thai nationhood, the king has little contact with commoners, except servants.

We met first for lunch in his royal palace, where we dined at a very long table—the king, his queen, and me. At the far end of the table sat an elderly aide-de-camp, the sovereign's most trusted retainer. Afterward this old admiral accompanied me to my car. It is quite a large palace and so we had a long walk; along the way he said, "Mr. Prime Minister, may I ask a question?" When I nodded yes, he said, "I am with my king thirty years. Where he goes, I go. I have been to many dinners and attended many state visits with my king.

"But in all those years I have never seen my king so happy as today. He drank with you, he smiled and he talked. I stood far away, and I could not hear what was said. Can you tell me what makes my king so happy?"

"Do you really want to know?" I replied.

"Oh, yes!"

I told the admiral that the king became very interested in my experiences as a pilot and as a fighter, and that he had many questions about my military service.

...

Before the opening ceremony of the Manila summit, Park Chung Hee invited me to his suite for a drink. "I came here to support you," he said. "So at the meeting, I will have nothing to say. Everything you want, everything you say, we will agree." I knew at once that this guy was different. For the last evening of the summit, Marcos organized a fiesta at Malacañang Palace. Earlier he had sent a tailor to measure us each for a hand-made *barong tagalog*, the Filipino national shirt. These fancy garments were delivered to us the afternoon before the party, but I decided that I would wear an ordinary business suit. At the fiesta, Marcos, President Johnson, and almost everyone wore the *barong tagalog*. Park wore a suit. When he saw that only we had ignored protocol, he laughed. He stood next to me and said, "You are right! You and me!"

The following year Park came to Vietnam to visit his troops. He invited Thieu and me to ride in his aircraft. As Park's English was very limited, so was our conversation. As we sat in silence, Park suddenly pointed at me. "All Korean people speak, 'You number one!' " he said.

I looked over at Thieu, sitting next to me, and I said, "No, no, I am not. President Thieu is number one."

"No, no, no, it is *you*! *You* number one," shouted Park, very emphatic. I could feel Thieu's embarrassment.

Despite an occasional faux pas, I made a sustained effort to win friends for my country. I was the first South Vietnamese leader to make state visits during wartime. Everyone before me, including Mr. Diem, either did not care about cultivating friendly relations with other states or feared to leave the country because they might be overthrown. Probably they also worried that if they went abroad nobody would want to see them!

I was also very well received in Kuala Lumpur, where Tunku Abdul Rahman, the George Washington of Malaysia, took a personal interest in me. Although he was a son of the sultan and his Thai wife, this prince disdained a life of bored leisure and became the first to unite the Malay, Chinese, and Indian peoples. He won election as chief minister of Malaya in 1955, and when the former British colony was granted sovereignty in 1957, he became its prime minister. Later he became the godfather of an alliance of Malaya with Singapore, Sarawak, and Sabah; in 1963 this new state became Malaysia. (Singapore later withdrew from the confederation.) On one of my official visits, the Malaysian government honored me with a royal title. To celebrate, the Prince entertained me in his private residence and toasted my health. Even now I may visit Malaysia without a passport!

Before my trip to Australia I visited Taiwan. One night President Chiang Kai-shek and I met privately, just the two of us in his residence. This was the man who had supported his brother-in-law, Dr. Sun Yat-sen, the father of modern China, in the struggle to modernize their country. Chiang had fought against Mao Zedong's communists for many years. He lost and, instead of seeking a comfortable exile abroad, retreated to an island province to continue his struggle. Then nearly eighty—I am younger than his son—he nevertheless treated me with respect and was very cordial.

"General, looking at you reminds me of when I was young," he said, seeming very wistful. "I remember when I attended the Whampoa Military Academy. I looked the same.

"Now I am an old man, and finished," he continued. "I hope that you will become the leader of anticommunism in Asia, because I think you can achieve what I tried to accomplish. I look to you as my heir in the cause that I have fought all my life."

I returned to Saigon determined to win the fight against the communists.

...

From a purely military standpoint, the Tet Offensive of January 1968 was a crushing defeat for the Vietcong. We destroyed or eviscerated the majority of the so-called Main Force units, organizations largely composed of southerners who over more than a decade had been trained and built into tough, battle-hardened fighters. The Vietcong were never able to reconstitute these units with southerners. Their loss meant sending in more North Vietnamese Army units.

But the most important element of our victory was the reaction of our people. The National Liberation Front, as the Vietcong called themselves, had always proclaimed that the people of my country hated their own government. The Vietcong positioned themselves as liberators and expected that when they appeared in the cities, people would stand up and follow them.

After Tet it was plain that the Vietcong were mistaken, that as much as people found fault with their government, they did not want to live under communism.

The foreign press should have been able to see what I had said from the beginning: The Vietcong were not holy redeemers, they were not popular among South Vietnamese people, they were not the wholesome nationalists they pretended to be.

The Tet Offensive invigorated the American antiwar movement. Fueled by a stream of U.S. casualties and proof that the Pentagon had lied about activities in Vietnam, it sounded a death knell for Johnson's administration. That was only the beginning: The Democratic and Republican political conventions of 1968 were besieged by chanting mobs, and despite Mr. Johnson's long efforts to reverse the tide of racism and bring equality to all his countrymen, race riots exploded in several cities. America seethed over the war in Vietnam. I have no evidence that international communism funded or in any way participated in the unrest and demonstrations, but in hindsight it is plain that nothing that the grim masters of Hanoi could have conceived would better have served their purposes.

The Democratic party nominated Hubert Humphrey, who had served as Johnson's vice president. The Republicans nominated Richard M. Nixon. Nixon's first trip to Vietnam was in 1956, when he visited the small U.S. military advisory group there and said on the radio, "The militant march of communism has been halted." He ran against John F. Kennedy in 1960 and lost. Then he ran for governor of California in 1962 and lost again. Nixon had served in Congress and as General Eisenhower's vice president, but he had been unsuccessful in his quest for another high office.

In the summer of 1965, a few months after I became prime minister, Lodge told me that his friend Nixon was planning to visit Vietnam and asked me to host a reception for him. I was happy to oblige. My first impression was that I liked this man.

He had a personality. Also, among most Asians, sounds have an effect on our thinking, like music. So perhaps it was Nixon's name, the sound of which evokes a strong image. Nixon was not as warm as Johnson, but he was different, and I got the feeling that he thought much differently from most politicians. For me, if you are different, I have some respect and interest in you. If you are average, I am not interested.

When we first met, we spoke about the necessity of stopping and containing world communism and of ways to do this. We discussed several geopolitical matters, and I found Nixon very well informed about many issues. He did most of the talking, but I saw that he knew how to listen as well. I was favorably impressed by all this. He won my respect.

Nixon did not seem to change that much when he became president. The major difference was that once he was in the White House, he no longer favored all-out war, as he had when we first met. He began to talk instead of accommodation, of reconciliation, of compromise. This was the first time that I heard an American president speak in such a way. Johnson was enthusiastic about Chieu Hoi, of reconciliation between former Vietcong, who had left the movement, and their countrymen. But that was different. After he became president, Nixon began to speak of compromise, of elections, of bringing the Vietcong into our government. He spoke about starting with elections in the hamlets and villages, then in districts and provinces, and finally at the national level.

That was when I said, "Why bother with all that? Let's challenge the communists in a general election for the presidency. North and South, the whole country. We'll field one candidate, they'll put up one candidate. Who wins controls Vietnam. Simple. The election is to show the world and the people, so let's do it. If we win, that's the end. If we lose, then okay, let the communists run things." Of course, if the communists had lost, we could be sure that they would have continued to cause trouble anyway. But my point was, let the world see who the people prefer, the communists or the anticommunists. I think we would have won.

Although I was young, I already knew that politicians cannot be trusted. So when Nixon began to change his word, began to show a new attitude reflecting a different idea, it was not a surprise. This is how politicians behave in every country. On the other hand, I never had that feeling about Johnson. I related to him as a man, as a friend, and not as a politician. That was his genius, and a quality that Nixon never had.

A few months after that reception, I slipped out of Saigon with my family to enjoy a rare weekend holiday. We went to Nha Trang, to a spacious, sparkling-white beach house that had been built for Emperor Bao Dai. Lodge called to say that another of his friends wished to meet me, a little-known Harvard professor who was visiting Vietnam for a few days. Henry Kissinger flew up and we spent a pleasant afternoon at the seaside, chatting about the war and enjoying the cool breeze. Dr. Kissinger is a brilliant fellow, very pleasant, and he made a great effort to charm my wife, to play with my children.

We spoke of many things, and he seemed very interested in my observations about the Vietnamese proclivity for conspiracy, about the often devious nature of my countrymen. Many years later, when I read the U.S. State Department summary of Henry's report, I had to smile. It said, in part:

Professor Kissinger emphasized the conspiratorial atmosphere which he said prevailed throughout South Vietnam. He had never visited a country which was so self-absorbed. During his two visits and countless conversations with Vietnamese he did not recall being asked a single question about problems outside Vietnam. He was also impressed by the amount of back-biting that went on among the Vietnamese and the value they attached to qualities like cleverness and cunning as opposed to attributes like probity and integrity which were esteemed in the Western World. He recalled a long conversation he had had with a Provincial Official in the First Corps area. The official had described with considerable pride the tricks and maneuvers he had employed at the time of the struggle movement crisis to avoid committing himself either to the Government or the struggle forces. To many Vietnamese, conspiracy had become a way of life making political stability that much harder to achieve.

As was the case with Nixon, I had no idea that Kissinger and I would meet again under such different circumstances.

As the American election of 1968 approached, neither candidate dominated. Humphrey, with his commitment to liberal policies and many years of public service, might have been more attractive to most voters, but his ties to Johnson undercut his record. Johnson was leader of the world's richest nation and commander in chief of its armed forces. In the purple prose of his political enemies, he had sent half a million well-equipped American boys to fight undernourished peasant guerrillas from tiny North Vietnam and failed to defeat them. Humphrey inherited the burden of this perceived failure.

While Nixon was known as strongly anticommunist, a distinguished public servant, he was also perceived by many Americans, and many in the U.S. media, as a stiffer, less appealing personality and as a sore loser. It was anybody's guess who would win the election.

One thing that would help Humphrey, however, was any sign that the war might soon end. To that end, U.S. diplomats fenced with North Vietnamese counterparts over commencing negotiations that could lead to peace. On May 3, 1968, not long after we had finished mopping up the last of the diehard

Vietcong in our cities, the two sides agreed to meet for talks in Paris.

Just what was to be discussed was vague. On the record, Hanoi was willing only to talk about a total end to American bombing of the North. Washington was willing to talk for the sake of appearing to talk. Washington appointed the elderly and much respected W. Averell Harriman to head its delegation, and Hanoi named Xuan Thuy. Before Hanoi would discuss anything else, however, they demanded an end to the bombing.

The bombing, of course, was the chief reason why they would talk at all. The bombing hurt Hanoi, and it strengthened the South Vietnamese cause. But the sort of bombing that the Americans engaged in could not lead to victory. The Johnson administration had carefully avoided bombing within four miles of Haiphong, where much of the ordnance fired at American and South Vietnamese boys was unloaded from Soviet and Chinese ships, and where other war matériel arrived on the ships of countries that America regarded as allies. Nor were American bombs allowed within a ten-mile radius of Hanoi. Many military targets were excluded from attack because of the possibility of civilian casualties. As they learned that the Americans were squeamish about hurting civilians, the communists sited antiaircraft missiles and other important military units next to hospitals and schools and in heavily populated areas.

The communists sent mortar shells and rockets into Saigon's residential neighborhoods. They machine-gunned refugees fleeing Quang Tri. In Hue they went house to house and rounded up innocent civilians, then shot them. In the countryside they butchered innocent children for the crime of being inoculated against childhood diseases by American medics. The Vietcong planted bombs in Saigon restaurants. Thousands of South Vietnamese civilians were killed or maimed by the communists. But the Americans did not want civilian casualties in the North.

The air war punished the North Vietnamese populace and made their lives more difficult, but it did not harm them enough that they would attempt to overthrow their government and demand peace. Instead, the bombing helped to unify support for the communist government. As long as the peasants of the North had enough to eat, they would not risk an uprising.

The Americans continued to handicap their pilots with all sorts of target restrictions. The United States lost hundreds of aircraft and pilots. While the bombing was unpleasant for the North—people died every day—even at its worst it remained for Hanoi a tolerable nuisance.

If Hanoi could get the Americans to stop the bombing without any concession in exchange, however, it would prove that America no longer had the will for victory. And if so, if the United States unilaterally stopped bombing the North, the communists believed that they could use the same lever to structure talks where the Americans and South Vietnamese would be forced to make all concessions. All they had to do was insist that no further discussions were possible until they got their way. In other words, they were willing to play with our money, but their own funds would remain in their pockets. This is classic communist strategy. Did not Stalin, as the price of allowing the creation of the United Nations, extort extra votes in the General Assembly by giving the Ukraine and Byelorussia—as much part of the Soviet Union as Texas and Minnesota are part of the United States—seats as independent nations? Surely the Americans saw it coming.

On the other hand, perhaps not. Maybe the Americans were simply unable to comprehend that there was no possibility of compromising with communists. Their way of thinking is so different. What had happened in Russia, Eastern Europe, and China and Vietnam during the years after World War II proved to doctrinaire communists that they were right, that time and history were on their side. Today, of course, a little more time and history have proven even to hard-core Marxists that while they could create a police state and control everything, and they could share misery more or less equitably, they could not make the lives of ordinary people better. Such revelation is recent; in 1968 most North Vietnamese remained true believers.

More to the point, among the powerful of Washington, just as in Saigon, were many who cared more for themselves than for their country and its allies. To put it more concretely, to them the details of a deal with Hanoi were less important than the benefits of retaining the presidency for their party. Any kind of a deal, any apparent progress toward that deal, could make a huge difference in the election—*and to them personally*.

A deal would be impossible, however, unless South Vietnam participated. Washington wanted a headline "Saigon Negotiators Head for Paris," or something like that, which would allow Humphrey to campaign on bringing the war to a swift end.

We were not quite ready for that headline. Hanoi had always demanded that the Vietcong have a place at the negotiating table, not as Hanoi's surrogate but as an independent entity. But to sit down with the Vietcong was to legitimatize them, and we South Vietnamese had spent too much blood and too many tears proving that they were not a legitimate political entity at all, merely a fiction created by Hanoi to hide its aggression.

If peace talks would help Humphrey to win the election, they would harm Nixon. Unlike Humphrey, whose supporters could apply pressure through the U.S. government, Nixon did not have access to the levers of official power.

He found another way.

He sent to Saigon the beautiful widow of a gallant airman to talk to Thieu and me: Madame Anna Chenault, whose husband had brought the Flying Tigers, American volunteer pilots, to fight the Japanese in China during World War II. She told us that Nixon was far more anticommunist than Humphrey and that if he was elected he would make sure that U.S. aid continued until the war was won. But, Madame Chenault explained, first he needed *our* help. We could help by not going to the Paris Peace Conference until *after* the election. If we refused to participate in negotiations, she explained, Nixon would be able to condemn the Democratic party and Humphrey as weaklings. There would be no light at the end of the tunnel, no hope for a quick peace.

Johnson was my friend. I trusted him to do what he said. If Johnson had asked me personally to help Humphrey, I would have honored his request and gone to Paris. But Johnson did not call me, and I did not know or like Humphrey as well as I knew and respected Nixon.

Moreover, from the outset the Americans had tried to bully us not only into going to Paris but into accepting the Vietcong as an entity equal to our government. I did not know with certainty that we could trust Nixon, but we did *not* trust Johnson's negotiators, Harriman and Cyrus Vance. I decided that circumstances were not yet right to go to Paris.

...

For many years, and even after 1975, I supposed that Thieu had been a patriot who merely succumbed to the temptations of power. I think now that from the beginning, even as a junior officer, he thought only about what was best for himself. I do not claim mind-reading skills, but he behaved exactly as if the only thing that worried him was the Americans. He seemed fearful that if they became unhappy with him, they would do to him what had been done with Diem.

Thus Thieu's primary goal became keeping the Americans happy. Each time that a confrontation with Ambassador Bunker or any senior U.S. official seemed imminent, Thieu pushed me to the forefront. I became the point man: If someone had to defy the Americans, it would be me. Obviously, Thieu hoped that if they got angry, it would be at *me*, and not at him.

I was aware that Thieu was hiding behind me. Even so, I

never objected. Whenever this happened, some friend or aide came to say, "Don't you know that Thieu did this deliberately to make you seem an enemy of the Americans?"

When I replied that I knew exactly what was going on, that I understood the game, they seemed incredulous. "Why do you do it? For Thieu?"

I did not do it for Thieu. I did it for Vietnam.

...

As the American election drew closer, the Americans, mostly through U.S. Ambassador Ellsworthy Bunker, continued to pressure Thieu to join the talks. Bunker went so far as to imply that no matter what the communists demanded as a precondition to negotiations, Thieu must agree and send a high-level delegation to Paris. Less than a week before the election, and with American help, Thieu drafted a joint U.S.–South Vietnam communiqué and attempted to slip it by both his cabinet and the National Security Council, which included, aside from Thieu and me, the prime minister, the minister of defense, and the chairmen of both houses of our congress. "If we sign this, all our difficulties with the Americans will end," Thieu assured us.

The others nodded. "Let me read that," I replied, and he passed me the document, written in English by Samuel Berger. He was a short, compact, and exceptionally quiet fellow whom I knew, only from a distance, as Bunker's right-hand man.

Intentionally vague, the document essentially committed us to negotiating with anyone about anything. "No, no, no, no!" I said. "We cannot do this!" The group discussed the communiqué and voted that Thieu should restate our objections to Bunker.

Later that afternoon Thieu asked me to come to his office. I arrived to find him with Bunker and Berger. Thieu showed me a cable from Mr. Johnson insisting that we drop all preconditions and send negotiators to Paris. "What do you think?" asked Thieu.

"No," I said. We talked a little more and then Bunker returned to his embassy to report our conversation to Washington and receive new instructions. It was not the first time that I realized that Bunker, despite the esteem in which he was held by official Washington, was no more than a glorified messenger boy, a functionary. In his memoirs, published many years later, Bunker said that he preferred dealing with Thieu, because I was "unpredictable." What he meant was, he could not control me as he did Thieu. Thieu never told Bunker no—he always had me do it. When I was unavailable, Thieu did not reply at all.

After an hour or so, Bunker returned to the Presidential Palace for more talk. He went back and forth to his embassy, and back and forth again. The sticky issue was ostensibly the shape of the table around which negotiations would take place. Hanoi demanded a round table, suggesting that all parties were equal. Of course we could not accept this. We wanted a square or rectangular table so that the two sides to the conflict, North and South Vietnam, faced each other. Hanoi could invite the Chinese or Russians, and we could invite the Americans or South Koreans or Filipinos. But the Vietcong, the NLF, was not Hanoi's ally, it was its weapon for waging war in the South, and to bring them to this table would be to support the communist lie that they were a legitimate and independent entity.

Our stubborn refusal to accept the Vietcong mirrored Hanoi's position. The North Vietnamese refused to accept the existence of South Vietnam as a nation. Our territory, they insisted, was merely the south part of their country, and our government an American puppet. They refused to engage in any discussion that would allow the continued existence of South Vietnam.

So why negotiate with a murderous enemy who insists that the only thing they will discuss is when and how you surrender? The Americans were desperate to get out. They did not care.

Food was brought into Thieu's office. I spent the night at the palace—my aide had to borrow a fresh suit for me to wear in the morning. Around 4:00 A.M. Bunker returned with a final message from President Johnson: If we did not agree to Hanoi's conditions and send a delegation to Paris at once, the Americans would halt the bombing, negotiate with Hanoi unilaterally, and cut economic aid to Vietnam.

Now we were down to the nub: an ultimatum. Thieu turned back to me and said, "What is your opinion?"

My cue. "Mr. Ambassador, we have already explained our position," I said. "We have already given you our last concession. We cannot go further. Now, if you have already decided to go forward on your own, what can I do? Tell your president to do as he decides to do."

The next day, November 1, 1968, Johnson halted the bombing and began bilateral talks with Hanoi. But nothing of substance transpired except that Hanoi had proven that it could bend America to its will.

Humphrey lost the election, but Nixon would not take office until early in 1969. By that time the Americans and the North Vietnamese had concluded tortuous negotiations to arrive at a formula for framing the negotiations. There would be three sets of delegates negotiating in Paris: the Americans, the South Vietnamese, and the communists. The communist delegation could include any people that Hanoi cared to bring, but if these included Vietcong, accepting their presence as individuals did not imply that the other delegations would recognize their affiliation as an entity. It was clumsy and deliberately vague, but we could live with it.

Thieu asked me to lead our delegation to Paris, not to participate in negotiations but to serve as the national authority so that our delegation would not need to cable Saigon for decisions. Once again he showed his cleverness. No matter how negotiations turned out—few expected that in the end the Americans would cave in to every Hanoi demand—it was plain that South Vietnam would have to give something to get something. Thieu, however, feared that if *he* accepted *any* concession, then I, backed by the military, would overthrow him. On the other hand, he also feared that if he refused *all* concessions, the Americans would kill him. By accepting the role of point man on negotiations, I became Thieu's bulletproof vest. I knew that it would take time before any meaningful negotiations transpired, so we dispatched a delegation to Paris, but I decided to wait before joining them.

Harriman was eager to start the peace process, desperate to end the war. He immediately began pressuring our delegation to accept American principles. Because of their instructions however, our diplomats would not budge. One day a frustrated Harriman asked our ambassador to the United States, Bui Diem, and Ambassador Lam Van Phat, the leader of our negotiating team, to his residence.

Then seventy-seven, Harriman had begun a long, distinguished career as an advisor to President Franklin D. Roosevelt. By 1968 he was nearly deaf, able to follow a conversation only with the assistance of hearing aids. When the two Vietnamese ambassadors were seated, he said, "For the last time, I will tell you what the American position is." He spoke for a few minutes, reiterating the American willingness to accept Hanoi's preconditions. When he finished, he reached into both ears and removed his hearing aids. He placed them on the table in front of the two ambassadors. "Now it is your turn," he said. "You can talk about the South Vietnamese position."

Had our Vietnamese diplomats been as courageous and clever at the art of deflating a tyrant as they were at attacking a soufflé, if they had responded with some brilliant riposte, I might never have heard about this incident. Instead, they called me to whine about Harriman and his bullying behavior.

I nevertheless tarried in Saigon a bit longer. When I at last decided to go to Paris, my expectations were that little good would come of these negotiations—and probably none at all. I expected a long and difficult journey, but I had to go because at this point I knew that the Americans were more inclined to side with Hanoi than with us. In other words, my purpose was to prevent the Americans from selling us out. Thieu was more than happy to see me go. Not only would having me out of the country give him more room to maneuver and further consolidate his position, but he knew that the Americans would listen to me. Also, I would be faced with the heavy responsibilities of being caught between the communists and the Americans. If I failed, and that seemed very likely, it would serve to diminish my stature, not his.

When I finally announced that I would go to Paris, Bunker was ecstatic. "Can you leave tomorrow?" he asked, and seemed very sad when I said that I could not go quite that soon.

"We will arrange an airplane for you to go," he said, when I named the day when I was ready to leave. Bunker did not seem to understand the implications of me arriving on an American aircraft: Here were the North Vietnamese insisting that there was no South Vietnam, that my government was a nonentity, mere puppets for the Americans—and he wanted me to travel to the negotiations in an American plane!

This insensitivity to appearances was characteristic of the American approach to the war. What had started as an effort to assist a struggling republic against an invasion—the original justification for U.S. intervention—had become an American war. There were hundreds of thousands of Chinese soldiers in North Vietnam, along with a significant Soviet presence, but neither the Chinese nor the Soviets called press conferences and issued statements about the progress of the war. They left that to the North Vietnamese. Instead of lowering their profile and deferring to the South Vietnamese, however, the Americans held daily press briefings, the so-called Five O'Clock Follies at the joint U.S. Public Affairs Office. The ARVN sometimes gave press briefings as well, but their content was often ignored by the American media. Of thousands of foreign correspondents who

BUDDHA'S CHILD · *297*

came to Vietnam for tours ranging from days to years, only a handful covered ARVN or VNAF combat operations. One of the few exceptions was Peter Arnett of the Associated Press—but he is from New Zealand, and was married to a Vietnamese.

In hindsight, however, I must accept some responsibility for the foreign press's disinterest in our combat operations and other newsworthy events. I met Dan Rather, Mike Wallace, and many other top U.S. newsmen, but I never bothered to discern their importance in shaping American public opinion and in turn national policy. My government should have given daily press briefings. We should have done a better job of cultivating the international media. We should have done more to show the world that we were an independent nation, not American puppets.

Even so, when Bunker offered to fly me to Paris, I replied, "I don't need your aircraft—and the Vietnamese delegation cannot go in an American airplane."

I arranged a special flight on Air Vietnam. The best plane they had was a Boeing 727, with a range of just over two thousand miles; we had to land to refuel several times. One stopover was in Tehran, where I found the foreign minister waiting with good wishes from the shah and boxes of the finest Iranian caviar.

Our next leg was to Tel Aviv. Although it was 3:00 A.M., the foreign minister received me in the VIP Lounge. Reporters were present, and when someone asked my opinion of the Israelis, I replied, without thinking, "You are very good fighters! Here you are surrounded by so many Arab countries, all by yourselves, and you have established an independent country," and so on.

A few months later, flying Air France for a second trip from Saigon to Paris, we made a stopover in Karachi. The other passengers disembarked during refueling, but I had fallen asleep and was allowed to remain on the plane. When I awoke, half an hour after takeoff, my two bodyguards told me that a group of about ten Palestinians with submachine guns had forced their way onto the plane and surrounded me, dead to the world in the last row of seats.

Facing automatic weapons, my guards decided not to draw their guns. I don't know the Palestinians' intentions, but apparently they were angry about my statement praising Israelis. Then the aircraft captain came down the aisle to confront the gunmen. "This is an Air France aircraft—French territory—and anything you do that violates French law will be treated as an act of war," he said. There was a lot of angry shouting, and finally the Palestinians got off the plane. And through it all, I slept like a baby.

But on my first trip, on Air Vietnam, when we landed at Le Bourget at 10:00 A.M., the entire diplomatic corps was waiting. After a press conference and tea, one of my aides told me that Harriman and Cyrus Vance would like to pay a courtesy visit at my quarters at 5:00 P.M.

The Americans had offered to provide the South Vietnamese delegation with everything needed for a comfortable stay in Paris, but again, because of appearances, we refused. Instead of using American autos, we bought several Mercedes-Benz sedans and rented a chateau from a French princess. I told my aide to tell Harriman and Vance that I was too tired, but he begged me to change my mind, to receive these very important men, and finally I relented. "Tell him to come," I said.

Promptly at five that evening the two ranking U.S. diplomats arrived at my residence. We shook hands and served refreshments, but before Harriman could say anything, I said, "Mr. Ambassador, I have received reports from my people about you. Before we continue, I would like to ask one question."

"Yes, what is it?" he said.

"I want you to tell me if, in these negotiations, you and the U.S. delegation remain our allies, siding with us. Or are you siding with the communist part of Vietnam? If you can confirm to me that you still are on my side, then you can talk. But we have the feeling that you're already on the other side. If that is true, you can finish the drinks and you can leave, because I have nothing to discuss with you."

Harriman stood up and shook my hand again vigorously. "General, you deserve your reputation," he said. Later he told our ambassador to Washington, "Your General Ky, the vice president. We know that when he says no, it is no, and when he says yes, it is yes. That's why I like him."

I stayed in Paris for several weeks, then commuted between Saigon and Paris for months. At that time there were many communists among the Vietnamese students living in France, and many southerners who had dodged the draft. There was also a vocal European antiwar movement, mostly among students, in Germany, England, and France as well as elsewhere. During my first stay in Paris these students demonstrated outside the building where the peace talks went on. They were countered by demonstrators with anticommunist sympathies, and often these two groups clashed. The communist sympathizers were led by a Vietnamese who earned his living teaching martial arts and who headed a street gang, and these toughs often inflicted heavy casualties on the anticommunist students. Because my bodyguards were also well trained in martial arts, the pro-Saigon element— without my knowledge—asked for their help in fighting this street gang.

Soon the street in front of the International Conference Center on Avenue Kléber was like a Chinese movie—dozens of kung fu masters whirling and leaping and pirouetting, slashing and kicking at each other. Reinforced by my men, the anticommunists chased the street gangsters away. Such battles continued for weeks.

I learned about this blood sport when my assistant came in to my office in our rented chateau to say that there had been a big fight and that French police had arrested all my bodyguards. It would have been very embarrassing if the authorities learned that these young men were part of the South Vietnamese delegation, so I asked one of my aides, who had friends among the Paris police, to try to find out what had happened. Before he could do so, however, my bodyguards came running into the compound. They had all been locked into a police van for transport to the jail; when the van stopped for a light, they broke the door down and ran away!

After more encounters, my men sent word to the gangster that they would kill him if he continued to attack anticommunist students. He moved to the South of France.

Several former French Legionnaires, veterans of the war against the Vietminh, heard that there would be an attempt on my life during a street demonstration that had been organized as a diversion for my bodyguards and the police. The Legionnaires, who knew by sight many of the key Vietnamese troublemakers in Paris, volunteered to join my bodyguard to provide additional security for our delegation. I was quite touched and accepted their offer.

I was also pleased and surprised to entertain a visitor from my past: Phan Thanh Van, the C-47 pilot who took my place flying a mission over the North. I had thought him dead, but he was living in Paris. Barely living, however, because he could find no work. I asked the Vietnamese ambassador to France to give him a job. Later I discovered that the ambassador, a Thieu appointee, feared that this brave pilot was my spy. He told Van not to bother coming to the embassy except to pick up his salary.

Negotiations, still over the shape of the table, continued daily. I remained in the chateau, where I met with my people to get their reports and to issue instructions. One day they reported a minor disagreement with the Americans, and the next afternoon Harriman asked to see me again. As always, the street outside the chateau was filled with newsmen and cameras waiting to record Harriman's arrival. Who can blame them? There was nothing else to report about the talks.

When we had finished our conversation, Harriman left. Outside he was surrounded by reporters. One asked if the dispute had been resolved. "General Ky agrees with me," Harriman said, then got into his limousine and was driven away.

When I came out later, the press asked me, "Is it true that you now agree with American position?"

"No," I replied.

"Then why did Mr. Harriman say that you agreed?"

Without thinking I said, "Well, maybe Mr. Harriman had trouble hearing me." The press peppered me with dozens of other questions, and by the time I went back inside I had forgotten about my first reply. A week or so later the Harrimans invited me to their home for dinner. I was seated next to his wife, and from her slurred speech I could tell that she had been drinking heavily. Suddenly she turned to me and said, "You know, Mr. Vice President, that you have hurt me. You also hurt my husband, but as I am his wife, you hurt me more."

I was dumbfounded. "What did I do?" I asked.

"You remarked that my husband has trouble hearing," she said, and went on to say that mentioning a person's physical disability in such a manner was hurtful.

At that moment I could not recall that I had made such a remark. I asked what I was supposed to have said, and to whom.

"It was in the newspapers," she said with a sniff, and then I remembered.

That was the moment when I realized that my words had hurt Harriman. Although, in a way, he brought it on himself by using his disability to screen out unwelcome views, it was never my intention to shame him. I wish now that I had thought to tell him that. All I could say was "Oh, you know the press. You can never trust them."

One thing I was able to accomplish was to assist Harriman in finally settling the business of the shape of the table. One day he came to our chateau on the Boulevard Maillot with a sketch of an oval table, but after one glance I knew that politically it was unacceptable. I immediately took out several sketches that I had made of tables and seating plans.

"Try these," I said. "But show them one at a time; let the communists believe they are rejecting them. At the end, take out *this* one," I added, making a small X with my pencil. "We will accept this, but make it your idea, not mine, and don't let the communists see it until they have rejected all the others."

Harriman agreed to try, and although it took a month of haggling, when he produced my marked sketch, Xuan Thuy, Hanoi's chief negotiator, bought it: a circular table twenty-six feet in diameter with no name plates, no flags, no markings of any kind. This was for the chief negotiators. The others would sit on either side at smaller rectangular tables placed eighteen inches from the center table.

Soon after this agreement was reached, however, Mr. Nixon took office. He preferred his own negotiators, and to my pleasure named Henry Cabot Lodge to head the U.S. delegation. Although I came to admire Harriman, I could never quite trust him. I had no such problem with Lodge.

...

As Thieu's term in office continued, American press and politicians began to perceive a struggle in the armed forces between what they termed the "Ky faction" and the "Thieu faction." In fact, each of us had supporters not only within the military but among the population. This reflected differences in our priorities and personalities, but it was also an indication of Thieu's steady consolidation of power. He created a political party, and although he was more subtle than Mr. Diem, he rewarded supporters with favors, promotions, and opportunities for graft. Those who owed their wealth and comfort to Thieu sought to consolidate his position. Since only I might have challenged him, they tried to undermine me.

But I personally did nothing to encourage anyone to choose sides, to support me instead of Thieu. As poor a president as Thieu was—and as his wealth and power grew his leadership stature seemed to shrivel—I knew from experience that staging a coup or promoting infighting would only make things worse.

Even though I had no formal party structure, many people continued to be attracted to my leadership. Most were relatively junior military officers. Many were students. But the illusion that there were two factions fighting each other was not true, because I would not permit my followers to undermine the war effort. Nor did I ever undermine Thieu, either in public or behind the scenes. In public I took great pains to show that I supported him, and if that meant sometimes serving as his flak vest, I did it. Whenever he was in trouble, he called on me for help, and each time I did what was asked.

...

As a top military man and the most visible leader in the national government, I felt the need to show American troops how much my nation appreciated their individual sacrifices. Thus I accepted many invitations to present medals to valiant American soldiers, sailors, airmen, and marines. While still prime minister, I was invited to visit USS *Independence*, a giant aircraft carrier operating in the Gulf of Tonkin. The navy sent an A-6 attack plane to bring me from Saigon, and after I settled into the right-hand seat, a young navy pilot, nicknamed "Bear," roared down the Tansonnhut runway and headed north. Perhaps he was a little nervous with me next to him, because after a few moments I realized that we were climbing much too slowly and the aircraft was slightly unstable. When I glanced downward, Bear realized that he had neglected to retract his landing gear.

Our flight was otherwise unremarkable until Bear began his final approach to the ship. It was to be my first carrier landing, and I was looking forward to the experience, but when Bear lowered the gear, one of the three wheels failed to lock down. We pulled up and flew over the *Independence*, whose flight deck was lined with a brass band and ranks of naval officers, all awaiting my arrival.

I found the emergency procedures manual, and together Bear and I went through the laborious work of manually lowering the gear. When that was done, we landed. The band began to play, an admiral stood waiting—and I peeled off my trademark purple silk scarf and gave it to Bear as a memento of our flight.

A few months later his wife wrote me: Bear had been shot down over the North, and was presumed dead. She said that he had called her to relate our little adventure aloft; when his personal effects arrived from the ship, she had found the scarf and wanted me to know how much he had cherished it. She also said that she was proud of her husband and understood the reasons for his sacrifice.

...

While I was in Paris as senior representative for the peace negotiations, I was invited by the Reverend Carl McIntyre to speak at a Washington rally sponsored by a group that supported South Vietnam's struggle. The antiwar movement immediately announced that they would hold a demonstration. "Don't go," advised Henry Kissinger. "If there is trouble between these two groups, if anyone is hurt, you will be right in the middle and will be blamed for any violence."

It was good advice, and I heeded it. Soon after that Nixon invited me to come for an unofficial visit to America in July 1971. I asked Bui Diem, the South Vietnamese ambassador in Washington, to plan and schedule my visit. When I told him how many staff members I would bring along, he objected that it was too many for the aircraft that the Americans planned to let me use. "You must reduce the size of your delegation and also reduce the amount of luggage," he said.

I replied that when after traveling such a great distance for such an important visit, I needed my full staff. "I will not make a trip with limitations or conditions," I said. "Why don't you ask the Americans to let me use *Air Force Two*?"

The ambassador almost choked. "Oh, I cannot do this, I cannot ask—they will never allow it. Never. Never."

"Just call them and tell them what I want," I replied. "I am not asking you, I am asking the American government." A few hours later he called to say that the Pentagon was only too happy to loan me *Air Force Two*. I was left pondering the limitations of the man who represented Vietnam in the capital of our most important ally.

I asked Nixon to add one stop to my official itinerary: the LBJ Ranch near Johnson City, Texas, where Johnson lived in retirement. Even now I don't know if I was wrong or right, but from the moment we met I believed that Johnson was a man I could trust.

My day at his ranch was wonderful, the best day of my trip, the best day I had spent in many years, the best for many to come. At lunch I was served the best steak I had ever tasted. It was so good that when I finished, I asked him, "if you don't mind, may I have one more?"

"As many as you like," replied Johnson. "The whole ranch, if that's what it takes."

Oh, that was tasty beef—and the second steak equally so. After lunch we got into Johnson's private helicopter and went to a cattle auction. I could not understand one word the auctioneer said! Afterward we flew back to the ranch and sat in rockers on the veranda, talking, rocking, talking—very pleasant. Once we were interrupted by an aide who brought papers.

"Look here," said Johnson, and I saw that the papers were

from President Nixon. Johnson was out of office, retired—and still they sent reports and asked his advice, his opinion, his reaction. I thought, How could something like this happen in my country: an ex-president, whose handpicked candidate is defeated by the opposition party, is then consulted by his political foe? I thought of Kipling, and realized that he was right, that East and West will never meet.

In those days most state visits began in Williamsburg, the restored Virginia colonial town where many of the patriots of the American Revolution met. Although I was vice president and this was not a state visit, Nixon's staff was sensitive to my feelings. I spent my first night in Williamsburg. When I arose the next morning, expecting to fly to the White House for breakfast with the president, the Secret Service told me that "several hundred hippies" were demonstrating in front of the hotel.

From the lobby I could hear them chanting pro-communist slogans. I told my Secret Service escorts that I wanted to meet with these young people. "Oh, they are very dangerous," they replied, but I insisted. I sent word that since it was very chilly outdoors, I would be happy to meet their delegation in the lobby, which was large enough to hold only about thirty people.

They came inside, apple-cheeked from the cold, boys and girls in scruffy, unwashed clothes. "Here I am," I said. "You may ask me any question."

At first it was much like Canberra: The youngsters mouthed the slogans of the Left, called me a dictator, a Pentagon puppet, a murderer. In response I told them the truth about the war, what we were fighting for. Then I replied to their questions in detail. The time flew by. After an hour, in response to repeated urging by my escorts, I held up my hand. "I am very sorry," I said, "but I am due at the White House to meet with your president, and I am already late, so I must go."

As I left the lobby, the demonstrators burst into applause!

In the car on my way to the heliport, one of my escorts said, "Our president needs someone like you to deal with demonstrators."

At the White House I was joined by Henry Kissinger, then National Security Adviser, Defense Secretary Melvin Laird, and other key members of the administration.

"What did you want to tell us?" said Nixon.

I had prepared no briefing. I thought that we would merely have breakfast, a purely social occasion. But since he had asked, I replied, "Mr. Nixon, there is a very serious problem with corruption in connection with the aid funds that the U.S. sends to Vietnam. These many millions of dollars are sent to help the poorest people improve their lives. Instead, I estimate that ninety percent of the money disappears into the pockets of corrupt American and Vietnamese officials."

An embarrassed silence hung over the table. "Um, that's a very serious matter," said the most powerful man in the world. "We need to know more about this. Send me a memo about it."

Then he changed the subject. With that, I understood that he was a complete politician. Even if I sent such a memo, he would take no action.

By this time I could see that the majority of Americans opposed continuing the war. Although I had not discussed this with Thieu or anyone in Saigon, later in my visit with Nixon, and then again with Vice President Spiro Agnew, I suggested that the United States should begin planning to withdraw its troops. "Because of the reaction of the American public against the war, someday soon you will have to make that decision. So why don't we agree that this will happen, and start planning now, so that when your troops are gone, they will leave behind very strong Vietnamese military forces that can continue the fight?" I said.

In 1966 I had made a similar proposal to Johnson in Honolulu, although couched in somewhat different terms, and he had ignored it. But as I glanced around the Oval Office I saw relief on every face, as if I had said aloud something far too difficult for any of them to mention. In fact, they responded as if I was a messenger from God! I came at the right time with the right message.

Nixon told Kissinger, I believe, to set up a meeting for me with the top Pentagon brass right way. The next day I sat down with Secretary of Defense Laird and all five members of the Joint Chiefs of Staff. As I explained my thinking, the generals became very happy. They immediately covered the table with all sorts of paperwork, contingency plans and such, all apparently written long before. Quickly we agreed on a policy of turning the war over to Vietnamese troops following a phased withdrawal of U.S. forces.

But in America you don't really have a plan or a program until it has a name. The generals began tossing out ideas, brainstorming for the right title. "We'll call it 'de-Americanizing' the war," said an army general.

"No," I said at once. "That is not the right word! To say 'de-Americanize' implies that until now it was an American war. But it is not. It is a war between the two Vietnams, and to say 'de-Americanize' gives the communists a propaganda victory. They will say, 'Until now, we have been fighting American colonialism and their Saigon puppets.'"

We discussed it a little further and then I said, "Not 'de-Americanization—'Vietnamization,'" and everyone agreed. The idea, simply put, was that the bigger older brother, America, would help the smaller, younger brother become strong enough to fight on his own. Of course, that was the original concept, dating from Dwight Eisenhower's administration, when the first American military advisors went to South Vietnam. But in those years no one recognized how big a task it would be or the size of the force that would need to be trained and equipped.

Of course, I would have preferred that the United States not only support a beefed-up ARVN but also send enough troops to allow the ARVN to invade the North and end the war on enemy territory. But I had to be practical: Given the political climate in America, the rising hostility to the war, it was unthinkable that any American president would support invasion of the North.

Over the next few years Nixon would employ massive bombing in North Vietnam. He would lift most restrictions on bombing Hanoi and Haiphong and invade Cambodia, but I am certain that he never considered that this would bring victory in the sense of a defeated enemy. No. His sole aim was to bring Hanoi to negotiate an honorable withdrawal of American troops. Like Johnson, Nixon never believed that we could win. The best outcome that they hoped for, I am sure, was a stalemate between North and South, as there was in Korea.

Later in my visit to America I flew to Los Angeles to speak to an overseas business association. The Secret Service had intelligence that an attempt would be made on my life by the terrorist group called the Weathermen. My bodyguards said that no less than three assassins, each traveling to Los Angeles by a different route, would try to kill me.

So when I arrived in Los Angeles, the police closed all the streets and freeways between the airport and the hotel. I traveled in a tight convoy of armored limousines. Over my objections, at the Ambassador Hotel, the place where Robert F. Kennedy had been assassinated a few years earlier, I was buckled into a bulletproof vest. I was brought in through the kitchen— the same route that Kennedy had taken. This time the security detail surrounded me, drew their guns, and escorted me to the auditorium.

Saigon was filled with tens of thousands of well-armed men. I usually moved around that town with only three or four bodyguards, and they never drew their guns.

I also visited the Air Force Academy in Colorado Springs, the Military Academy at West Point, and toured several other places. It was my first chance to speak with ordinary Americans and to see the wealth and vast beauty that is the United States.

Not everyone I met agreed with me. My hosts set up a Washington meeting with about a dozen leading senators; they were polite but questioned me quite sharply. Senator Ted Kennedy asked if I had any plan to help minorities, specifically Montagnards. I reminded him that as premier I had appointed a Montagnard to serve as secretary of minorities, the first such cabinet appointment. I described how I had ended armed resistance by meeting with Montagnard leaders and sending food, medicine, teachers, and many other things to improve their people's lives.

That seemed to satisfy Kennedy—but then up spoke the leading voice of the antiwar movement, Senator J. William Fulbright. "I read the history of your country and I understand that your people are very proud, very anticolonialist—you fought the French, the Chinese," and this and that, he said. "Your people don't like the presence of foreigners. So what do your people think about the presence of America?"

"You read Vietnamese history," I replied. "I read American history. During your War of Independence you called upon foreigners to help you to fight the English—Frenchmen named Lafayette and Rochambeau, Poles named Pulaski and Kosciuszko, the Prussian Baron von Steuben—and many others.

"As for the presence of Americans in South Vietnam, my people think the same way—that when we meet a friend we call them friend. America comes to Vietnam as a friend, not as a colonialist."

This seemed to make Fulbright happy.

The press was waiting outside, and a reporter asked me about my meeting with him. "Very good," I said, smiling. "We are now comrades in arms."

The next day, however, I gave a speech at the Marine Corps base at Quantico to about a thousand senior officers, including many veterans of Vietnam service. Afterward, I took questions. The Marine Corps commandant growled, "Can you explain to us how you become a comrade in arms with Fulbright?"

Fulbright was not popular among the American military, and the audience seemed anxious to hear my reply. I explained that my remark was a joke. "I have had so many nice times with politicians, you know," I said.

Near the end of my stay in America I hosted a dinner at our Washington embassy. I invited the diplomatic corps and all the American general officers who had served in Vietnam. At almost the last moment I had a thought, and I asked our ambassador to invite Henry Kissinger to this dinner. I should have known better than to ask him for such a simple thing. "Oh, we cannot," replied the ambassador. "Cannot! The dinner is tomorrow and Dr. Kissinger is a very busy man, a very important man. It is not easy to schedule an appointment with him. We can't invite him on such short notice . . ."

He went on and on for five minutes about why Kissinger could not, should not, be invited.

"Just call Dr. Kissinger and say that I, General Ky, have invited him," I interrupted. An hour later the ambassador called to say that Kissinger had accepted.

But his acceptance created a protocol problem. Where was the ambassador to seat Dr. Kissinger? Here is a man that had appeared on the cover of *Time* magazine as "the Second Most Powerful Man in America," but held no elected office. As a presidential advisor, he ranked below ambassadors and generals.

As I had half expected, the ambassador bucked the seating problem back to me. Henry Kissinger was one of a kind, I thought, no one else could compare. Then it came to me. I told the ambassador, "The table is U-shaped. I am the host, so I sit in the center of the U. My guests sit on either side, in order of rank. But we are all on the same side of the table.

"Inside the U, directly across from my seat, put one chair

for Mr. Kissinger." We sat face to face, and I believe that Kissinger appreciated the arrangement. Protocol aside, everyone knew that he was the number-one guest. We related to each other as men, exactly as we had before he was the president's advisor. I liked Kissinger, and I felt that when we spoke privately, just the two of us, I could take him at his word. He was very frank, and that was unusual, especially in a politician. And I had the sense that he trusted me.

The long flight back to Saigon gave me plenty of time to reflect on the challenges that awaited me. At the top of the list was how to transform the armed forces into a modern fighting machine that could resist the communists without American troops. The Americans were not leaving immediately, but one day they would all be gone. Would my countrymen be ready?

15

DEBACLE

EARLY on the cloudy morning of March 10, 1975, an ARVN helicopter landed at my farm and the chief of Khanh Hoa Province, Colonel Ly Ba Pham, jumped out. "General, you must help me," he said.

"What has happened?" I asked.

"Ban Me Thuot is surrounded and under attack!" he replied. This provincial capital of about 100,000 people was some forty air miles north. "The enemy has blocked the highway from Nha Trang," he continued. "The relief column from Nha Trang [on the coast south and east of Ban Me Thuot] cannot get through!"

The colonel explained that he did not have enough forces to break through from the south and that although the II Corps commander in Pleiku had ample reserves, he had refused to send help. His efforts to get reinforcements from the high command had likewise been in vain; the Saigon generals did not want to hear his pleas. "It is your responsibility to clear the road!" they told him. But most of the province chief's forces were bottled up in Ban Me Thuot. Frustrated, he came to me.

This was my first inkling that the North Vietnamese were attacking Ban Me Thuot. Defending the city, I would learn, was one understrength regiment of the Twenty-third Division, supported by a single tank battalion, a few artillery batteries, and lightly armed paramilitary troops of the so-called Regional Forces. Enemy infantry, reinforced by Soviet-made light tanks, had cut both main roads into Ban Me Thuot. Reinforcement by air was impractical: The field could not accommodate enough aircraft even to land urgent supplies.

To the enemy, Ban Me Thuot was a great prize. Its Mai Hac De supply complex held huge stores of artillery ammunition that they were eager to turn against us. Worse, this largely Montagnard city was South Vietnam's solar plexus: It straddled the junction of Route 14, which ran south from Kontum to Saigon's northern approaches, and Route 21, connecting the highlands with the coastal plain. From Ban Me Thuot the communists could roll north to take Pleiku from the rear, east to the coast to slice South Vietnam in half, or south to seize Saigon. If the city fell, national disaster loomed.

I cranked up my own helicopter and headed for Saigon.

...

Almost three years earlier, disgusted with politics, I had left Saigon to pursue the quiet life of a farmer. As the end of Thieu's first term drew near, I had inquired if he intended to run for reelection, and if so, if he wanted me on the ticket again as vice president. Characteristically, he never replied. When he announced his candidacy a few weeks later, Thieu named as his running mate Tran Van Huong, a frail, elderly schoolteacher and former Saigon mayor—a man who posed no threat to his power.

Even before this it had become clear to every member of the secret military council that far from safeguarding army solidarity and cultivating political stability, Thieu, the sly, self-serving politician, had splintered military unity by maneuvering cronies into key positions of authority. As his grip on power solidified, he no longer gave allegiance to the army, to the people, or even to his country.

Still terrified of the Americans, however, he often took Bunker's casual suggestions as orders. In a 1980 interview for the LBJ Presidential Library's Oral History Project, Bunker described me as articulate, voluble, and flamboyant, while Thieu was "enigmatic" and had "a certain solidity" that I lacked. What he meant was that if he wanted Thieu to do something that Thieu knew was bad for him, Thieu would agree but do nothing. Eventually Bunker would ask me to press Thieu for action. But if I thought that what Bunker wanted was wrong, I said so. So Thieu was thoughtful, while I was articulate and voluble.

The secret document that the council had forced Thieu to sign in 1967 was worthless: As an elected president, he was backed by the legal force of a constitution ratified by an elected congress. At best, attempting to enforce this agreement would have meant exposing a clandestine society that sought to evade the constitution. At worst, it meant a coup. Either way, the fact that Thieu had signed such a document before running for office might discredit him—but using it against him would have been construed as an army vendetta, exposed the military to ridicule, and allowed our enemies to paint our real progress toward democracy as a sham. Making such a document public probably would have sent the Americans packing. Thieu had outfoxed us.

So I kept the secret—and explored the possibility of running against Thieu. Big Minh, back from comfortable exile in Bangkok, also considered throwing his hat in the ring. Thieu used his special kind of influence with the congress to ram through a law restricting presidential candidates to those who could get written endorsements from hundreds of elected officials—congressmen and province and village leaders—a trick borrowed from Moscow and Hanoi, where opposition candidates are chosen by the party in power. Thieu had spent four years putting his own people into these positions.

In 2001 Nguyen Van Ngan, among Thieu's closest political advisors in 1971, told the Vietnamese-language newspaper *Ngay Nay (Today)* that the primary purpose of the law was to eliminate me as a candidate.

Nevertheless, with effort I was able to get sufficient endorsements to qualify as a candidate, but the process disclosed how deeply Thieu was entrenched and the lengths to which he was

willing to go to prevent competing candidates. I began to reconsider my position. I had the support of many, many people
around the country, but I suspected that Thieu would not allow
a fair vote. He had enough control over the election apparatus
to rig the results, and I felt that he would not hesitate to do
whatever was necessary to remain in power.

Before I had made up my mind about running or not, Bunker himself came to my home. I knew that the United States
was comfortable with Thieu in the Presidential Palace. He
mouthed the buzzwords that made Americans salivate, spoke in
support of democratic ideology, endorsed internal solidarity to
counter communist aggression—all the small talk that endeared
him to American politicians. There had been no coups or even
attempts since I came to office, and in Saigon sat a democratically elected president and congress. On the surface, and especially viewed from Washington, South Vietnam's political
situation was much as the United States had desired since Eisenhower sent in the first advisors.

In contrast, I had often challenged Bunker, and my re-
sponses to American criticism were sometimes vehement and
public. For example, after U.S. senator George McGovern's out-
burst describing me as a tin-pot dictator, I replied that if Mc-
Govern came to Vietnam, I would kick his ass. American officials
protested that I had used language inappropriate to a prime minister; I am told that McNamara described me as an *"unguided
missile"* (author's emphasis). Maybe so, but I was responding to
a U.S. senator. No American challenged *his* right to free speech.
How could they object to the leader of an allied country exercising the same privilege?

America's political leadership praised Thieu to the skies,
comparing him with George Washington and Simon Bolívar as
Asia's twentieth-century champion of liberty. Such statements
were received by Vietnamese and many other Asians as the sort
of syrupy pronouncements one makes over a loyal servant to

encourage his continued cooperation. Thieu was a *guided* missile, controlled by American hands to satisfy American goals. So the more I was publicly insulted by American politicians, the happier I felt. When Americans called me petty, nasty names, it signaled to the masses that I was nobody's yes man, no one's slave.

If Bunker had read any of the reports filed by Edward Lansdale, the CIA official who provided an unofficial American ear and escape valve to frustrated, out-of-power Vietnamese politicians, he knew that many Vietnamese, and especially politicians, detested Thieu.

Lansdale had been involved in the Philippines and with Diem and Nhu. By the time we first met, about 1964, he was in his late fifties but looked and spoke like someone much older. He seemed rooted in the past, unable to keep up with the pace of change. Even so, his reputation as a CIA spymaster and as a grand conspirator had preceded him. The way he talked made it plain that he was too much a thinker; I am not so much a thinker. Instead of deliberating and consulting, I act. Lansdale looked for empty vessels to pour his thoughts into, men whom he could shape—but I would not accept his advisors, I would not consult him on policy matters. When he learned that I was not receptive to his ideas, he distanced himself to concentrate on others. The first time we met, I said, "You come here with a reputation as a king maker, but don't bother yourself with me—I do not want to be king!"

Lansdale told Bunker that I was the only one who stood up to Thieu: I scared Thieu almost as much as did the Americans, and for much the same reason: He knew that if I believed that he had done something to imperil our country, I could stage a coup and shoot him.

Bunker did not have to tell me that it would look bad if Thieu ran for a second term without opposition. Such a one-candidate contest would appear little different from an election in Hanoi, Moscow, or Beijing—a sham that would erode Thieu's international support and embarrass the United States whose vast presence in South Vietnam was predicated on fostering democracy.

I never threatened Thieu, never said anything against him in public, never tried to undermine him, concealed my contempt for him from even my closest aides. I was as loyal to him in word and deed as anyone could be, and even as I gave him good advice I allowed him to use me as a political lightning rod, diverting the wrath of American officials. Many Americans, however, and especially those in the media, seized on the remarks of my friends and supporters to make it seem as if Thieu and I were at each other's throats.

There came a time when this illusion of competition could serve American goals, and that brought Bunker to my door. He said nothing about the unseemliness of a president running for reelection against himself. He merely asked me to run against Thieu. In other words, he wanted me to be window dressing, Thieu's fig leaf, the guarantor of his appearance of legitimacy. I told him that I had not made up my mind to run. "If you need money," he said, "we have two million for your campaign. We'll channel it through General Loan."

I was deeply offended at this stupidity. All I said, however—taking care to be neither voluble nor flamboyant—was "Thank you, Mr. Ambassador. The day that I decide to run, I will have no trouble raising sufficient funds from my Vietnamese supporters. I don't need your money, but thanks for offering."

After Bunker was shown out, my aides said, "Why not take it! Two million U.S. dollars!" But if I took the money and ran, I would be seen as Bunker's puppet. If I took it and didn't run, I would be a thief.

In the end I decided not to run. Doing so would have been an exercise in futility, not because I couldn't get enough votes, but because Thieu would stop at nothing to win. Also, for four years I had lent this man the legitimacy of my public support. I had had more than enough. On his own, and without consulting me, Big Minh came to much the same conclusion: that even if he got the most votes he would probably lose. According to the journalist Stanley Karnow, Bunker also tried to bribe Big Minh to run against Thieu.

Thieu ran unopposed in 1971. His election sealed Vietnam's fate.

With thirty years to ponder my judgment, and after countless discussions with other exiles, including many who once opposed me, I now wonder if my decision to withdraw from politics was correct. In 1971 I enjoyed widespread popularity and high name recognition, and with international election observers, such as those who came in 1967, perhaps Thieu would not have dared to cheat enough to make a big difference. Maybe the election would have been fair enough that I would have stood a chance. I will never know, but I add this decision to my regrets.

Thieu was cunning. He craved power, and he knew how to hold onto it. I never cared about power, and my personality was never comfortable with anger; I do not allow the triumph of foes to make me unhappy. After I decided not to run against Thieu, I also resolved not to involve myself with politics any longer. I knew, however, that if I remained in Saigon, close to supporters and friendly sources within Thieu's government, if I continued to hear the laments of disillusioned military officers and outraged politicians and to observe Thieu's behavior, sooner rather than later I would succumb to temptation; I would stage a coup and get rid of Thieu for good.

I could not return to my beloved air force; doing so would have meant either accepting a subordinate role to the officer whom I had placed in charge or pushing him aside; he deserved neither scenario. So I decided to insulate myself from temptation, to take a time out, to rusticate myself, to slip into a sort of internal exile.

As I was making arrangements, the "peace talks" in Paris drew to a conclusion with an agreement on January 27, 1973. The U.S. troop withdrawal had begun in June 1969; around the time when Thieu started his second term, in 1971 the United States removed the last of its ground combat forces. Naval and air support, however, continued until the signing of the cease-fire agreements.

Naturally, the American media asked me what I thought of the treaty. I replied, "A debacle," using the word as I had learned it in French: a fiasco. I did not say "defeat," but since the outcome of the war now depended on Thieu's leadership, I told reporters that even with nearly a million men under arms, when the time came to test its mettle, the ARVN would be no better than its commander-in-chief, that the "peace treaty" virtually guaranteed Hanoi's triumph. Thieu and Bunker responded through the media that I was jealous, that I disliked Thieu. Only half right. "Wait and see," I said, hoping I was wrong.

Soon after that I went to Khanh Duong, a tiny hamlet in the jungle-clad mountains of the Central Highlands. Vietnam then had no dairy herds and few beef cattle; most peasants, and especially children, did not get enough protein. Undernourished mothers gave birth to underweight babies. Infant mortality was so high that peasants felt the need for large families to ensure that at least one son survived into adulthood: this fact doomed most of the peasantry to poverty.

I wanted to break this cycle by growing soybeans and corn, which would eliminate the need to import them with scarce hard currency, build a factory to process grain into animal feed, then raise beef and dairy cattle, chickens, sheep. By showing my countrymen the path to modern agricultural techniques, I hoped that when the war ended the Central Highlands would become a vast agricultural center, and all Vietnamese could look forward to better nutrition and longer, more prosperous lives.

Thieu seemed glad to see me leave Saigon. He told his minister of the interior to allow me to homestead as much government land as I needed and told the ARVN to lend any equipment I requested. I borrowed operating capital from a Government development bank; I imagine that Thieu told it to approve my application, because it sailed through in days.

For three months, night and day, I read pamphlets and books from American universities and the U.S. Department of Agriculture. I learned about farm equipment, about the many different types of crops, and about using fertilizer and insecticides safely.

About a dozen military officers, likewise overdosed on war and Saigon politics, came up with me. With a borrowed army bulldozer and hand tools, we knocked down trees, cleared brush, and transformed the wilderness. Together, we set out to build Vietnam's first modern farm.

Our first big problem was water. Unlike California, with thousands of miles of aqueducts and canals to irrigate its arid regions, in the rainy season we had too much and in the dry season too little. Without consulting anyone, I designed and built a dam. Our maps were useless, so I flew over the area in my helicopter, took pictures of the topography, and in this way chose a stream. We bulldozed dirt to fill a narrow point in its canyon; in about two weeks a lake had formed behind this dam. After another month, however, there was so much water behind the dam that it burst. Fortunately, no one was hurt in the flood.

Now I realized my mistake. When we rebuilt the dam, we installed big corrugated pipes just below the top. When the lake rose to that level, the excess spilled into the streambed. Soon I had a beautiful lake and all the water we needed year round.

I had little money for machinery, but fortunately I knew a French Vietnamese businessman who had imported farm equipment before the war. There were no big farms in Vietnam, nowhere to sell such items, so he parted with his inventory very cheaply.

The jungle was full of hardwood, and we used some of what we cleared to build houses. After weeks in tents and rude shelters, we hired local people to help us, and soon I had a cozy little bungalow. The ARVN loaned me generators and a portable morgue—two large refrigerators. After cleaning and disinfecting, we used them to store meat and other perishables.

As word of my project got around, a trickle of newcomers asked to join us; soon we were about thirty men. After I taught them how to work the land and to grow specific grains, some brought their families up. My own children were still in school, and my farm was deep in the jungle so my family remained in Saigon. I used the two Hueys that General Westmoreland had given me to commute to Saigon every few weeks.

We organized ourselves much like an Israeli kibbutz, working the fields with rifles strapped to our backs and in constant radio contact. At night we sent out hunting parties, not only to put meat on our table but also to scout for signs of the Vietcong. It seems incredible, but for more than two years we had no trouble. I do not doubt that guerrillas were around, but they left us alone. This led to talk in Saigon, rumors that the Americans had made a deal to protect me. But what could you expect from politicians for whom even Saigon was not safe? When I was asked about this supposed deal, I decided to let people think what they wanted. "Of course, of course," I would reply. "Washington and Hanoi worked out the details."

In addition to corn, soybeans, and vegetables for our own use, we grew sweet potatoes and Vietnam's best sugarcane. I even got some seeds from a Brazilian and sowed big pink tapioca plants. By using machinery for everything, from preparing the ground and planting seed, to fertilizing and harvesting, we were able to plant 10,000 hectares—the biggest farm in the country.

Each morning I stepped from my bungalow to see the plants, incredibly green and healthy, sprouting and growing up, up, up. It was beautiful. After about a year, the Taiwanese ambassador—Taiwan was then known as the Republic of China—offered to send me a group of agricultural specialists. I accepted, with thanks. After their visit, however, the head of the delegation said, "General, I think we need you in Taiwan as our advisor on advanced farming techniques."

I found farm life very satisfying. Never have I slept better. People came by the thousands at harvest time to help bring in the crop. They drank my wine, slept in the fields, and made love under a full moon. Our first harvest was so big that I gave much of it to the local people who helped bring it in. Our intention was to sell the rest in Nha Trang for animal feed, but early one morning, as we were processing corn and soybeans, the province chief's helicopter landed and I learned of the communist attack on Ban Me Thuot. I got into my own Huey and headed south to Saigon.

In Saigon I went to the ARVN chief of staff, General Cao Van Vien. As we discussed the situation, he confirmed that there was an attack on Ban Me Thuot and that he feared a general offensive.

"So what about Ban Me Thuot?" I asked.

"Very difficult," he replied. "We can't spare many troops because we need to defend Saigon."

"I don't need a lot of troops. Just give me a couple of battalions of marines or paratroopers and a column of tanks—twenty or twenty-five, one armored company—and I will try to break through."

I went on to explain that there were ARVN tanks near my farm, and fire support was available from the VNAF and from II Corps artillery units. "I will ride in the first tank, not buttoned up out of sight but standing in the hatch with my flag so everyone knows who it is, and go directly to Ban Me Thuot," I said.

The troops knew me, appreciated my war record, and I was sure that my presence would lend them courage. They would follow me. "Wherever I meet the enemy I will fight them," I said. "This is the only way to break the siege or at least reduce the enemy pressure and buy time for Ban Me Thuot.

"Do you think that I could succeed?" I asked Vien.

There are never guarantees on the battlefield. I might die in the first minute of the attack. But as I had been ready to die leading the first air strike on the North, so too was I ready to die leading this tank column. What was the alternative, do nothing?

"If it is you leading this force, I think so," said Vien.

"Then let's do it," I replied.

"Unfortunately, I am not in a position to make such a decision," said Vien. "That is up to President Thieu."

"Okay, call Thieu, say that I am here with you, and tell him what I have offered. Give me a time, give me some tanks, and I will go to Ban Me Thuot. I am ready to die for you, understand?"

Vien called Thieu, but the chief of staff could not speak to his commander in chief. Vien left a message with an aide, who called back to say "The president thanks General Ky very much for his offer, but he needs time to think about it."

Is twenty-seven years long enough for such a decision? I am still waiting for Thieu's answer. Probably he was more afraid of what I might do in Saigon with a column of tanks than of what the enemy might do to his country.

In fairness to Thieu, however, years later we would learn that ARVN intelligence reports coming into Saigon at this time passed through the hands of a certain senior sergeant in ARVN headquarters. This Vietcong spy created fictitious North Vietnamese divisions that he showed occupying positions near Pleiku. The II Corps commander thought that he was surrounded.

On the other hand, months earlier, CIA intelligence reports indicated that the highlands could not be held unless the ARVN dramatically altered its defensive strategy. The American CIA chief did not send these reports to Washington; for unknown reasons, he held on to them. But the CIA gave Thieu an American plan to evacuate Ban Me Thuot. Thieu agreed to consider it. He never responded.

Even as far back as the war against the French, every military expert considered the highlands the key strategic area, far more important even than Saigon. Thieu's response, once the attack on Ban Me Thuot began, was to pull the Airborne Division, his best troops, back from I Corps in the north to defend Saigon, where *he* was, along with all that he held dear. As remaining I Corps units began to realign themselves to defend the area vacated by the Airborne Division, they came under attack. Few, if any, fought for very long. Most began pulling back, heading for Saigon. Thus the debacle began.

Soon after Thieu spurned my offer to open the road to Ban Me Thuot, the city fell. Among its residents were the families of most of the Twenty-third Division's soldiers. Thieu then ordered a counterattack to retake the city "at all costs"—but sent no armor. With the roads in enemy hands, the II Corps commander, General Pham Van Phu used helicopters to put five infantry battalions of his Twenty-third Division into a landing zone east of Ban Me Thuot. They landed in the open, exactly where the enemy expected them. In four days the North Vietnamese Tenth Division, supported by tanks and with plenty of artillery, destroyed what was left of the Twenty-third Division and the Twenty-first Ranger Group.

Instead of sending the still powerful II Corps forces at Pleiku to fight their way south through enemy forces holding Ban Me Thuot, on March 14 Thieu ordered these units to withdraw from Pleiku to the coast down Provincial Route 7B, an abandoned and almost impassable track clogged with refugees. This stupid act of desperation was aimed at saving what was left of our forces in the highlands. Once the troops started heading south, however, the enemy repeatedly ambushed the column. Officers deserted their commands, and their troops scattered to the winds— the "strategic withdrawal" became a rout. Hanoi's estimate, made weeks earlier, was that it would take at least three more years to win. The communists expected to fight their way south, paying a price for every mile. As ARVN resistance in the highlands evaporated, the enemy began maneuvering to attack Saigon.

I could not return to my farm with so many enemy forces menacing the area. More importantly, I was needed in Saigon. I did not yet suspect how quickly things would end. We had nearly a million men under arms, and I expected that many would fight well. Surely, I thought, America would not allow a slaughter. The terms of the Paris Treaty allowed the United States to replace Vietnamese military stores existing before the treaty was signed—but the U.S. Congress had refused to vote much money for spare parts, fuel, and ammunition. Surely now, I thought, they will send assistance. It never came to my mind that I might someday have to leave my country. I saw a fight to the finish, win, or die on the battlefield trying.

In Saigon, I spent my time trying to regroup, telling anyone who would listen not to run away, to stand their ground. As quickly as Thieu's pullback began, the politicians and even many in the army realized that he was a politician, a schemer, but no fighter—and that he was finished. When word got around that I was back in Saigon, a river of civilian politicians, leading Catholics, important Buddhist monks, colonels and generals, labor unionists—all of whom had supported Thieu—came to my home. Even my worst enemies begged me to do something. "You are the only one who can!" they said.

I held a press conference to call upon Thieu to form a new

cabinet, a "National Preservation Government," and to appoint ministers representing opposition parties, including me. For this and other constructive suggestions, Thieu had immediate answers: No, no, no. That was the only response from one who kept his suitcases ready. Thieu was preparing to flee the country. Sharing power would only complicate his escape.

Thieu was unhappy with my words. A few days later one of my pilots burst into my home. Gasping for breath, he said that he had seen a man lurking nearby, and challenged him. The man took off and the pilot went after him, eventually bringing him down with a football-style tackle. This fellow was armed and carried a pass that allowed him to enter any area on the base.

So why did he run?

I had the man brought to my office. After he understood that we meant business, he admitted that he had been sent to watch me and to kill me when I left my house. Who sent him? General Dang Van Quang, the former warlord of IV Corps whom I had fired years before for corruption and who now worked out of the Presidential Palace as Thieu's advisor. The VNAF commander, General Tran Van Minh, told me that Quang had requested fifteen identity cards of the type normally issued only to security police. Perhaps Quang's intentions were mercenary: With the access permitted by these cards, he could have put almost anything on an aircraft, and he could have taken almost anything off the base. Suspecting that he had something else in mind, however, I sent my men around to round up all Quang's infiltrators.

By April even the Americans could see that Thieu was finished. Major General Charles Timmes, who had made a lot of friends among the Vietnamese military, began acting as a sort of liaison officer between me and the U.S. Embassy. Timmes was CIA, and every week he came to my house to brief me on the military situation. One day he called to say that he would like to see me that afternoon. When I agreed, he dropped the other shoe: He wanted to bring "a friend."

This "friend" was U.S. Ambassador Graham Martin. When I opened my office door and saw who it was, Martin said, "I think you are surprised to see me here."

"No," I said. "Why would I be surprised? I have been expecting you, and I know just why you came."

In truth, I was a little annoyed by Martin's delusions of grandeur. He was not the first U.S. ambassador to visit my home, and every such emissary whom I had met was no more than a glorified messenger acting on his government's instructions. America was not Imperial Rome, and Martin was no proconsul. Henry Cabot Lodge and Averell Harriman, two very different sorts, each had the grace to understand this, but Martin seemed very impressed with himself, as if he were a god, an incarnation of the Buddha, mingling with mere mortals. He should have been surprised that I agreed to see him.

He sat down and asked, "If you were to become premier again in the present circumstances, what will you do?"

"First we must stop the enemy advance," I replied. "Stop them, and from there we can talk, offer concessions or accommodations, whatever—but first we must stop them. But if this debacle continues, there will be nothing to discuss."

"What would you do about Thieu?" asked Martin.

"I don't have time to think about Thieu or anyone else, and I don't care if he stays or goes."

As he said good-bye, Martin turned back and said, "I'm very happy with your response. Give me a few days to get Thieu out."

Three days later General Timmes returned, alone. "Is it true that you and some of the other officers are trying to do something against Big Minh?" he asked.

"No," I replied. "But why Big Minh? Why would I move against *him*?"

"I'm happy to hear that," he replied without answering my

question. "Because if anything happens against Big Minh, Washington and Hanoi will blame you."

"Ah. Now I understand," I replied. After Thieu bailed out, Minh was to act like the receiver in a bankruptcy: Sign the papers and hand over the assets. "If Big Minh becomes leader of South Vietnam, the communists will arrive in Saigon within twenty-four hours," I added.

When Timmes did not argue the point, I knew that America had washed its hands of its problems in Southeast Asia. We Vietnamese were on our own, but it was not necessarily the end. There were things that might yet be done to save at least a remnant of my country. This was not the time to argue or even to think about the symbolic slap in the face Timmes had delivered. As I would learn later, Washington had brokered a deal with Hanoi via the president of France. The communists would accept Minh in the Presidential Palace: They knew that he wouldn't be there long. It would have been difficult for them to accept someone like me. So Minh made his own deal, and I could do nothing about it.

After my earlier conversation with Martin, when he had raised the possibility that I might again lead the country, I had called my closest military friends. We came up with a plan. It was too late to consider trying to retake the northern provinces, so we borrowed a page from Chiang Kai-shek's playbook. With most of his forces intact, he had withdrawn across the strait to Taiwan. *We* would move south to the Mekong River Delta and take up positions south of the broad Dong Nai River, which formed Saigon's southern boundary. Then we would destroy all the bridges, so that the enemy could not follow us across.

But there were at least 150,000 enemy troops converging on Saigon, and we would need time to get across the river. I made a speech in which I called upon the young and able to volunteer and to turn Saigon into a second Stalingrad. We would evacuate the old and sick, women and children, but everyone who could fight would stay in the Saigon area to fight one more big battle, to punish the enemy and stall the offensive long enough for our troops to reorganize and establish a strong line of resistance. We would give our lives, if necessary, to prove that Vietnamese are not cowards. We would fight on, house by house, street by street, until the world had to admire what we were trying to do. As I spoke, many young officers began to weep. They said, "Oh, yes, we are ready to die with you."

After my speech an American reporter laughed in my face. The press lampooned my idea. My volunteers evaporated, and an air of desperation gripped Saigon. Those with money stood in line to flee the country. Anyone who could wangle a seat on an outgoing flight did so.

Meanwhile, VNAF aircraft from Da Nang and other bases that had been captured landed in Tansonnhut. Some of these were cargo planes commandeered by ranking army officers to haul their furniture and personal belongings, but others were flown by combat pilots hoping to save their planes from the enemy. About ten Skyraider pilots from other bases landed at Tansonnhut, where they flew sorties all day and into the night, returning to rearm with ammunition and bombs. They bedded down in my house, and my home office became a sort of un-official operations center, an annex with telephonic liaison with base operations. One night while we were eating, Operations called to say that the enemy was attacking the vast army head-quarters and supply depot at Long Binh. Our defenders needed air support. I turned to the pilots sitting around my kitchen ta-ble. "You, you, okay, you, pom, pom, pom!" After they came back to rearm, I sent them out again. Thus I spent my last days in Vietnam as an air force officer, doing what I knew best: carry-ing the fight to the enemy.

The most powerful weapon in our arsenal was an American-made cluster bomb. As this half-ton bomb sailed over its target, it released hundreds of small bomblets, which spread over a very wide area before each exploded into hundreds of pieces of shrapnel. One aircraft with a few cluster bombs could kill everything within a square kilometer.

Because it was so powerful, however, Thieu feared that someone might drop one on his palace; permission to use a cluster bomb required his personal order. One day Operations called to say that an enemy division had encircled one of our bases. Our people asked for air support, but there were so many enemy troops that only a cluster bomb would be of any use.

I had none on hand, so I asked the air force commander. He said that he had no authority to authorize their use. I asked the chief of the joint general staff; his answer was the same. I called several generals, and each said they had no authority. I knew that if I were to ask Thieu, he would have to consider his answer for a while, so I called the prime minister, Tran Thien Khiem.

"It's up to you," he replied after I had explained the situation. "Tell them that I'm okay with it."

I called the chief of operations back and said, "Okay, use it." He accepted my authority, and the resulting air strike was the last time we inflicted major casualties on the enemy.

I share this story to illustrate the sad state of our military. No one was in charge. No one accepted responsibility. And when a decision was needed there were no fighters. In a crisis, everyone came to Marshal Ky.

This was not because my countrymen are stupid, lazy, or cowardly. It was not because the Vietnamese soldier was incapable of fighting. It was partly due to Thieu's leadership, of course, but mostly it was the legacy of Vietnam's long, bittersweet relationship with America.

America is the leader of our world. Because its national destiny is its great and unrivaled strength, people around the world must rely on the United States. If Americans knew how to deal with other people, they could bring peace to the world. Alas, they have not learned enough yet. The true American feels that he is 100 percent welcome anywhere he goes; the way Americans understand and treat other peoples almost guarantees that the world will suffer more trouble. I say this not as angry critic but as sorrowful friend, as one who understands and admires America and Americans, as one who has enjoyed America's great generosity and warm American friendships in ways that no other Vietnamese leader can claim. I have been blessed often by Buddha, but equally by America.

So when I am offended by an ignorant American, I remind myself that he probably means well, that if his behavior is not entirely correct, it is because his cultural expectations and experiences are mostly limited to dealing with other Americans, who share similar sensitivities, priorities, and history.

Of course, there were many in Vietnam, as in other nations, who rarely reflected on how Americans saw things or on what was wrong or right. People like Thieu and his cronies, for example, were willing to accept the American point of view because it offered them a path to personal enrichment. But Americans should understand that for every Thieu there are thousands more who expect to be treated as equals, even if they were not born in the United States, even if they are small and brown and eat strange foods and worship gods of whom Americans have never heard.

When the American military left Vietnam, they pointed with pride to an ARVN of 1 million men, a VNAF that was the world's fifth-largest air force, and second or fourth in this or that capability. They had much less to say about the leadership of these forces. They could never admit, even to themselves, that a million armed men were led by a group of venal toadies, with Thieu serving as the prototype, officers who could never say no to

America and who felt that if they did not please the Americans, they would lose their positions.

When Westmoreland first came to Vietnam in 1965, I was still the air force commander. On a courtesy visit to my office, he asked my opinion on ways to improve the ARVN. My answer: "You have to demobilize or retire all the old general officers—every one of them." I thought he would ask why, but instead he just stared at me as if I were crazy, then changed the subject. Here is what I wanted to tell him, although he should have known it:

All those senior officers had served the French. They belonged to the era of colonialism, when the French promoted not those who displayed courage or initiative but those who served as their most loyal puppets. The French taught them that what was best for France was best for Vietnam, that white Europeans had a monopoly on brains, that the French way was the right way. A few of the brightest officers went to the military academy, but even they got no significant military experience. They were administrators, lower-level staff officers—bean counters. Most dressed and acted like French officers. When the French went home, they became comic-opera generals: extraordinary drinkers, graceful dancers, masterful chasers of girls. They spoke beautiful French, though some had trouble with Vietnamese, and few had any idea what it meant to be a fighter. The best would have struggled commanding a division or even a regiment. And they were, to a man, corrupted. From this group came Thieu and those in charge of his million-man armed forces!

Every military man knows that if you have 1 million brave soldiers but put them under cowardly commanding officers who run away from battle, the million will run right after them. That was our situation: We had many brave soldiers—I know that from personal experience—but when it came to leaders, we had too few. Under Diem and later under Thieu, promotion did not reward the best fighters. The officer who stood up to his American advisor when that advisor was ill informed or muddle-headed often did not retain command.

Proof of the Vietnamese fighting man's prowess was the Tet Offensive. Surprised, initially outnumbered, and under fierce attack, the ARVN closed ranks and fought. From the top down, senior officers led by example, sharing the risks of battle. All the way down the line, Vietnamese soldiers fought bravely. We kicked the Vietcong out of our cities, we kicked their asses. The little Vietnamese soldier will fight hard under good leadership.

I believe that nearly every American advisor came with honest and pure intentions to advise his Vietnamese counterparts. But over the years a few dozen advisors grew to become tens of thousands, and as the American commitment became bigger and bigger, their own chain of command put pressure on them to show results. The higher the level at which an advisor worked, the more that was expected of him. Each advisor prepared regular reports on his activities and sent them up his chain of command. American captains and majors learned that if the colonels and generals whom they advised were described as intelligent, cooperative, and eager to fight, these qualities would reflect, in part, their own performance as advisors. Advisors whose Vietnamese counterparts were brave tigers got medals and career advancement. If the commanders they advised was stupid, corrupt and cowardly, however, those advisors risked poor efficiency reports and being passed over for promotion.

Even so, I think that most U.S. advisors had the integrity to resist these pressures. At the highest levels, however, where the U.S. advisor was a colonel or a general, the pressures were greater, and he had far more to gain or lose. Most senior Vietnamese officers were concerned only with pleasing their advisor. They told the American advisor whatever they thought he wanted to hear. When advisors went home, they usually received the highest decoration, a medal that only their Vietnamese counterpart was in a position to recommend. Such decorations were important to careers, so many American advisors promoted their own interests by reporting that an ARVN general was terrific and ran a crack unit. Ninety percent of senior Vietnamese commanders were repeatedly lauded by their Americans advisors.

These were the officers who presided over the debacle that started with Ban Me Thuot and ended with enemy tanks crashing into the grounds of the Presidential Palace less than two months later. A famous wire service photograph tells the whole story: A long stretch of asphalt highway, otherwise vacant, is littered with hundreds of pairs of empty combat boots. If Thieu had kept even five or ten smart, brave generals—just a few good men—the million-man army that the Americans trained, equipped, and left behind would not have melted away, its terrified soldiers tearing off uniforms and boots and desperately trying to pass themselves off as innocent farmers.

There is another lesson to be learned from our debacle: Americans come from a wealthy and confident army. We Vietnamese regarded them as big brothers who had come to help us. There was a language barrier; few Vietnamese spoke good English, and far fewer Americans spoke understandable Vietnamese. Often it was faster and easier for the big brother to do something than it was to show the little brother how to do it well. Especially at higher levels of command, many Vietnamese officers lacked the knowledge or courage even to attempt most modern military procedures. They preferred not to embarrass themselves by failing, so often they simply let the big brother do it for them.

This happened every day in the army, the navy, the air force, the marines. Fire support planning? Maintenance? Facility construction? Combined arms operations? The Americans were well schooled in such matters, had trained for years in the small details that are crucial to success. It was mostly new to us Vietnamese. But if you have a big brother who knows how to do everything and is impatient to put into practice what he has learned in training, let him do it! Maybe not everything, but 80 percent, and you do the rest. It is like a relationship between husband and wife. If the husband does the dishwashing well and enjoys it, the wife says Okay, you do it. It is a small thing. But do these small things day after day and they become routine. Thus the ARVN became dependent on its advisors.

Worse, the U.S. military introduced the Vietnamese to warfare, American style. American soldiers fought hard, and no one can disparage their courage or individual commitment. But while we towed artillery behind trucks, and were thus confined to roads, the Americans slung guns beneath choppers and dropped them on inaccessible mountaintops to fire down at the enemy. That this consumed much expensive fuel and precious jet engine hours did not trouble them; they had plenty of resources.

The big, strapping American GI carried a light, fully automatic Colt M-16 rifle into combat with hundreds of rounds of ammunition, a match for the enemy's AK-47 assault rifle. Until after the Tet Offensive of 1968, our small soldiers carried heavy, eight-shot American M-1 rifles so obsolete that the U.S. National Guard did not want them.

While our troops in the field were often forced to forage for food, American combat troops got a hot meal nearly every day—on Thanksgiving, every GI in Vietnam dined on turkey and all the trimmings! A U.S. combat ration, one meal, contained 3,800 calories—almost twice what a typical Vietnamese soldier got for a whole day.

Americans built bowling alleys and movie theaters on their bases, stocked their post exchanges with the best and cheapest consumer goods, made sure there was plenty of cold beer when the troops came out of the field. And after a year, the American soldier went home to his family. We had no post exchanges, no movies, no cold beer, and we fought for the duration, for twenty years, for however long the war continued, until death, disease, or disfigurement ended our service.

So we let our big brother, who was capable and eager, do as much fighting as he cared to. When the Americans finally went home, they left us knowing that there were easier and more comfortable ways to fight—but they were not available to us. This did not elevate troop morale. Quite the contrary.

I must add that the air force was much different. We had USAF advisors, but in general our pilots and commanders were their equals in intelligence and flying skill. Most Vietnamese pilots had more flying time than their American advisors, and certainly we knew the terrain and flying conditions far better. We were true comrades in arms; the USAF advisor's role was not about guiding our day-to-day operations, it was about making it easier to integrate our combat and logistical activities with American forces. Provided with consistent good leadership, our airmen fought to the bitter end, displaying not merely technical proficiency but the greatest courage. Here is more proof that with leadership, we Vietnamese fight well. But of course, even the VNAF had a few traitors.

...

On the morning of April 8, 1975, VNAF First Lieutenant Nguyen Thanh Trung, flying a Northrop F-5E Tiger II fighter-bomber, took off from Bien Hoa, flew south to bomb Thieu's palace, then headed north to land at Phuoc Long, where he defected to waiting Vietcong. The bombs did little damage.

Nevertheless, by late April Thieu was gone, along with, I am told, seventeen *tons* of luggage and many millions in cash. Contrary to rumor, he did *not* abscond with the national gold supply. He did not need it. When Big Minh became president a few days later, on April 27, I realized that I might soon find myself fighting him as well as the communists. I did not want to have to worry about my family, so that night I told my wife, "Tomorrow, take all the children and leave the country." At that time six children, from both of my marriages, ages ten through twenty, lived with me. My other daughter was in America with her mother and stepfather.

But how was my family to get out? American planes, commercial and military, still flew out of Tansonnhut. But because we had not anticipated leaving, we had no plan, no reservation, no tickets, no papers, hardly any money. Exit visas and airline tickets were changing hands at astronomical prices; anyone with money enough for a ticket even at regular prices was desperate to leave. Even I could not arrange a ticket. But my wife is very resourceful, and her face was known by many Americans. I told her, "Just go to the civilian air terminal and find something." So I put them in Buddha's hands, and we said good-bye.

Soon after they left, I heard a powerful explosion. With two or three bodyguards at my heels, I jumped into my Jeep and went to see what had happened. Tansonnhut was a ghost town. No air traffic moved on its runways, roads and streets were empty, not a living soul was in sight; my Jeep was the only thing moving. The eerie calm was shattered by the bruising shriek of jet engines at low altitude. I looked up as a pair of A-37 Dragonfly attack planes shot by. I didn't know it yet, but they had been captured when Da Nang fell; the lead plane was flown by Nguyen Thanh Trung, recently of the VNAF, and the newest captain in the North Vietnamese Air Force.

Driving an empty highway, I saw the lead plane bank to line itself up on the road. In the blink of my mind's eye, I saw myself at the A-37's controls, hunched forward, peering though the gunsight, gloved trigger finger caressing the firing button of my 6,000-round-per-minute electrically driven minigun, aiming the aircraft. No way I could miss that Jeep.

My Jeep.

Ayah!

I stood on the brake, then threw myself into a roadside sanitation ditch. An instant later my Cambodian Vietnamese bodyguard landed on top of me. Over the distinctive, low-pitched growl of the Gatling minigun, he chanted Buddhist prayers in some incomprehensible dialect. A lethal whirlwind whined down the road, then Thanh Trung howled by.

No bullet hit my Jeep; Trung's bombs had missed Thieu, and all his shots flew wide of me. After flunking bombing, he struck out strafing! Had I been his commander, he would have been flying a desk. He is now chief pilot for Air Vietnam.

Minutes later I encountered Major Dam Thuong Vu, an F-5 pilot. I told him to find a wingman and bring down those A-37s. The F-5s scrambled in minutes, but without ground-based radar to help locate them, the A-37s escaped.

By late that afternoon about four hundred civilian refugees had packed themselves into my house. It was wall-to-wall bodies, barely enough room for everyone to lie down. But I could not turn them away. These desperate people had heard rumors: If you want to escape, go to General Ky! If you need help, find General Ky! All these years later, I marvel that so many people felt that they could rely on no one else.

I had not slept in days, so at nightfall I lay down and fell at once into deep sleep. I was jolted awake by the impact of dozens of huge Soviet-made incendiary rockets raining down on the air base. These were followed by enemy artillery firing hundreds of high-explosive and antipersonnel shells that burst on and above the base. Among the first buildings hit was the hospital, which erupted in flames. The barrage went on and on, my house shaking and shuddering with each nearby concussion.

The launchers were so close that we could hear the *whoosh* of the rockets as they took flight, dozens at a time. In the other rooms women and children wailed in terror, knowing that death was coming, that nothing could stop those rockets. Many lost control of bowels and bladder. Soon the stench was overpowering. The bombardment continued through the night; many base buildings, including the homes of all my neighbors, were consumed by fire or demolished by blast. By Buddha's grace, my house and all in it were spared.

Early in the morning I received a radio call from a paratroop unit commander. "Sir, I am now at your farm," he said. "My men are hungry, and you have a lot of meat in your refrigerators here. Will you allow us to use some of it?"

"Of course," I said. "Take all you want. Take it, eat it."

"Thank you, sir. This is such a beautiful place. And I congratulate you on the dam—the engineering is wonderful."

There was a polite fellow. I wonder what became of him.

The rocket bombardment resumed at nightfall on April 28. After half an hour I had had enough of being a target. I found my helicopter, miraculously unscathed, and with a few bodyguards took off. Aloft I made radio contact with two Skyraiders coming up from the delta. I had no codes, none of the usual radio operating instructions, not even a call sign. I spoke in the clear: "Here is General Ky, do you roger?"

"Oh, yes!" came the response.

I showed the pilots where the enemy rocket battery was and told them to annihilate it. After their bomb run, they came back on the air and said that they had two bombs left. "Go back and drop them—make sure that you destroy them," I replied.

After they had done this, I said, "Land and come to my home and have a drink with me." But the runway was littered with burning aircraft; much of the airport was in flames. I radioed again to say "Okay, then tomorrow. Either I will come to see you, or you come back here and have a drink with me."

I put down for a few hours' sleep. At dawn I returned to the air and flew the whole day and the whole night, watching South Vietnam's death throes, giving target guidance to our remaining warplanes, landing to talk to our troops, watching the enemy's inexorable advance.

By 6:00 A.M. I was nearly out of fuel. I still could not land at Tansonnhut; the fueling area was afire. Just outside Saigon, I knew, was a Shell petroleum depot. As I approached it I counted ten helicopters, some circling, some on the ground. By the time I had refueled, we were more than twenty. I had everyone land and gathered the crews together. They sat or knelt in a semicircle around me. I told them that those who had no ammunition were to refuel and head south, find a place in the delta to set down and wait for orders. Those who had machine-gun ammunition or rockets were to fly around Saigon and look for enemy targets of opportunity. "Fire off all your ammunition," I said. "Make every bullet and every rocket count. Then go south and wait for orders."

About 8:00 I flew back to Tansonnhut and set down on the football field near Air Force HQ. Lounging around the area were hundreds of officers and airmen. I found the VNAF commander in his office with about ten other top generals, mostly ARVN, and a U.S. liaison officer. They were waiting for a signal so they could leave on a U.S. flight.

Now I felt that it really was the end. In desperation I got back into my Huey and flew to the headquarters of the general staff, landing in an empty parking lot usually full of staff cars and Jeeps. I went upstairs to the office of the chief of staff. Gone. Only one general remained, and when I asked him about the situation, he said, "It's the end." I asked him to call the navy commander. No one answered the phone. We called the marine commander. No answer. I called the VNAF commander, with whom I had spoken less than an hour earlier. The sergeant who took the call said, "The general has left for the American side of the base."

I sat behind a desk and tried to contact someone I knew, anyone, to see if we could still continue the fight. Around 2:00 P.M. one of my aides said, "You see, General, everyone has gone. The enemy is here already." I listened for a moment and the faint rattle of small arms seemed to come from every direction.

With me were my staff and bodyguards. "We think it is also time for you to go," said one. "What more can you do now?" I realized that he was right. There was no point in staying, no use in further resistance. But go *where*? Earlier, when I had telephoned army headquarters in the delta, someone there said, "It's too late, the enemy is all around us." My Huey's range was just over two hundred miles, not enough to reach Thailand. But unless I had a death wish, I had to leave Saigon soon.

We climbed into my aircraft, thirteen Vietnamese in a gunship built to haul six or seven Americans. Men perched in the doorway, feet dangling over the side. Before the engine was warm enough for flight, General Ngo Quang Truong appeared. He saluted me. Here was the I Corps commander, extolled, lauded, glorified—all but deified—by his American advisors as the second coming of George S. Patton. His crack divisions had melted before the enemy advance like summer snow.

"What are you doing here?" I shouted over the engine.

He shrugged his shoulders. "I don't know."

"Has your family left?"

"Yes."

"So you have no way to get out?"

"No."

"Come with us," I said. "We will make room."

"But I have my aide—can you bring him too?"

Somehow, we did.

Without a destination, we lifted off. Swooping low over Saigon, we had our final look at the city we had called Hon Ngoc Vien Dong, "the Pearl of the Orient." Smoke from a thousand fires soiled the sky, and the broad avenues, always choked with traffic, were vacant and littered with rubbish.

I headed toward the sea. When there was a little altitude

beneath us, I tuned to the international distress frequency and called, "Mayday, mayday, mayday."

In moments a U.S. Navy radioman on the aircraft carrier *Midway* replied. I identified myself as a VNAF helicopter pilot, and he gave me a heading. Eyeing my compass, I flew south and east, the sea fading from clear emerald to dark blue. Behind us Vietnam dwindled to a dark smudge on the horizon, then vanished, leaving only water and sky. Finally, I had time to wonder if my family had somehow escaped Saigon.

On and on we flew; more than an hour passed, but the sea remained limitless and empty. At the point of no return, when there was not enough fuel to go back, I began to consider that I might have to ditch. I thought about the procedure, about hovering to let the others jump out, then moving away so they would not be cut to pieces by the rotor blades, about how long a Huey might float upright. We had neither life jackets nor rafts, and in a few hours it would be dark, but I was confident that the U.S. Navy would search for us. Well, fairly confident.

Suddenly a faint blotch appeared. Half hidden by cloud shadows, it resolved itself into the *Midway*, its bulk and speed throwing a foamy bow wave, escort vessels splayed out over the deep to either side. Was ever there anything more beautiful?

As the *Midway* grew big in my window, I unbuckled my old .45, the ivory-handled revolver that I had carried throughout the war, a gift from actor John Wayne. Our hosts would have to disarm us, I realized, and I wanted to spare my men this indignity. I tossed my prized sidearm into the sea, and the others threw their weapons after it.

I stepped onto the deck of the *Midway*, and when everyone had followed, a dozen sailors unceremoniously shoved my Huey over the side. Peering westward, I saw dark specks approaching from every direction, dozens of planes, and I understood: There was no room aboard for so many aircraft.

An American officer said that his skipper wanted me to come to his office. The captain's chest displayed the gold wings of a naval aviator and below them rows of ribbons denoting combat decorations.

"You gave this to me," he said, fingering the top ribbon.

My eyes filled. Great sobs wracked my body. The captain withdrew, quietly shut the door, and left me with my tears.

16

EXILE

WHAT is there to say of exile? After twenty-seven years abroad, I conclude that in my case it was far better than the alternative: years of prison and so-called reeducation camp. Since leaving my homeland, I have learned that Americans, in general, are the kindest, most trusting, and most generous people in the world— and yet, among them, more often than one would imagine, is every sort of idiot and mischief maker. In short, Americans are very much like everyone else, except that usually they are nicer. *Usually.*

Not long after I was reunited with my family in Fairfax, Virginia, a suburb of Washington, D.C., a friend whose car needed a tuneup asked me to accompany him to a garage; my English was better, and he asked me to help.

Across the street was a Cadillac dealership, so while mechanics worked on my friend's car, we crossed the road to look at those beautiful new cars. All the salesmen recognized my face and my name, and the sales manager said that he would be honored to sell me a car and promised a big discount. Even after I explained that I had neither money nor job, he insisted that I take a new Coupe DeVille for a test drive.

It was a gorgeous convertible, red with white leather upholstery, and I wanted to show it to my family, so I headed toward the home that friends had rented for us. Along the way a motorcycle officer stopped me. He said it was because there was no license plate, but more likely his reason was that this was a prosperous neighborhood and behind the wheel of a flashy new car he saw a barefoot, tousled Asian man in a rumpled T-shirt and shorts. "Do you live around here?" asked the cop.

I wasn't sure of the name of my street.

"You have a driver's license?"

I had no wallet, nor any identification.

"Do you have a job?"

"No," I replied.

"What kind of work do you do?"

When asked questions that require complex answers, it has long been my habit to gather my thoughts before replying. The cop took my brief silence for a negative response.

"Have you *ever* held a job?" he barked.

Again I considered how best to answer. My thoughts drifted back to my escape from Vietnam, my visit with the captain of the USS *Midway*. After the skipper returned to his office, he said that I was to be taken to USS *Blue Ridge*, a command ship.

With a group that included my aides and General Truong, I stepped out of a navy helicopter onto the *Blue Ridge*. We were herded to a table where American officers attempted to conduct individual interviews with hundreds of refugees. Pandemonium reigned—officers shouted orders and petty officers forced people into lines and told them to be quiet. I waited at the table, but before anyone spoke to me, a navy lieutenant who had been bellowing commands at the top of his lungs came over to whisper, "Please come with me." I followed him.

After ten paces or so he glanced at me and said, "Are you Marshal Ky?"

"I think so." We walked a little farther.

"You're coming from Saigon?"

"I think so."

While the rest of my countrymen were forced to sit crowded together on a hard deck under a blazing sun like so many farm animals, I was shown to a tiny cabin with a marine guard outside. The lieutenant sent for food and asked if I needed anything. I asked him to find out about my family. In half an hour I had a radiogram from Washington: My wife and all my children were safe in Virginia. A few hours later, about nightfall, the lieutenant returned in dress uniform. He said, "I'm sorry that this afternoon I didn't recognize you, sir."

"Don't worry," I replied. "But because you are here, I want to remind you I am *not* a prisoner of war. I am your ally. So also are the others, all those little Vietnamese soldiers. For so many years we fought together! Is this the way to treat comrades in arms? I hope that from now that you will treat Vietnamese military officers in a better way."

Evidently this officer carried my words to his superiors, because later the senior Vietnamese officers were treated with more respect. One came to see me, a colonel, who asked if I had any cash. I went through my pockets, discovering, not entirely to my surprise, that I had no money at all.

The colonel produced two American ten-dollar bills. "Maybe you'll need cigarettes or something," he said, handing me one.

So how is it that a general officer, former prime minister, and vice president had no money? First, understand that in most Vietnamese households, and especially among military families, the wife serves as chief financial officer. This is custom, and prudent: No soldier can predict the time of his death, and if his wife did not control family finances, in Vietnam, where there was no life insurance, few banks, and virtually no consumer credit, the family might easily starve.

Even though I had every opportunity to enrich myself through corruption, except for my little farm bungalow, I never owned a house. I lived in a military camp, and that was enough for me. Even if I had wanted a house, on my salary I could not have afforded to buy one. I used a military Jeep or staff car;

until I came to America I never owned a car. I never had a bank account in Vietnam or elsewhere. My possessions were uniforms, clothes, and a few personal things—and I left them all behind.

I was exhausted, so after the colonel left I lay down. Images, odors, and sounds of the last days and weeks spun nonstop through my mind like a multimedia kaleidoscope; after a time, I asked the guard to get me a sleeping pill. Soon a doctor appeared. He asked me to open my mouth, then put a capsule in it and watched as I swallowed.

"Thank you," I said. "I will need a few more."

"Any time you need another, just let me know," he said. The next day I realized that they were afraid that I might commit suicide. I began to consider it. I felt empty, almost hollow, as if I had left some vital part of my self in Vietnam. What kind of life awaited me in America? After dwelling on this for a few hours, however, I decided to live. I would fill my emptiness with activity, by going on with life. My family needed me, and I hoped that one day, perhaps, Vietnam would need me again.

After I slept a little, I asked to see the ship's captain. The evacuation of Saigon was in high gear, and because I knew many places where Vietnamese might be hiding or awaiting help, I volunteered to work with the rescue operation. The captain agreed, and I remained in the operations center.

In this way I learned that Ambassador Martin was also on the *Blue Ridge*, along with about four hundred newsmen, mostly Americans. When they heard that I was aboard, they requested that I hold a press conference. Martin sent a man to tell me this, adding, however, that the ambassador had already told reporters that this was not an appropriate time for such an event— which of course made the journalists very angry.

"Personally, I don't want to see you or anyone," I told Martin's emissary. "But don't tell me what the ambassador wants. If I choose to speak with reporters, I will do so. You Americans are always wailing about freedom of the press—if I want to talk to reporters, do you think your ambassador can prevent me?"

The next day after the last American helicopter had left Saigon, I was offered the opportunity to take a VIP flight to the United States. Instead I decided that my duty lay in remaining with my brethren; I wanted to be treated as they were. We were taken to Camp Pendleton, a Marine Corps facility near San Diego, California. We arrived at night; I was led to a big tent, empty except for myself. It was very chilly, and all I had was a tropical-weight khaki uniform. I asked a marine captain if he could take me to a field kitchen, someplace where I could warm myself, because even with several blankets I was shivering.

"I'm not allowed to bring you to the kitchen," replied the young officer. He peeled off his own flight jacket. "Sir, I once served under your command. Please take this."

"Oh, no," I said. "You still have to fly back and forth to bring in the refugees. You will need your jacket."

The captain insisted until it would have been rude to refuse him. The next night, however, going from tent to tent to lend at least moral support to the others, I encountered an older woman who was shivering, and gave her the jacket. Later that night I had a surprise visitor—my old girlfriend, the lady who lived with me after my first marriage ended, who had borne my daughter. With her American husband, she lived nearby. She brought me good wishes and a bottle of Martel Cognac.

When I got to Washington, some of my friends suggested that I might earn a living, at least for a while, as a speaker. I was booked for speaking engagements at colleges and universities, and elsewhere, where I earned $2,500 to $3,500 for each appearance—over four times my annual VNAF salary. I also sat down with people in New York who interviewed me for a couple of days and then published a book, *Twenty Years and Twenty Days,* about how the United States and Vietnam lost the war.

Much of this work is factually correct, but when I read it carefully, I discovered that the editors sometimes put words in my mouth and invented events that never took place. That was one reason that I decided to write this book.

Soon after my exile began, Madame Anna Chenault invited me to a private dinner at her Watergate penthouse, just the two of us. She had just returned from Taiwan. "I went to tell Mr. Thieu that he cannot come to the United States," she explained. "President [Gerald] Ford asked me to say that because of his reputation, he is not welcome here." I believe Thieu lived in the United Kingdom for some years, and after Mr. Carter was elected president, he quietly applied for a visa. Until his death in 2001, he lived in New England, where he undoubtedly discovered that all that money won't buy a single real friend: He was shunned by most Vietnamese.

After a few months on the speaker's circuit, I was invited for a television appearance in Los Angeles. Afterward I stayed a few days with a Vietnamese friend in Orange County, and one morning after breakfast a real estate agent came by. After a time he revealed that he knew of a beautiful house for sale, and invited us to see it. I liked this home, so I dickered with the owner and finally made a deal. From my speaking tour I had acquired enough cash for a 10 percent down payment.

After my book was published, I had some money and went to a bank near my home to open an account. The bank president came out of his office to introduce himself. He invited me to lunch, where I met the board of directors. Of course, they asked what I was going to do now that I lived in America.

I replied that I was not sure, but I was thinking about finding a small business, perhaps a car wash. Among the directors, however, was Jack Hanshaw, the king of Orange County liquor stores—with his brothers, he owned about seventeen. Jack suggested that I consider buying my own liquor store, and offered to help teach me how to run it profitably. Because of his position, the bank loaned me enough to buy a store.

The way one turns a profit from a liquor store is to keep it open from early in morning until late at night. Although I often spent fourteen hours a day on my feet, I never became too tired to remind myself how fortunate I was to be living in a free country along with my entire family.

When a former national leader becomes a storekeeper, it is news. Journalists of every sort visited my store. One day a bus driver came in to ask if his passengers, German tourists, could enter and see me. I discovered that my business was a standard stop on his tour, which ended at Disneyland. Among my regular customers were many Mexican Americans. They usually addressed me as "El Presidente." Vietnam veterans drove miles to buy my beer. One day a police SWAT team arrived, each man wearing the steel helmet that he had worn in Vietnam. Tourists came in for nothing but my autograph.

One day a burly Mexican American man bought three cases of beer. Usually I had a box boy to bring large orders from the back-room cooler, but that day he was out. I told my customer, "Watch the counter, I'll get your beer."

"No, please," said the man. "Allow me to get it. I served as a marine in Da Nang, and it's not right that you should have to work so hard."

I let him go in the back. "Why are you buying so much?" I asked when he returned.

"Tonight is my wedding party."

"Congratulations!" I said. "Allow me to repay you, in a small way, for all that you have done for my country. Please accept the beer as my wedding gift." That big, tough ex-marine stood there for several minutes, tears rolling down his cheeks.

From such customers and events, little by little, I built a business and a life in America. At first I was depressed over my circumstances; in 1977 I told a *New York Times* reporter that to end up selling liquor in Orange County meant that my life was a tragedy. But such doubts were rare. I fed and clothed and educated my seven children, and if we never lived in luxury, neither did we suffer. When we needed something beyond my means, one of my friends, or several joining together, would provide it.

I visited Nixon twice at his home in San Clemente, both purely social calls. And after tens of thousands of my countrymen took to leaky boats to flee Vietnam, I went to see John Wayne in his Newport Beach home about getting land in Arizona to resettle Vietnamese refugees. My brother-in-law wanted to meet Wayne, so I brought him along. After our meeting, he asked for an autographed picture, and the Duke graciously gave him one. Then he said, "What about another for Mr. Cao Ky?"

"No, the general doesn't need a picture of me," replied Wayne. "Any time he needs me, he gets *me*—just call."

Wayne was by then quite ill, however. We met a few more times before his death from cancer in 1979.

In 1983 I visited New York for a few days on business. I took lunch one day in one of the city's better restaurants, and when I looked over at the next table, there among a group of dark, Levantine men sat Henry Kissinger.

We had become friendly a decade earlier in Paris. After long, painful wrangling over the vital issue of the shape of the negotiating table, I told Kissinger, "The main thing is a guarantee that the North Vietnamese stop their aggression and infiltration. All we want is assurance that they cannot send their troops to the South. There must be some effective international control, perhaps under the United Nations, which already polices the DMZ between South and North Korea."

Kissinger agreed that what I asked was minimal and, moreover, that it was right. Unlike most other senior U.S. officials, he always treated me as a friend. When I said something that struck a chord with him, he would immediately declare whether he thought I was correct or not, and I always had the feeling that he was straight with me. But as a practitioner of *realpolitik*. I knew that I could trust him only to act always in the perceived interest of his own country, just as I would always defend the interests of mine. We stayed on good terms, but I cannot say that we were truly friends.

When Kissinger saw me he came to my table. As we shook hands, he said, "General, I owe you an apology."

"It's too late," I replied. But I have to like this guy; he needed no prompting to acknowledge the need to offer his regrets. Among gentlemen, there was no need to say more.

While in Tokyo to deliver a lecture a few years later, I stayed at the Imperial. Kissinger, who was visiting with President Ford, was also at this hotel. He called my room and in his inimitable voice told me, "I always tell my friends that you are a patriotic Vietnamese." He left his phone number and an invitation to call at any time.

Not long after my New York meeting with Dr. Kissinger, I bought a second store and opened a boutique in Southern California's Westminster Mall. My timing was bad, however: This was the early 1980s, when inflation was rampant, the U.S. economy faltering, and unemployment rising. The boutique did not do well, yet I was locked into a long lease. There came a time when I had to file for bankruptcy.

Around this time muckraking Washington columnist Jack Anderson reported that I was among a group of former ARVN officers who extorted money from businesses, mostly those owned by Vietnamese. I knew some of these bandits and had condemned their activities, but I had no power to stop them. Knowing that lurid accusations make headlines and that he could attack a public figure with impunity, Anderson also wrote that I had left Saigon with $8 million in gold, diamonds, and currency!

President Reagan's Commission on Asian Organized Crime

launched an investigation into Anderson's allegations. They published a report that said that there was no evidence of any kind that I had ever been involved with criminal activities.

Before that report was published, however, Joseph L. Galloway, the *U.S. News & World Report* bureau chief in Los Angeles, decided to investigate as well. He found my name and address in the White Pages and knocked on my door one Saturday morning. I invited him in. Galloway came right to the point: Was I involved with kidnappings and extortion? Was I head of a Vietnamese Mafia?

In reply I suggested that he walk through my home—search it carefully, if he cared to—to see that I was alone and unarmed. "If I was kidnapping people for ransom and extorting businessmen, don't you think I'd have to keep a few bodyguards around? Or at least a gun?" I asked. I had been invited to attend a community event in the largely Vietnamese part of Westminster known as Little Saigon, and I asked Galloway to accompany me. He rode in my car and saw how my countrymen treated me: with courtesy and dignity, often with affection, never with fear. Those who had been my political opponents or who blamed me for the loss of our country simply ignored me. Galloway came to the same conclusion as the Asian Organized Crime Commission. *My* conclusion was that Jack Anderson writes from the wrong city. With such a vivid imagination, he should be in Hollywood writing what everyone knows is fiction.

Even after the crime commission gave me a clean bill of health, however, my problems were not over. At the invitation of a group of Vietnam veterans, in 1985 I went to New Orleans to join General Westmoreland as grand marshals of the Armed Forces Day Parade. Organizers used our names to attract sponsors, including several banks, and so I met many local people. Over dinner we discussed the difficulties of Vietnamese fishermen along the Gulf of Mexico. They struggled to find credit sources to finance new boats, to market their shrimp and fish at fair prices, and to get along better with local government and business. We discussed forming a coordinating body to help deal with such problems and to ease friction with American fishermen who believed that Vietnamese overfished, depleting stocks.

Both Americans and Vietnamese suggested that perhaps I could help promote the fishing industry. After a lot of talk, I said that I would take a look around and assess the situation on my own. I drove through the Gulf Coast region with a few Vietnamese fisherman, and what I saw attracted my interest. My home and my stores had been sold to satisfy my creditors, so I was looking for a new venture. Why not shrimping?

Then I was approached by a lender in Houma, a port about forty miles southwest of New Orleans, which had an old factory that packed and froze shrimp. The plant was important to the local economy, but it was losing money and the group running it had many problems, including little management experience. After visiting the facility and discussing it with the bank, the lender sold me the plant and a boat, *The Morning Star,* for one dollar and a mortgage to cover the balance.

I became a shrimper during the worst fishing season in ten years; those tiny crustaceans were far more elusive than I had believed. On one voyage of twenty-one days my catch was so small that by the time I paid my crew and operating expenses, my profit came to five dollars.

The next year was worse. Many Vietnamese, descended from generations of professional fisherman, moved to Hawaii or elsewhere in search of a living from the sea. It was soon obvious that the plant was worthless without shrimp to pack. The bankers who held the mortgage were only a mile from the plant and understood the situation perfectly. When it became obvious that the facility could not turn a profit, the bank took it back; on paper they showed a foreclosure on a bad loan, but as it had been from the start, our transaction was amicable.

As it happened, however, this was a time of crisis for the

U.S. lending industry. After Mr. Reagan's administration pushed through deregulation of savings and loan institutions, mismanagement and fraud ran rampant. Many lenders failed or were forced to merge with others. When the one in Houma was taken over by the federal government, they reviewed its loans, especially the bad ones. Eventually, an auditor looked at the document dealing with the packing plant. He sent copies of the paperwork to the FBI in New Orleans.

There a particularly ambitious FBI agent began to wonder "Why did Nguyen Cao Ky go into the fishing business down *here*? Maybe it's a front for something dark and dirty. After all, this fellow was investigated by the Asian Organized Crime Commission! Maybe he is really smuggling drugs from Mexico!"

As I would learn, this agent is from Eastern Europe and tends to see conspiracies in even the most casual transaction. Perhaps he thought "Nguyen Cao Ky is like all those other Asian dictators. He must have at least a few hundred million salted away. Why would he sail a fishing boat from the middle of nowhere? Why does he keep sending boats out when there are no shrimp in the gulf? Something is fishy!"

FBI agents began going around asking questions about me. They interviewed my friends and business associates. An agent even approached one of my relatives. He said, "We don't want you, we're after a bigger fish. We want Nguyen Cao Ky! Can you tell us about him? What is he *really* doing in Houma?"

If an investigator had called me, I would have told them the whole story. But the FBI never asked me. For many months I was unaware of this investigation. As the probe continued, however, my friend Jack Hanshaw was summoned to New Orleans. He told the FBI, "All I know about General Ky is that he is a good man, an honest man. That's it—I have nothing more to say about him. Now I have business. Good-bye."

Eventually I learned that a federal grand jury had been convened to consider an indictment against me. Angry, I hired a

New Orleans attorney and asked to meet with the prosecutor. For two years this worthy put me off, played games with my lawyer, made lame excuses. The investigation continued, and in the end the FBI found convincing evidence that I was a poor fisherman—but nothing to support any allegation of illegal activity.

Somehow this made that FBI agent even more suspicious! Convinced that he was on the trail of a master criminal, he had told the U.S. attorney and the grand jury that he had hooked a very big fish, the Moby Dick of lawbreakers. It must have been very hard for him to admit that he had found nothing.

Until this time, whenever I came through Immigration and Customs I was treated as a king. After the FBI began investigating me, I returned from an overseas trip to discover that my name was on a blacklist. Customs questioned me at length. My luggage was torn apart and searched thoroughly. Immigration officials demanded to know details of my itinerary.

Furious, I instructed my attorney to tender the U.S. attorney an ultimatum: Meet with me at once, or I will call a press conference. The G-men caved in, and I went to the sixteenth floor of the Westwood Federal Building in Los Angeles for a first look at my tormenter. My first impression was that he would have been Central Casting's choice for some sinister character, perhaps an informer, for some old French movie.

In contrast, the U.S. attorney was smart and elegant. I told him everything I knew, holding back nothing. When I finished he said, "To be frank, we cannot make any decision concerning your case. That is up to higher authority."

I saw at once that this prosecutor was telling me, in a roundabout way, that the FBI agent was acting on his own authority, that there was no case for the grand jury.

While I no longer had to worry about being investigated, I had to find some way to earn a living. I decided to go to Bangkok, where my friend Tay Chung-Hai, Singapore's most important purveyor of liquor and tobacco products, had recently acquired a spacious condominium. He invited me to stay as long as I liked. His place was staffed with a cook and a housekeeper, and Hai saw to it that the pantry was always well stocked with my favorite food and drink.

Except for a few brief visits, I had been away from Asia for almost fifteen years. I soon learned that my name and face remained widely known. An especially pleasant surprise was the discovery that many top Asian leaders, and especially those in finance, trade, and governmental posts, men who had been my juniors when I served as prime minister, looked upon me with fondness and respect. I learned that they listened when I spoke and that they would pay for my advice. Basing myself in Bangkok, I made extended visits to Hong Kong, Singapore, and Tokyo and became a traveling consultant, offering counsel or asking hard questions of those seeking business around the Pacific Rim. Word got around quickly: In less than a year, I became busy.

As Vietnam relaxed restrictions on travel and opened itself to visitors and expatriates, I met with more and more of my countrymen, including those heading for Saigon or Hanoi and those who had just departed. In oblique and sometimes elliptical ways, I began sporadic conversations with some of the younger, more progressive members of Vietnam's ruling regime, a dialog that continues to this day. On the surface we seem to speak of many things, but beneath the pleasantries I say, in a thousand ways: "Uncle Ho would spin in his mausoleum if he knew what a mess you made of our country! You won the war, you kicked my ass out—but if communism ever held any value, surely you must see that it has done nothing for the people of Vietnam! Communism is dead—so bury it, say a prayer, move on. Change your ways, get rid of those old grandfathers who are stuck in the past!"

Their reply is always some variation on a single theme: "Oh, yes, you are right—but we have a dozen Deng Shao-pings to

contend with! They hold no office but cling to party power, obstruct every effort at reform—we can do nothing now."

Not long after moving to Asia, I met my present wife. Some
years my junior, she is lovely and smart, and as industrious as
she is kind. After I obtained a divorce from my previous wife,
we married.

Soon afterward, on a visit to Singapore, my new wife took
up golf. I had thought myself much too young for this sport, but
because I enjoy spending time with her, I decided to try it. It
was a fortuitous decision. Tiger Woods has little to fear from
me, but I have come to enjoy this game very much.

These days I often stroll the links with millionaires and even
a few billionaires. Most usually wager a small sum, perhaps a
dollar a hole, "to make things more interesting." I *never* play for
money: When you bet on a match, it is not enough that you
want to play well: You also want your friends to play poorly. So
I tell my golfing pals, "I am sure that before the match you hope
that your friends do well. But if he plays better than you and
beats you, then you are unhappy, right?" Why kill a friendship
for one dollar!

When I am not consulting or golfing—or both at once—I
spend as much time as I can with my fourteen grandchildren
and one great-grandchild. I will be in my seventy-third year
when this book is published in America, but my health is excellent, my energy high. I still eat and drink as in my youth, and
my weight is almost as when I commanded the VNAF. If I have
the benefit of many more experiences than I had on the day
when I agreed to serve my people as prime minister, my passions
and ideals are unchanged. Most of my friends in America are
average people living commonplace lives; I treat them and all
others exactly as I did before I came to power, exactly as I did
while I was in office, and exactly as I did after leaving government. I have less hair and more wrinkles, but inside I am the
man that I have always been.

When I am awake I am content to play golf five hours a day for the rest of my years. But each night sleep comes wrapped in a cloak of visions. I dream of returning to Vietnam, of helping to rebuild and reshape my nation to meet its destiny.

As for my own destiny, so far the blind fortune-teller has been correct: I have never gone to jail. On that spring day in suburban Virginia, the police officer looked me over. My borrowed clothes were ill-fitting hand-me-downs, and I sat behind the wheel of a gleaming new Cadillac convertible. "What kind of work you do?" he asked, ready to take me in.

"I used to be prime minister of South Vietnam," I replied.

Before I became prime minister there was chaos and internecine conflict. Buddhists and Catholics fought one other, northerners struggled against southerners, political parties elbowed and clawed for advantage—even the army battled itself. After I took office came stability, continuity of government, a transformation to constitutional rule, a legal foundation for the beginnings of democracy. That was my achievement, the thing of which I remain most proud.

In these pages I admit to errors of youthful inexperience, to blunders of my naive and trusting heart. But if I tripped over a few miscalculations, never did I err from greed or grandiosity. My biggest mistake was allowing the wrong man the opportunity to lead a guaranty of defeat. For this I beg forgiveness of those who fled into exile, of those who remained, and from those then unborn.

The motorcycle officer became excited. "You're Nguyen Cao Ky!" he said. He apologized, then requested my autograph.

The next day I bought the Cadillac, no money down, on the strength of my own good name.

17

FORTUNE-TELLER

VIETNAMESE folklore is sprinkled with myths and monsters, sometimes so intertwined with history that it is impossible to say where one begins and the other ends. So it is that turtles, symbolic of long life and virility, are revered as divine messengers, conveying the gods' wishes to mortals.

Many Vietnamese believe that our nation enjoys the protection of the Turtle God, who appears in times of national crisis to provide magical weapons to our leader. For example, about 225 B.C., he is said to have given King An Duong Vuong one of his claws to use as a crossbow trigger. One shot of this magical bow killed thousands; so long as Vuong kept it, Vietnam remained invincible. Alas, it was stolen, then lost.

More recently Le Loi, leader of guerrilla resistance to Chinese occupation, was empowered by a magic sword delivered by the Turtle God. With it the young warrior drove out the invaders and restored Vietnamese independence. Le Loi became king and established a new dynasty. As the king was cruising on Luc Thuy, a lagoon near the center of Hanoi, then and now the capital of Vietnam, his sword leaped from its scabbard and into the mouth of a giant turtle, which plunged underwater. The sword was never seen again. The lake, now one of Hanoi's tourist attractions, has been known ever since as Ho Hoan Kiem—the Lake of the Returned Sword.

Legend says this happened around 1428; in recent years, however, many in Hanoi—hundreds of people—have reported sighting a giant turtle in this lake. It is likely that several huge softshell turtles actually live there, but whether they are creatures of flesh and blood or mythic manifestations is a question that I leave to others.

I am no Minh Loc, the sightless fellow favored by Saigon's superstitious, who relies on astrology to see a man's fate. But if no living being can predict another's future, one may yet foretell the general outlines of events by examining past and present, and in this regard my record is good. When Washington and Hanoi put ink to paper in Paris in 1973, I told a *Newsweek* reporter what I thought would happen: In two years the North would launch its final offensive, and if Saigon's leadership did not change, a debacle was inevitable. Thieu and Bunker huffed to the media that I was jealous of Thieu. Thieu remained in charge, and two years and three months after my prediction, the communists were in Saigon.

Several years later I was presented with another opportunity to foretell the future. In 1985 several American soldiers were killed in the bombing of a Berlin nightclub. Within a few months, U.S. President Ronald Reagan concluded that Libya's Colonel Qaddafi had supported and financed this and other acts of terrorism. Reagan filled the Mediterranean with warships. Undaunted, Qaddafi then claimed the Gulf of Sidra as Libya's territorial waters. In April 1986 the United States and Libya moved toward a confrontation. Three American aircraft carriers deployed to underline the American position that the Sidra was international water and that ships of any nation had the right of free passage. They were backed up by a fleet of amphibious ships loaded with U.S. Marines.

Libyan pilots in Soviet- and French-built planes probed the U.S. Navy defenses; these aircraft were intercepted, challenged, and escorted by American naval aircraft. For days there were near collisions, and several Libyan fighters were shot down.

In the midst of all this, while visiting Tunisia as the guest of a member of the Saudi royal family, I was invited to play golf in the Canary Islands with a group that included ranking Arab diplomats and politicians. They were understandably anxious about undeclared hostilities between Libya and the United States. "What will Mr. Reagan do about Qaddafi?" inquired my hosts. "Will he send marines to invade Libya, or just bomb military targets as they did before?"

"The Americans might try to kill Qaddafi," I replied. When that happened the very next day, my hosts thought I had a pipeline to the Pentagon.

Well before 1990, when the Berlin Wall came down and Eastern European communism folded its tent, I began telling fellow exiles that Vietnamese communism was dead, strangled by its own inefficiencies and corruption, that the Hanoi regime must seek reconciliation with America.

The group who had controlled Vietnam for thirty years was in trouble. Our nation remained poor, underdeveloped, stagnating in a region where others were becoming wealthy. As communism expired in the Soviet Union, as even China's leaders proclaimed that it was glorious to be rich, few of Vietnam's gray old men tried to change. Either they were incapable of understanding the new realities, or they were desperate to cling to power, to retain the personal perquisites that enriched them and their families. Whatever their reasons, they refused to leave, refused to make the hard choices.

Had they been men of vision, they would have taken the lesson of Boris Yeltsin, renounced communism, embraced capitalism, and basked in the admiration of politicians and businessmen from Taipei, to Berlin, to Washington. Instead, they behaved as they had under American bombing: They hunkered down and waited. Now most are dead or have been forced to retire. Younger, more able men have taken their places and opened the door to American tourists, cooperated with Americans searching for MIAs. When U.S. president Bill Clinton signed a trade treaty with Hanoi, even my critics began calling me a fortune-teller.

I am not a fortune-teller.

But what will happen in Asia over the next few decades may be perceived. A personal note: Just as I respect America and I admire many Americans, I respect China and admire many Chinese. What I see is what I see, not what I wish for, not what I hope to see, not what I need. In making private thoughts public, I hope to ease painful transitions, to allow friends to plan for peace by avoiding war.

Southeast Asia of the twenty-first century is very different from the struggling, economically depressed colonized region of my youth. Thailand has become a bustling business and communications center. Hong Kong, Singapore, South Korea, and Taiwan are each small dragons, exercising comparatively great economic power for their size. In recent years Hong Kong has reverted to China, and Japan will soon put aside pacifism and revert to a regional military power.

But some things do not change. For millennia, the grand dragon that is China has been the geographic, political, and military center of the East. Inherently expansionist, by turns it influences, then controls and finally dominates its neighbors. When economic and political means have failed, force has always followed. Therefore, economic rivalry between East and West is inevitable; America and its European allies, with economies heavily dependent on Pacific trade, must eventually deal with Chinese expansionism.

As much as China's present leadership seeks peace and friendly trade with the West, that could change. If in fifty or one hundred years China is a military and economic giant controlling Asia, it will bring another world war. The West will therefore move to stop China *before* it becomes strong enough to threaten its interests.

America, leader of the West, will attempt to cage the dragon behind a wall of military alliances. The north end of this wall is Korea, a politically bifurcated peninsula with people starving under communism in the north and prospering in a free-market south. Eventually, however, Seoul and Pyongyang must again pickle cabbage together. After a period of adjustment, a reunited Korea will flourish as never before.

From Korea, the Western Wall runs south through Taiwan. As it has for generations, Taipei will artfully straddle the diplomatic fence between the dragon and the West. But Taiwan has married itself to the West, and when it becomes necessary to restrain China, Taipei will hold the center.

America no longer has bases in the Philippines, Singapore, Indonesia, Malaysia, or Thailand. So America's southern line of defense must begin in Vietnam, at Cam Rahn Bay, the huge base built by the U.S. Navy. From there the United States can participate in a global version of *weiqi,* the 4,000-year-old Chinese board game sometimes called *go.* Instead of black and white pebbles on a ruled board, America will base ships and planes, make strategic alliances, counter the dragon's moves. A U.S. base in Vietnam will tell the dragon, "As long as you seek only trade and friendly relations, we will get along. But if you start to make trouble, we will not permit it."

Just as important, over the next few decades, disagreements will arise between Asian nations. Not as the world's policeman, but as its magnanimous leader, a permanent military presence in Southeast Asia will allow America to act as an impartial referee to maintain regional stability.

But how can two countries that fought so bitterly put aside their past and take a new road together?

It really is simple. The *idea* of America—its freedom, its financial and educational opportunities, the lifestyle, wealth and beauty of the country, and its people—remains the envy of the world, emulated at every opportunity. In Vietnam today the sons and daughters of those who fought America and its soldiers for two decades love everything American. Tens of thousands of American veterans have visited Vietnam and encountered a populace that welcomes and admires them.

When President Clinton visited Vietnam in 2000, people in both the north and south turned out in droves, eager for even a glimpse of him. Because whatever Vietnam's communist leadership may say in public, the great masses of Vietnamese people, now numbering 83 million, are for America. The United States represents a better life, opportunity, hope—everything that American and South Vietnamese soldiers fought to bring to our country thirty years ago. The tremendous outpouring of affection for Mr. Clinton, no less than for all Americans, is proof that those who fought for freedom and democracy were on the right side.

For this reason, the veterans of that lost war, Vietnamese and American, Australian and South Korean, and all the others who supported our fight for freedom, have no cause for shame. Thirty years of communist rule have proven that we who opposed the communists were right. Now we must all put aside our feelings of guilt, the so-called Vietnam war syndrome, and be proud of ourselves and our efforts.

Today Vietnam is run by a new generation, leaders ready to let go of the past, to forget about communism, to adopt free market principles in the national economy. So it is time for the so-called anticommunist Vietnamese, the older generation now living mostly in exile, to let go of their pain and anger and allow the younger generation, our sons and daughters, to have their chance to bring Vietnam together. It is time for my generation to stop preaching hate and bitterness.

Like most of the old anticommunists, I am a fighter. I understand how my brothers and sisters suffered under communism. I know how they endured the agonies of so-called reeducation camps, that they lost loved ones, lost their personal liberty, lost their homes and property. It was unjust. It was humiliating. It was painful.

But our time has passed. We are too old; the future of the country no longer depends on us. What is the point in arguing about who was right and who was wrong? Let the new generation find the path to the future without having to carry burdens created by their parents. Let us put aside our own feelings and allow the new generation to find its own way, because Vietnam will realize its potential only through unity.

If Vietnamese communists and American veterans can forgive each other, surely American vets can now forgive Jane Fonda. Naive and ignorant, she had no inkling of the suffering that communism's triumph would bring upon all Vietnamese. I am sure that she is much wiser now.

...

Vietnam now approaches a crossroads. Should it turn toward China, source of much of our cultural heritage, or, by establishing an enduring partnership with America based on a new paradigm of mutual respect and shared interests, remain independent? What most ordinary Vietnamese want is clear from the friendly reception given to visiting Americans, but national choices will be made by the national leadership over the next years. And these leaders face many problems.

Ironically, Vietnam's most difficult problem is the same that confronted me when I became prime minister in 1965: corruption. While the present government describes itself as communist, the leaders of Vietnam, like leaders in the defunct Soviet Union and in present China, have used their official positions to enrich themselves, their families, and their friends. Since 1955 Vietnamese communist propaganda has promised a dictatorship of the proletariat, equality, representative government—a socialist utopia.

Now everyone knows that communism is a fraud. The most

powerful men in Saigon, hard-line, doctrinaire communists who hold top party positions, now live in luxurious villas and own Vietnam's most successful restaurants, factories, construction companies, tourism agencies—businesses of every sort. The ranking Vietcong officials of the 1960s and 1970s, men who owned nothing and mouthed slogans about social justice, are now rich beyond their wildest dreams.

Yet Vietnam remains economically depressed, a poor agrarian nation that needs to develop modern industries. Virtually everything that Vietnamese consumers want to buy, from textiles to telephones, from canned goods to hand tools, bicycles to brooms, is produced very cheaply by China. In order to develop and protect domestic industries, Vietnam's leadership banned import of most Chinese products.

Nevertheless, throughout the country, from Ha Giang in the north to Cahmau on the delta's southern tip, virtually everything displayed in markets is made in China. In one place that I know, the border between Vietnam and China is a canal. All day long thousands of people step over that narrow channel. On the backs and in the arms of those heading south from China are boxes and cartons and bags holding every sort of manufactured item. Above them on the bridge are Vietnamese border police, watching themselves get richer with every load of Chinese goods that enters their country. How can their superiors also fail to profit?

From time to time, Hanoi newspapers report that a smuggler has been arrested. But each one who is caught is as a drop of water to the sea. Chinese goods smuggled into Vietnam have destroyed the lives of Vietnamese craftsmen and ruined many small industries. Vietnam cannot compete with cheap, good-quality Chinese products, and yet these goods today pour into Vietnam by sea, by land, even by air.

We Vietnamese like to say that our culture is 85 percent Chinese, that the 15 percent that is different defines us as Vietnamese. If there is no end to corruption, if Vietnam does not get honest and clean leaders, my homeland will revert to what it was a thousand years ago: a Chinese province. A Chinese governor will run my country.

It does not have to be this way. If Vietnam cleans its house and reduces corruption to internationally accepted norms, then the transformation of its economy and institutions can begin. My country needs modern highways and a telecommunications system. It needs a modern national airline to bring the world to our markets.

All that will cost billions of dollars. Wise Vietnamese leaders will ignore government loans and development banks and avoid the raft of restrictions that accompanies such funds. They will go directly to the private sector, which has the expertise to match its financial motivations. Much as nineteenth-century Americans granted land to railroad companies in return for creating a national transportation system, an enlightened Vietnamese leadership will engage the world's largest multinational companies with long-term concessions in return for modernizing our infrastructure and training Vietnamese to manage and expand what they build.

All this economic activity will also encourage many exiles to return. There are more than 3 million of us, two-thirds in North America, and compared to the average Vietnamese, we are better educated and have superior skills. Some worry that the younger generation, those born in exile or who left Vietnam as small children, may not want to give up their comparatively easy lives in the United States, Canada, France, and Australia. Even so, they will find that their language skills and cultural heritage will make them valuable to companies seeking business in Vietnam.

Vietnam can someday provide opportunities to use their education and skills, and I believe that many young Vietnamese will want to help develop the land of their fathers. I have crisscrossed America for years, meeting and spending time with this younger generation, telling them that they are important to the future of Vietnam, that the country needs their brains. And I am happy to report that making money is not their top priority. Many young men and women, motivated by patriotism no less than personal ambition, will return to their homeland when they see ways to employ their skills.

Americans who come to Vietnam to pursue business opportunities will find a much different situation from the soldiers who came during the war. They will not be big brothers come to help fight. They will be partners, contractors. Helping to bridge the inevitable misunderstandings between East and West will be the generation of Vietnamese born or educated in America. In ten or fifteen years, most successful Vietnamese enterprises will be run by those who have learned American techniques and American thinking.

I am optimistic about the next generation of Vietnamese leaders. Now that the trade agreement has been ratified, there will be a sharp increase in contacts between the two countries. As Communist party officials see more of America and meet more Americans, they will see the wisdom of moving Vietnam toward the West. I believe that they will soon change the economic rules that have limited Vietnam for decades.

It is axiomatic that changes in political rule will follow, because political systems are built on a foundation of economic rules. As state ownership gives way to private capitalism, the effects will ripple through every corner of society, including the courts and the legislature. Instead of party hacks, bright technocrats and entrepreneurs will make the day-to-day decisions of government and business. Once Vietnam embraces capitalism, democracy and the rule of law will follow. If even ten bright, dedicated, and honest Vietnamese could work together, they could well reinvent the whole country.

...

Not long ago I went to Louisiana to visit an old friend. As young boulevardiers in Saigon, we came to know each other's favored delicacies, so when I arrived at my comrade's farm he led me to his barn. He showed me a wooden box with five turtles that he had caught.

"We can have these tonight, with a fine cognac I saved for you," he said, recalling our custom of long ago.

I looked at the turtles. Their shells were perhaps twelve inches across, a far cry from the five-foot carapace of the legendary denizen of Hanoi's Ho Hoan Kiem. But still, fine turtles.

"I don't think so," I heard myself say. "Let them go."

"I'll keep them one more night," replied my friend. "Tomorrow you may change your mind."

As the hour of my departure approached, my host displayed his cognac bottle and renewed his offer.

"No, let them go," I said.

He carried the crate to the water's edge and turned it on edge. The first turtle made a beeline for the water, but once immersed, it loitered near the bank. The second followed at a more leisurely pace, and it, too, surfaced near the bank.

The third and largest turtle cocked its head and stared at me through unblinking eyes. It was still looking when the last two captives ambled into the water. Finally, like a conscientious commander overseeing his troops' escape, the big turtle edged toward the creek. Every step of the way, those tiny black button eyes burned holes in mine.

A sluggish current carried all five creatures downstream. As it floated away, the third turtle continued to stare at me. The distance between us slowly widened, and it craned its extended neck back over its shell, staring, staring, staring into my eyes until at last neck, eyes, and turtle vanished around a bend.

I will not be too surprised if we meet again some day.

EPILOGUE

MY mother died a few months before I became prime minister, and even though I was busy trying to cope, trying to survive a week, a month, a year, I found time to mourn her passing. She was buried in Mac Dinh Chi, Saigon's only cemetery. Until I fled Vietnam in 1975, I made sure her grave was well tended.

A few years after the communists took over, it was decided that because those buried in Mac Dinh Chi had been wealthy or prominent, instead of using this space to honor the elite, the area would become a public park, available to all. Relatives were given only a few days to move the remains of their loved ones. Thousands converged on the cemetery, among them a few of my kin, who dug up my mother's casket and took it to a Buddhist temple.

As they cleaned the earth from her bones, monks stopped to stare. They had no idea whose remains these were, nor even if they had belonged to a man or a woman. But the cleansed bones, they told my relatives, were like very few others. They had not decomposed in the warm tropical soil, they had not turned black and fragile. Instead they remained hard and strong, and glowed with the soft white of old ivory. "Like Buddha's bones," said the monks, and begged to be allowed to keep them. Some day, when I return to my homeland, I will go to this temple and perform the ceremonies that honor my mother's memory.

INDEX